Every Bit of Who I Am

Every Bit of Who I Am

Devotions for Teens

James C. Schaap

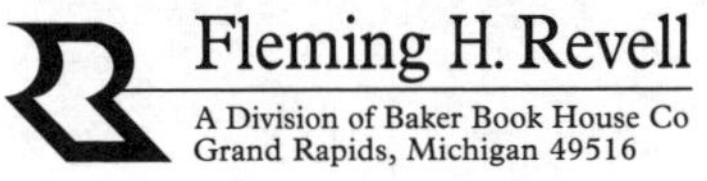

Published by Faith Alive Christian Resources
2850 Kalamazoo SE
Grand Rapids, MI 49560

and

Fleming H. Revell
a division of Baker Book House Company
P.O. Box 6287, Grand Rapids, MI 49516-6287

Printed in the United States of America

Library of Congress Cataloging-in-Publication Data

Schaap, James C., 1948–
Every bit of who I am : devotions for teens / James C. Schaap.
p. cm.
ISBN 978-1-56212-788-6 (Faith Alive Christian Resources)
ISBN 978-0-8007-5790-8 (Baker Book House Company)
1. Christian teenagers—Prayer-books and devotions—English. 2. Reformed Church—Prayer-books and devotions—English. 3. Heidelberger Katechismus. I. Title
BV4850 .S3192 2001
242´.63—dc21 2001040406

10 9 8 7 6 5 4 3

Every Bit of Who I Am
is dedicated to:

Matt Ruter,
who made it clear such a book would be useful;

Andrew Kuyvenhoven,
whose *Comfort and Joy* guided me wisely through the Catechism;

and a teacher from Ontario, Canada,
who met me on an elevator in a downtown Toronto hotel,
lowered her pointer finger, and said,
"You have to write more devotionals for kids."

Thanks to all of you.

Contents

Introduction: "Every Bit of Who I Am" 11

1 Spitwads
2 Friends
3 Count on It!
4 Just Imagine
5 Confession
6 No Hoax
7 What You Can't Do
8 Every Last One of Us
9 It's Natural
10 Face It
11 Unless . . .
12 It's Not My Fault
13 Hell
14 More Than a Wink and a Nod
15 Self-Preservation
16 Powerball Dreams
17 Heroic Canaries
18 The Supreme Sacrifice
19 No Mere Mortal
20 Perfectly Stupendous
21 Breaking Up the Ice Jam
22 Fundamentals
23 Good News, Bad News
24 Tough Love
25 The Lessons of History
26 Grafting
27 Head Knowledge
28 No-Brain Faith
29 What Is Truth?
30 The Leap of Faith
31 The Gift
32 Sheer Grace
33 At-one (ment)
34 More Than Just a Warm Heart
35 The Whole Thing
36 Discuss—But Don't Fight!
37 A Creed Beyond Doubt
38 It's Simple—and It Isn't
39 Into Three Parts
40 The Trinity
41 So Big
42 Awesome
43 The Old, Old Story
44 What Do You Need?
45 Mourning to Gladness
46 Breathtaking
47 Providence
48 God and the Weather Channel
49 An Intrusive God
50 Despair
51 Hitting Bottom
52 Sovereignty
53 Savior
54 No Other Name
55 The Real Thing
56 Messiah
57 Lunatic Prophets
58 In Our Place
59 The Lion and the Lamb
60 By Faith Alone
61 You're a Prophet
62 You're a Priest
63 You're a King—Now
64 You're a King—Forever
65 Begotten
66 Belonging
67 Jesus Gives a Quiz

68 Born in a Barn
69 Magnificat
70 Away in a Manger
71 Suffering and SUVs
72 Then Is Now
73 Cursed and Crucified
74 A Cross and a Crooked Chunk of Cement
75 Ghosts and Old Graves
76 Just the Beginning
77 No Scars
78 The Kingdom of the Dead
79 Bad, Bad Places
80 Winners
81 Voted Off the Island
82 Humpty Dumpty and God
83 God's Headquarters
84 History—and Old Baseball Gloves
85 Lifted Up in Prayer
86 One of Us
87 Chicken Little
88 A Thousand Years
89 A Carry-Out Faith
90 Puppies and Other Gifts
91 On Patrol
92 Unimaginable
93 Faith and Sight
94 The Last Judgment
95 He Is Lord
96 Stones Rolled Away
97 The Holy Spirit
98 Head and Heart
99 A Personal Savior
100 The Catholic Church
101 Harvest Time
102 Scowling in Church
103 Better Than Bucks
104 Bowling Alone
105 Forgive and Forget?
106 Want a New Body?
107 Whispers of Eternity
108 What No One Knows
109 So What?
110 'Fess Up Time
111 "Nobody's Perfect"
112 At the Heart of Things
113 The Tower Experience
114 No Bragging
115 Un-American
116 What Peter Earned
117 What God Does
118 How We Come to Faith
119 The Preaching of the Word
120 Are We All Preachers?
121 On the Job
122 Eating and Drinking
123 Swooshes, Signs, and Sacraments
124 Show-and-Tell
125 What's Sacred and What's Not
126 Only Two
127 Reminding
128 Saul Sees the Light
129 Ritual
130 Why?
131 Lydia's Story
132 The Command
133 Blood Brothers and Sisters
134 Commemoration
135 Horror Movies
136 Nourishment
137 Post Toasties
138 Some Mayn't
139 Supervision
140 King of Kings
141 In Our Lives
142 Carry the Keys
143 When People Are Wrong
144 Keys and Swords
145 Forever Thankful
146 From the Inside Out
147 Doing Good, Feeling Good
148 By Our Love

149 Conversion Software
150 Getting Cranked
151 Death of the Old Self
152 Hear the Joy
153 A Wildfire of Joy
154 Love and Hate
155 "Only What's Done for Christ Will Last"
156 Here's the Story
157 The Ten Commandments—for Israel or Us?
158 The Cross and the Ten Words
159 Foundations
160 Other Gods
161 God and Money
162 Fashioning God
163 The Cathedral at Canterbury
164 Snake Worshipers
165 Drivel
166 Abusing the Name
167 Blasphemy!
168 Anachronism
169 Saint Christopher
170 A Matter of Freedom
171 Church—Who Needs It, Really?
172 The 24/7 Sabbath
173 Deadbeat Dads
174 Honoring
175 Respecting Mystery
176 Growing Up
177 No Sweat
178 Loving Ourselves
179 Capital Punishment
180 Community
181 Adultery
182 Commitment
183 Unfaithful
184 Unchastity
185 Trying to Manage Things
186 A Little Number Crunching
187 Loving Things
188 The Love of Money
189 Even in Our Families
190 Raisin Bread
191 False Witness
192 Reasons to Lie?
193 The Cynic
194 Strictly Speaking
195 Desire
196 Media, Marketing, and Coveting
197 The GQ Christian (and Spouse)
198 Billy Graham
199 Losers and Winners
200 Bar Mitzvah
201 When to Pray
202 Close to God
203 Beggars to Givers
204 Keep in Touch
205 How to Pray
206 Chums
207 "Know Thyself"
208 The Bottom Line—It's Simple
209 Everything We Need
210 How, Not What
211 Kids
212 "'Death Spiral' Around a Black Hole"
213 Definition
214 Like the Hypocrites
215 Whatever You Do
216 The Battle and the War
217 Couch Potato
218 Listening for God's Voice
219 The Iron-Pumping Church
220 "Marching Along"
221 Lord Jesus, Come Quickly
222 Obedience
223 Self-Denial
224 *Zaniken*
225 Modesty
226 Compassion

227 Confidence
228 The Miracle of Forgiveness
229 The Forgiven Forgive
230 Forgiveness and Godliness
231 Lead Us Not
232 The Devil
233 Temptation Island
234 "The Flesh and the Spirit"
235 Our Only Comfort
236 Grumbling and Singing
237 Raised Hands
238 Amen

Afterword: "Every Bit of Who We Are" 251

Introduction: "Every Bit of Who I Am"

He looked professional in his sport coat and tie, his silver hair neatly combed. We introduced ourselves and both sat down in the small conference room on the campus of Arizona State University. He had a job to fill; I was applying.

Small talk? Maybe a little—I really don't remember. What I'll never forget is his first question. "Mr. Schaap," he said, "if there was one thing you'd like me to know about yourself, what would it be?"

It wasn't my way—and it still isn't—to preach to people the moment I meet them. What's more, I hadn't been such a glowing believer for the last several years, even though I'd come back to the church after a couple of years away.

What's amazing to me yet is that I didn't really hesitate. Even though I understood that what I was saying just might end my chances for the job, I said what I did almost as if the words were written on my heart—because they likely were.

"I suppose I'd fall back on the old Catechism I learned as a kid," I told him, looking him straight in the eye. "I belong in body and soul, in life and in death, to my faithful Savior Jesus Christ."

The man with the silver hair was a public school administrator from the city of Phoenix. I was applying for a job as an English teacher. I knew that saying such a thing might not be smart, but what I'd blurted out, almost without thinking, was the best answer, the best truthful answer I could think of. I was claiming my identity.

"You're hired," he said.

We talked for another half hour, but he told me in less than two minutes that he wanted to hire me. This public school administrator—his name was Robert Sterrett and he's now gone to live with the Lord—was a Christian. He wanted a Christian believer with a master's degree in English, and the guy who'd stepped into his office that morning was exactly what he was looking for.

That story still stuns me because a hundred different scenarios could have played out. I could have found another way of answering the question "Who are you?" He could have been someone who hated Christians. He could have laughed. He could have winced. But he hired me.

Now if you believe that giving the same answer I gave that morning on the campus of Arizona State University is going to mean, for sure, that God will bless you with the job you wanted more than anything else, then I've got a bridge to sell you.

For some cosmic reason, the Lord God Almighty wanted the two of us to click, I guess, and we did. I got the job. For two years I taught high school English at Greenway High School in Phoenix, Arizona.

But there was a bigger lesson in that morning's conversation for me. I'd given the answer not because I'd planned it—I had no idea that he'd ask something like that. I didn't do it to impress him; after all, the odds were against me, given the way public education can be hostile to the Christian faith.

I'd answered the way I did because those words—"That I belong, body and soul, in life and in death, to my faithful Savior Jesus Christ"—were absolutely and undeniably the best short answer I could give. And for me, then and now, they are dead-on true. That's who I was and who I am. I belonged and I belong. I knew it then and I know it now.

What I'd done is answered his question and given him my identity, "every bit of who I am," you might say.

That's what's at stake here in this book of devotionals: identity. Who am I? I don't know that there is a more fundamental question in life itself.

Who am I?

That's where I begin. That's where we begin. That's where it all starts.

"I am not my own, but belong, body and soul, in life and in death, to my faithful Savior Jesus Christ."

That's where we start.

Spitwads

Q&A 1

What is your only comfort in life and in death? That I am not my own but belong—body and soul, in life and in death—to my faithful Savior Jesus Christ.

For none of us lives to himself alone and none of us dies to himself alone. If we live, we live to the Lord; and if we die, we die to the Lord. So, whether we live or die, we belong to the Lord.

—Romans 14:7–8

Get soft paper—that lined stuff—get it wet and sloppy, roll it out of your mouth, and whip that blob up at the statue of Abe Lincoln. Or else take a dozen little ones and stick them against the ceiling like a colony of white ants. Spitwads were a ton of fun when I was a kid.

One day when I thought the teacher wasn't looking, I whipped one across the room, where it smacked up against the window and stuck like white mush.

Perfect.

Not quite.

"Jim," the teacher yelled. The clock on the wall stood still.

"I saw what you just did," he said. Then he said something I'll never forget. "You threw it," he said, "and you, a Schaap."

My father was the mayor of the small town where I lived. My grandpa, not that long before, had been the preacher in our church. What the teacher was saying was that he thought such barbaric behavior would never come from someone with such a holy family.

When I walked home that night I was really steaming. After all, I told myself, what did my spitwad have to do with my dead grandpa?

But with those words, the teacher taught me something very important: I was part of a family, part of something bigger. I wasn't a kid who could do what he felt like, whenever he felt like it. Why? Because I belonged to something, to a family.

We belong. The apostle Paul says so, and so does the first answer of the Heidelberg Catechism. We are not our own. I am named. You are named. We all are named.

We belong—not only to our parents, our communities, our churches, our schools. We belong, far more importantly, to our Lord Jesus Christ.

I am not my own. I belong. So do you.

Lord Jesus, thank you that we have names, families, and friends. Thank you even more for loving us, because we know that we belong to you first of all. We are children called by your name. Amen.

2

Friends

Q&A 1

. . . in fact, all things must work together for my salvation.

And we know that in all things God works for the good of those who love him, who have been called according to his purpose.

—Romans 8:28

Emily wasn't sure exactly when the fighting began. But it seemed that the older she got, the worse it grew—Mom and Dad were constantly yelling at each other. Peace was almost worse. They wouldn't talk to each other and the whole house seemed like a tomb.

One Saturday her father took her out for breakfast. He and Mom were breaking up, he told Emily. "Maybe you've heard us fighting," her father said, as if she had been deaf for the last five years.

At school the next day, Emily didn't want to talk to a soul. She didn't want to think about tomorrow or next week. Whatever came into her mouth came up like that sour stuff from a rancid stomach.

Two months later, at play practice, she saw her friend Sarah walk off the set, right in the middle of a scene. Emily ran after her.

"I'm quitting," Sarah said. "I don't need this hassle."

"You crazy?" Emily said. Sarah was a natural—great voice, great presence, quick to learn her lines. If she left, who would take her place?

And then Sarah looked at her in a way no friend of hers ever had. Her face turned into one big scowl, her eyes into slits.

"What's the matter? You hate the play or the director or something?" Emily said.

"I hate my dad," Sarah said.

The two of them walked away from practice—just the two of them. All of a sudden Emily understood what had put the hatred in Sarah's eyes. At home the two of them were going through the very same horror.

God can use the worst things, the Bible says, even the very worst, to bring some good. The day Emily talked to Sarah was the day God used Emily's worst nightmare to help her love someone else. Emily understood what Sarah was feeling very, very well.

God Almighty will do things like that. Some people call them miracles.

Lord, in the worst of times, help us to remember your promise—that you will never leave us and you'll use even the worst of times to make us stronger. Help us to never give up. Thank you that you will never walk away, even when we feel like it. Amen.

Count on It!

Q&A 1

Because I belong to him, Christ, by his Holy Spirit, assures me of eternal life. . . .

Now it is God who makes both us and you stand firm in Christ. He anointed us, set his seal of ownership on us, and put his Spirit in our hearts as a deposit, guaranteeing what is to come.

—2 Corinthians 1:21–22

People like my own great-grandparents used to think that buying insurance was a sin.

That idea seems silly today, even stupid. Take a farmer out here in Iowa. If he doesn't buy hail insurance and some July storm drops destruction on his corn, he's history as a farmer.

But my great-grandparents used to think that if they bought insurance, they were saying God wouldn't take care of them, and that would be turning their backs on God's Word. Buying insurance, they thought, was an act of unbelief.

Insurance does take the worry out, right? If you back Dad's Chevy into a telephone pole, you might be in trouble, but your dad (or you) won't be out hundreds of bucks to replace the back bumper. The policy is paid for and the accident is covered. Insurance *assures* us that we won't have to foot the bill.

Assurance is what Paul is talking about in our passage for today—after all, God *guarantees* what is to come. Assurance is also what the Catechism says in one of its most memorable answers: "Because I belong to him, Christ, by his Holy Spirit, *assures* me of eternal life."

Unfortunately, not everyone is so sure they're saved. Maybe you're not. Lots of people sometimes wonder, even though they've likely said this line from the Catechism hundreds of times.

Perhaps people wonder about their salvation because they don't pay for it. God assures us of eternal life, but some of us aren't altogether sure because it's not our own hard-earned bucks that paid the bill.

OK, if we've really got this eternal insurance policy, then who *did* pay for it?

You know. Jesus Christ spent his blood for us. Eternal love didn't cost us a dime. He loves us. He died for us. And that's hard to believe.

But it's true. We've got assurance of eternal life because his blood paid our bills.

All you've got to do is believe. That's your only investment. Count on it.

Help us believe, Lord, that you paid the bills. Help us believe that all our sins are washed away eternally by your blood. We thank you for paying that bill. We thank you that we don't have to worry, that now we're free to serve you in our world. We're counting on your promises. Amen.

4

Just Imagine

Q&A 1

Because I belong to him, Christ, by his Holy Spirit, assures me of eternal life and makes me wholeheartedly willing and ready from now on to live for him.

[Jesus Christ] gave himself for us to redeem us from all wickedness and to purify for himself a people that are his very own, eager to do what is good.

—Titus 2:14

Here's what I'm offering—and it's all for nothing at all. It's free. You just get. What a deal!

You want looks, snap your fingers and you're Jennifer Lopez. You'd rather be Leonardo DiCaprio? OK, we'll work on that.

Want bucks? How about this? Snap your fingers and you've got Bill Gates's mega-billions waiting on you, hand and foot. Look behind you—there's a barn full of cash.

Athletic ability your thing? Snap those fingers and you get the legs of Mia Hamm, the jazzy moves of Kobe Bryant, or the bulging biceps of Sammy Sosa. Snap them again and design the whole frame yourself, to spec.

Brains? Once more, lift those hands, snap those fingers, and you get an instant injection of the best of Albert Einstein. Want to sing? In a second you're Britney Spears.

Wouldn't that be grand?

But hold on. Skin wrinkles. Muscles weaken. Minds wander. Memories fade. Knees buckle. Bellies lop. Bones creak. Voices get gravelly. What's real is death.

I'm dreaming and so are you. There's only one Britney Spears. No finger-snapping is going to make you into what she is.

Now here's the real deal. What you *may* have for nothing is everlasting life with happiness greater than you can imagine in a place where there are no bad knees. No kidding. And it's free. It's our gift. It's God's grace. What God offers is like nothing we can get here, and it's a flat-out gift. That's how much God loves us—just imagine! That's how much God wants us to belong to him.

What do we say? Simple. We say thanks. What do we do? Simple. We give God thanks in everything we do, in every area of our lives—from hoop dreams to history tests. Give it all to God for what he's given to you.

For the greatest gift of all, thank God today and every day of your life.

Lord, we'd love to be prettier, quicker, or smarter. We'd like to love ourselves more than we do. But we know you love us. We know you've given so much for us. Thank you for what you've done, once and forever. Thank you, thank you, thank you. Amen.

Confession

Q&A 2

What must you know to live and die in the joy of this comfort? First, how great my sin and misery are. . . .

If we claim to be without sin, we deceive ourselves and the truth is not in us. If we confess our sins, he is faithful and just and will forgive us our sins.

—1 John 1:8–9

Get this—sinners can now confess online. On a website called "The Confessor," people can type in their sins in the blanks provided. "This is between you and God," the web page says, "and your privacy is totally respected." The people who run it claim that whatever sins are listed will be erased immediately.

I think it's kind of silly actually, and so do Roman Catholics. "Confession cannot be done by telephone, e-mail, or by proxy," a spokesperson for the Roman Catholic church said recently. Catholics believe confession has to be done to a priest, face-to-face. I wouldn't go that far, but the idea of a cyberspace Jesus seems a bit goofy to me.

There's nothing goofy about confession. Think of the worst thing you've ever done—the worst. I'm serious. Go ahead. Think about something you've done or thought that's really awful. Whatever it is, it probably smells wretched and feels like hot tar in your heart. We've all got things we wouldn't tell a soul.

The Catechism says the first step every one of us has to take to know real joy in God is to know inside and out, up and down, through and through, how full of sin we are. We're just fooling ourselves if we think we're without sin, says John in our passage for today. And that's not easy for anyone to confess. Nobody wants to look bad. I don't want you to know what I'm thinking, and you don't want me to know what you're thinking. But if we own up to what we've done and what we are, then—and only then—can we begin to understand joy.

Brutal, isn't it? But that's what the Bible teaches.

Knowing our sin is necessary. The reason is simple—if we don't know in the depths of our hearts how much we need God, we will never know how incredibly much God loves us. We have to know what we absolutely *can't* do in order to understand the miracle of what God *can* do.

Jesus Christ takes us, with all our ugliness, and washes us perfectly clean. That's the gospel truth.

It hurts, Lord, to have to think of us at our horrible worst. It hurts terribly to think of ourselves as scummy sinners. But help us to confess that we aren't perfect, not at all. Help us to confess that we don't deserve the joy you give us. Help us know your love. Amen.

6

No Hoax

Q&A 3

How do you come to know your misery? The law of God tells me.

Therefore no one will be declared righteous in his sight by observing the law; rather, through the law we become conscious of sin.

—Romans 3:20

There's this poor guy, full of open sores, a beggar who doesn't have dirt his whole life. He eats by rummaging through rich people's garbage. His name is Lazarus.

Lazarus dies and goes to heaven, "to Abraham's side," Jesus says in his parable. This rich guy dies too, the one who used to throw out the garbage Lazarus gobbled. But the rich guy doesn't make it to heaven. He's in a place where the temperature is about four hundred degrees hotter. What's more, he sees Lazarus over on the other side not even breaking a sweat.

"OK, OK," the rich guy says to Father Abraham, "why don't you send Lazarus back to my five brothers to tell them this whole hell business isn't some cheap hoax. Please?" he begs.

"They have Moses and the prophets," Abraham says. In other words, they already have the whole truth.

"Wait a minute," the rich man says. "If I come back from the dead, that'll shock them into reality—a dead guy walking? That'll get 'em."

Abraham shakes his head—and this is the part that's unforgettable. "If they don't believe Moses and the prophets, they won't believe a dead guy either."

Amazing. Imagine this. Five wealthy drug lords—all brothers—out by the pool sipping drinks. Suddenly, out of nowhere, their dead brother walks up, smelling like a bonfire.

"Boys," he says, "I'm here to say you've got to change your ways."

Abraham says these brothers would laugh it off. They'd figure it was some kind of hoax. Why? Because they've already laughed off "the law and the prophets." They've already chucked the whole God business. A dead guy walking wouldn't mean a thing.

How do you know your sin? the Catechism asks. How do you know that you don't deserve God's love? The answer is short and to the point: "The law of God tells me." The Bible says the same thing in different words: "Through the law we become conscious of sin."

Believe me, that's no hoax.

Your law, Lord, is in our hearts. We know that you want us to live in ways that bring glory to your name. We know there are things we shouldn't do. But we also know that all too often we do them anyway. Have mercy on us, O Lord. Help us do better today and tomorrow. Amen.

What You Can't Do

Q&A 5

Can you live up to all this perfectly? No.

Love the L*ORD your God with all your heart and with all your soul and with all your strength.*

—Deuteronomy 6:5

When I was a kid, I wanted to be a high jumper. I wanted to defy gravity. It looked easy: you just take a couple steps, break into a trot, angle in toward the bar, put your left foot down really close to the pit, and jump up and over the bar.

So I worked at it. I studied the movements of Olympic stars, went out to the track, and worked hard at it. I approached the bar with their in-depth concentration, marked my steps so I'd come down perfectly, then shoved off with every bit of strength I had. My technique was probably OK. But I rarely made it over my bicycle.

Then I started to notice that real high jumpers' long, long legs start growing somewhere out of their rib cage. High jumpers are skinny, too—long rubbery legs and no butts. They're gangly and loose-limbed, not short and stumpy.

I'd seen enough mirrors in my life to know I wasn't outfitted in a high jumper's package. It was painful, but one day I realized I could have spent sixteen hours a day at the high jump pit and never have cleared more than five feet of gravity.

People tell kids to dream, and that's a good thing. People tell kids they can be whatever they want to be, and that's a good thing too. But it's not the whole truth, really. One of the toughest lessons of life is learning there are some things we'll never do, some dreams that will never come true.

The Bible and the Catechism say that we're supposed to love God with every last square inch of who we are. But then, like a slap in the face, comes the bad news.

"Can we live up to all of this perfectly?"

"No."

Ouch. No, we can't high jump into glory. No, we can't get our posteriors up and over the bar.

To win eternally, to high jump eight feet and come down an eternal champion is going to take more than what we've got. Taking the gold is going to require help.

We need a Savior.

Every day, in every school in the world, Lord, there are some people who don't make the team, don't win the contest, don't get the scholarship. When we don't make the grade, Lord, relieve our sadness. We don't measure up, so help us remember we're on your team. Thank you for cleaning up the mud and making us shine. Thank you for what your Son did for us. Amen.

8

Every Last One of Us

Q&A 6

Did God create people so wicked and perverse? No. God created them good and in his own image.

So God created man in his own image, in the image of God he created him; male and female he created them.

—Genesis 1:27

This week Leonardo DiCaprio graced the front of *Time* magazine. DiCaprio's face will be forever imprinted on the hearts of millions and millions of moviegoers because he was the star of the most-watched film of all time, *Titanic*.

DiCaprio's latest film—or so says *Time*—is a real dog. Every review I've seen says the same thing. Not even DiCaprio's famous face can keep this movie from going down like the real *Titanic*. But his face is still on the cover of *Time*. Why? Most likely because his face sells magazines. *Time*, like Hollywood, isn't stupid.

We all love a pretty face. Watch some movie with Julia Roberts or Hugh Grant sometime, and count every second they're seen close up. You'll be shocked how much of the movie is a portrait gallery.

So what do you think? When the Bible talks about people being made in God's image, is it talking about our looks? Or about our central nervous system, our bones and muscles, our mysterious eyes? Or about our ability to think or talk or make decisions? Just exactly how are we an "image" of God, like God?

I don't honestly know. But isn't it fascinating to think that God, the Creator of the universe, chose to make us ordinary human beings here on planet earth in his image? Yes, I know—we lost a lot of that image back when Adam and Eve ate that forbidden fruit. But we all still resemble our Maker. We can look at each other and discover something of what God is like.

Think of the kid most despised by all of your friends. Think of the kid you walk away from when school is over. Think of the kid you wouldn't date if it were just the two of you on earth.

Then remember this: each one resembles God. That makes every last one of us loveable, every last one valuable and important.

Your face may not look much like Leonardo's. But you—and every last one of us—look something like God. And that's even better.

Thank you for the image you've given us, Lord—every last one of us. Thank you that you made each person resemble you, the almighty Creator of the universe. Help us to remember that when we look at others. Amen.

It's Natural

Q&A 7

This fall has so poisoned our nature that we are born sinners. . . .

Therefore, just as sin entered the world through one man, and death through sin, and in this way death came to all men, because all sinned . . .

—Romans 5:12

- Faye Bolson's brother got picked up for driving drunk. The judge put him in the slammer overnight, and he can't drive for six months.
- Did you hear that Maria Fadiman is pregnant? You-know-who's the father, but they're not even going to get married and Maria's thinking of adoption. Can you imagine?
- Natalie's sister was in a drug bust at a party. She claims she's never once smoked a thing.
- Gregg's parents don't even know that he's sending this dirty Internet stuff to all his friends. He can get away with anything.

It's almost fun, isn't it? Wherever two or three are gathered, it's not hard to come up with an honor roll of sinners, because people mess up. And when they do—in public—they get all the headlines. We can have a lot of fun with sin, except when it hits us; then it's not so funny.

The Catechism doesn't talk much about sins—with an *s*. It talks instead about *natures*, and there's a humongous difference.

Rob's dad goes off for treatment for alcoholism, and everybody and their dog knows about it because it's easy to pick on the fallen. But what about me?

The Catechism doesn't focus on our flub-ups; instead it talks about what we *are*—all of us. We are "born sinners." That's our condition. Our very humanity—even though we look like God—has the mud of sin spattered all over it.

Spotting sin across the block is easy, interesting, and sometimes even fun.

But sin is in all of us. And looking for sin "over there" can comfortably keep us from looking within. Other folks' messes can make us feel good. That's called pride. And pride is nothing less than capital *S*, capital *I*, capital *N*.

Pride is Adam's sin—he wanted more and better. So did Eve. They did what God said they shouldn't. They ate of the forbidden tree.

Ever since, we've followed suit. Me first. We all sin, the Bible says. Every last one of us.

But we don't talk much about that, do we?

Forgive us for wanting the best for good old Number One, Lord. It's so easy to do, and sometimes it feels so good. Help us to see for ourselves that we're not as holy as we might think we are. Help us to see the potholes in our character that only your love can fill. And thank you for filling them. Amen.

10

Face It

Q&A 8

Are we so corrupt that we are totally unable to do any good and inclined toward all evil? Yes. . . .

We all, like sheep, have gone astray, each of us has turned to his own way. . . .

—Isaiah 53:6

Benji's in hot water. He's always been a good kid, never in trouble; but he and his buddies spun out of control last night and broke some windows at school. He didn't think they'd get caught. But they did. Benji says he sinned and he's sorry.

Jasmine gets irritated with Carolyn, who talks too much and constantly follows her around. Yesterday, she'd had enough. She told Carolyn she was sick of her. Told her to bug off—and worse. Now Jasmine's feeling awful. She knows she lost it. She knows she sinned.

Both Jasmine and Benji know that they sinned—that is, both know very well that they did something wrong. Now it's your turn. Fill in the blank: "I sinned yesterday when I ______________________." Chances are, most of us can fill in something without working up a sweat.

But when the Catechism talks about our sin here, it's not talking only about our screw-ups. It's not talking about sneaking a beer or putting our hands where they shouldn't have been or walking out of Wal-Mart without paying for the CD in your pocket. These are sins—don't get me wrong. But if you want to know the truth about you and me and the guy down the street, the Catechism says you've got to start with this—we sin. Now. In a half hour, even in a half minute. Sin is what we do, same as breathing. Same as eating and drinking. Because we are sinners, sin is what we do.

Today Jasmine told Carolyn she was sorry for saying all those mean things. And in his room, Benji prayed like he'd never prayed before, asking God to please forgive him. Both learned a lesson. Both are committed to staying out of trouble. But that doesn't mean they're not sinners. That doesn't mean they were dirty yesterday and today they're clean. That doesn't mean they're perfect.

The truth is, nobody's perfect. All of us—even the best of us on our best days—are sinners. It's what we are by nature.

Face it.

It would be great if we could decide not to sin, Lord, just for today. It would be great to think that we could do it, or that with your help we could be perfect. But we know we can't. We'll always—every last day of our lives—need your love to win. Thank you for being with us—always. Amen.

Unless . . .

Q&A 8

Are we so corrupt that we are totally unable to do any good and inclined toward all evil? Yes, unless we are born again, by the Spirit of God.

Jesus answered, "I tell you the truth, no one can enter the kingdom of God unless he is born of water and the Spirit."

—John 3:5

Years ago, my wife and I were youth counselors. One night we brought our group to a real revival in downtown Phoenix. The preacher, whose name I've forgotten, did a whole lot of jumping up and down and wailing, if you know what I mean.

During the altar call, one of our kids—one who wasn't known for his saintly behavior—decided to go up and, in the words of the revival preacher, "get saved."

On the way home that night, this kid—let's call him Mark—didn't say much. During the rest of the year, he didn't change much either. Sometimes he came to youth group, sometimes he didn't. When he was there, half the time he was goofing off.

I don't know if something big happened to Mark that night. He must be in his forties by now. I wonder if Mark's a Christian.

The Catechism asks, "Are we so corrupt that we are totally unable to do any good and inclined toward all evil?" And then it gives us one of those really blunt answers: "Yes"—but there's a comma, not a period. There's a catch.

"*Unless* we are born again, by the Spirit of God," it says. We need to be born again. That's what Jesus told Nicodemus in a secret meeting one night (John 3:1–15). So what does it mean to be "born again"?

Let's imagine that Mark is now a preacher at a small church in rural Arizona. He's married, three kids, plays a good game of golf. His wife plays keyboard at church and his kids are in the praise team. They're great people.

Is Mark finished sinning? Did he leave all his sin back at that revival? Has Pastor Mark reached perfection? Of course not. Even if that revival meeting changed his life completely, he still has to tell himself not to get ornery when people say stupid things. He still has to fight sin, just like everybody else.

But if Mark is born again, sin doesn't rule his life. It can still make his life miserable, but it doesn't rule. It isn't king. In Mark's heart, where sin still hangs out and always will, God Almighty is King. He rules. That's what it means to be born again.

And that makes all the difference.

When we do the right thing, Lord, and when we don't do the wrong thing, we know it's because you're piloting our lives in the right direction. Thank you for loving us, for not only being a lighthouse, but for being a whole direction system inside our very soul. Thank you for giving us a second birth. Amen.

12

It's Not My Fault

Q&A 9

[Humans] . . . in reckless disobedience, robbed themselves and all their descendants of these gifts.

God saw all that he had made, and it was very good.

—Genesis 1:31

My parents used to visit a state prison once a month. With a few other retired couples, they'd do a Bible study, sing some hymns, and munch down some of the goodies they brought along. They loved visiting prisons because the prisoners were so loveable.

Find that hard to believe? Not really. Lock yourself up in a room day after day with no one to see except other prisoners, and you'll understand how a visit from the outside world, not to mention triple portions of homemade chocolate fudge cake would seem almost heavenly.

But there was just one thing. Just about all of the guys my parents visited swore they were innocent. "Nope, didn't do it," they'd say, shaking their heads. "They got the wrong man."

The truth is every last one of us—in prison or out—will do every last thing we can to avoid that "guilty" label.

Think of it this way. You have a midnight curfew. One night you've got this great thing going with your friends, and nobody else is supposed to be home as early as you. All of a sudden it's late. Really late.

When you get home you open the front door as if you were cracking a safe, tiptoe upstairs in bare feet, then slip into bed so silently you don't even wake the cat.

Hall light comes on.

"That you?" your dad asks. "It's two o'clock!"

"I couldn't get a ride." The excuse leaps into your mind so fast you couldn't stop the words if you tried. You'll do every last thing you can to keep from getting nailed.

God demands that we be pure, but honestly and truly, we're full of sin. If that's true, the Catechism asks, then isn't God asking for something that's flat-out impossible? How fair is that?

The answer is hard to swallow. It's fair, all right. "God saw all that he made, and it was very good," says Genesis. Then we messed up. "In reckless disobedience, we robbed ourselves," the Catechism says. Our sin is our fault.

We shouldn't try to hang our troubles on God. We're the ones who made a mess we can't clean up. We need a Savior.

We admit it, Lord. We mess up. If we lived perfectly pure lives, we'd never have headaches; but we mess up. It's amazing how much you love us, Lord, how much you care. Thank you for your love. Help us to spread that love around. In Jesus' name, Amen.

Hell

You are not a God who takes pleasure in evil; with you the wicked cannot dwell. The arrogant cannot stand in your presence; you hate all who do wrong.

—Psalm 5:4–5

Q&A 10

As a just judge he punishes [our sins] now and in eternity.

Warning: parental discretion advised. Some violent content may be offensive.

Ever grab a hot plate just after it came out of the oven? You could spend the next hour with your fingers knuckle-deep in ice water and still not shake the pain. Ever burn the roof of your mouth on hot pizza? Could still hurt the next day.

When most of us think of hell, we don't think of a blizzard. We think instead of searing, scorching, scalding heat—lakes of fire, oceans of red, snapping flames. We think of people being hung over forest-sized flames like human hot dogs. We think of weeping and the awful sound of gnashing teeth.

Which is not to say we think about hell all that much. Most every night on TV you're likely to hear "Go to hell" a dozen times, but nobody means it—not literally. Few people really believe in hell. Even some people who profess faith in God don't like to think about hell, whatever hell is.

The truth is, we don't know exactly what hell might be like. If we believe the Bible, then we have to assume that hell is as real as the neighborhood we live in. But what's it like? All we know is that it makes the worst Stephen King nightmare look like a Disney weekend. That's because hell is forever. No bell dings after a fifty-year sentence; there's no possibility of parole; no death penalty will ever end the horror. Hell is an eternal place made unflinchingly desolate by the absence of God's love.

Here's the deal. Our holy God cannot let our sin—which is very real—go unpunished. No way. "He is terribly angry about the sin we are born with as well as the sins we personally commit," says answer 10. Much as we'd like to, we're not going to duck this. We can't blame someone else, and we can't clean up our own act. Apparently, hell is what we've got coming.

Thank God, there's more to the story. Stay tuned.

It's hard to imagine living without you, Lord. When you've been in our lives so close and lovingly, it's impossible to think of life without your love. Keep us forever in your hands, your loving hands. Amen.

14

More Than a Wink and a Nod

Q&A 11

God is certainly merciful, but he is also just.

And [the Lord] passed in front of Moses, proclaiming, "The Lord, the Lord, the compassionate and gracious God, slow to anger, abounding in love and faithfulness, maintaining love to thousands, and forgiving wickedness, rebellion and sin. Yet he does not leave the guilty unpunished. . . ."

—Exodus 34:6–7

Last week a student of mine sent me an e-mail. He thought he deserved better than the C he received. That C, he said, means the end of his scholarship. "Dr. Schaap," he wrote, "please check the grade book again, will you?"

I like this student. He isn't all that great at writing essays, but he comes to class regularly. He plays hockey and he's an all-around good guy. I'd really hate to see him lose his scholarship.

My heart says to change the grade. Who cares anyway? No one else in the class would ever know. Isn't keeping this great guy here worth more than one lousy grade hike? With a wink and nod, I could just change the grade.

What he wants from me, you see, is a break. And I want to give it to him. The fact is, he worked hard. He wrote papers over when I asked him to. "Schaap," he's saying, "show some mercy."

The trouble is, his grade book numbers don't add up to a B. What's more, I already did him some special favors when I allowed him to redo papers rather than receive what he should have for some pretty shabby work.

My heart says give him the B; my head says he doesn't deserve it. My merciful soul sheds tears for him; my sense of justice to the other students insists he didn't make the grade.

So did I change the grade? No. It hurt not to, but it wouldn't have been fair to the others in the class.

What do we do when a sense of justice and mercy conflict? We wince and worry; we don't sleep well.

Today's Catechism question is a smart one: How can God—who is merciful—send people tumbling off into hell? Shouldn't God's divine love simply excuse our measly little sins? How can God be both just and merciful?

The answer is unequivocal: God's justice demands that our sin be punished. We can't slip and slide out of what's coming to us. We earned hell (gulp!) with our disobedience. It's going to take more than a wink and a nod to save us from getting the penalty we deserve—a whole lot more.

Our disobedience is something that doesn't go away easily. We know that. We had choices, but we chose the wrong direction. Still do. But you graciously gave your Son. What a gift! Thank you, Lord, for saving us. Amen.

Self-Preservation

Q&A 12

According to God's righteous judgment . . .

But because of your stubbornness and your unrepentant heart, you are storing up wrath against yourself for the day of God's wrath, when his righteous judgment will be revealed. God "will give to each person according to what he has done."

—Romans 2:5–6

What do human beings want most out of life? Some people might say it's the perfect pizza. Others might suggest it's driving a Land Rover or having a condo in Mazatlan. Still others might opt for a loving family, a fun job, or a nice house.

Biologists would have a different idea. What humans want more than anything else, they'd say, is to stay alive. In other words, self-preservation. For instance, we can't live without breathing. But have you ever tried to stop breathing? Can't be done. The body won't let you.

Good old self-preservation. It's in all of us. Often it's a real blessing. We'll do everything we can to keep ourselves alive.

Self-preservation ought to be on our mind if we're paying attention to where the Bible and the Catechism have been taking us. Think about what we've learned so far. First, God Almighty created us good. Second, we didn't want the goodness God was offering, so we helped ourselves to the forbidden fruit. Third, God's mad. Fourth, we're doomed.

I know of more heartwarming stories.

But now listen to the questions:

Q. My goodness, how can we get out of this disaster? A. You can't; live with it.

Q. Isn't there anything we can do? A. Nope.

Q. How about we find someone else to take our rap? A. Grow a brain.

To me, the questions sound like they come from somebody who's doing every last thing possible to stay alive, somebody who's into self-preservation. In fact, they sound a lot like me. I'll do just about anything to get out of trouble.

But the answers are stingingly clear. There's nothing I can do. If I'm going to get something better than what I deserve, I can't make it happen. For any of us to escape the horror, something completely strange is going to have to happen. Something perfectly unbelievable. Something supernatural.

That's our real hope.

We can build houses. We can make freeways five layers high. We can do a lot of things, Lord, but we can't change ourselves. Only you can do that. Only you can find a way into every bit of who we are and change us. And you have. You are. Every day, help us to thank you for what you've done in our lives. Amen.

16

Powerball Dreams

Q&A 13

Can we pay this debt ourselves? Certainly not.

For all have sinned and fall short of the glory of God.

—Romans 3:23

Just for kicks, let's assume that I won last month's Powerball jackpot—a cool 225 million. (No, I don't play, but let's dream anyway.)

What do I do with all that cash? Well, taxes grab off 60 percent or so. No matter. I've still got almost 100 million to play with.

First I buy time. I quit my job to write books, but I need a nest egg to do that. Ka-chunk, ka-chunk (that's the sound of the cash register): 20 million tucked away in a stash.

Our two cars are getting old, so I want a new one—a BMW for long trips. Ka-chunk: 40 thou. Last week my son didn't buy a Honda Accord he liked because it cost too much money. Buy it: 12 thou. How about a really decent cottage at Lake Okoboji: figure 200 thou. Oh yeah—got to have one of those great bass fishing boats. Ka-chunk, ka-chunk—another 25 thou.

I've always wanted an addition to our house so my basement office admits more natural light. Ka-chunk, ka-chunk. Twenty thousand more.

Three scholarships for writers at the college where I teach (300 thou), ten gifts to the charities of my choice (500 thou), and a new set of golf clubs—another thousand. Oh yeah, a good laptop (my screen is kaput)—two thousand.

Even though by my tally, I've spent about one-fifth of the 100 million I raked up in that lottery windfall, I've got plenty left and my wish list is pretty much depleted.

Just imagine you were so rich you could have every last thing you wanted. Everything. You make the list.

You know something? I'm typing this while lying on a couch because not long ago I had back surgery and I'm not supposed to sit in a chair. I really wish I could buy a new back and end all the pain tomorrow; but I know there are some things that money can't buy.

For sure, you can't buy joy, not the eternal kind at least. You can't swap 100 million clams for deep-down happiness.

"Can any of us pay this debt?" the Catechism asks, and the answer is an unequivocal no. Not even the fattest of the fat cats.

Joy, forever, is going to cost a ton more than the greatest Powerball payoff.

All the big sales in the world, all the best cars, all the finest clothes finally mean nothing because the only thing that will be with us forever is your love. Dear Lord, thank you for giving us the most expensive gift of all—for nothing, for free. Your love makes us all rich. In your Son's name, Amen.

Heroic Canaries

Q&A 14

Can any other creature . . . pay this debt for us?

No man can redeem the life of another or give to God a ransom for him. . . .

—Psalm 49:7

I don't know anyone who has a canary. Parakeets, sure—lots of them. But then, parakeets are so ugly they're cute. They do strange little nodding dances, sing, growl, and grouch.

Canaries are yellow and they sing. Big deal. But maybe it's a shame there aren't more around because, after all, canaries are heroes. Someplace in North America there ought to be a big canary museum honoring yellow-jacketed heroes who gave their lives for others. For a lot of years, miners—those dirt-faced, lamp-helmeted workers who blast away in the bowels of the earth—wouldn't have gone below without their beloved canaries.

You see, someone figured out that the gases that arise from earth's innards could be deadly. What's more, some of those gases can't be detected by human beings. In other words, a whole company of miners could be jack-hammering away when—bingo—they'd just all die. No warning, no long periods of coughing or nausea—just sudden death.

Then someone else figured out that those deadly gases reach up and grab the throats of canaries much quicker than they grab human beings. So if miners hung a cage full of canaries way down in the earth somewhere, they'd always know if those sneaky deadly gases were hanging around. If they'd drop their picks for a minute, have a look at the cage, and find those canaries dead as doornails, they'd know to get out of the shaft, pronto.

Today, the people at PETA (People for the Ethical Treatment of Animals) wouldn't like the practice. Since animals have as much right to their square inch of creation as humans, they'd argue, those miners were doing a bad thing. Me? I don't like the idea of a whole cage full of dead canaries, but I like even less the idea of a whole mine shaft full of dead parents and spouses.

Whatever. I still think that someone should build a canary museum and dedicate it to those bright yellow heroes who gave their lives in the darkness of a hundred mine shafts, canaries who sacrificed themselves for others.

But all the canaries in the world—indeed, all the birds in the world and all the animals in the world—says the Catechism, won't be a sufficient sacrifice for the weight of God's eternal anger against sin, our sin. To get rid of the darkness of our hearts, it's going to take a whole lot more than a museum full of heroic canaries.

Not what my hands have done, Lord, can save my guilty soul. No hero is big enough or tough enough or loving enough. It took someone really special—it took the death of your own child, your own Son. Thank you, Lord. Amen.

18

The Supreme Sacrifice

Q&A 15

. . . one who is also true God.

In the beginning was the Word, and the Word was with God, and the Word was God.

—John 1:1

Every May, my grandma used to insist that our whole family attend the Memorial Day commemoration at the local cemetery.

In small towns today in the United States, these ceremonies are pretty much the same as they were when I was a kid. Usually the high school band plays and then a preacher or war veteran talks, often about the "supreme sacrifice" paid by those who gave their lives for freedom. Sometimes the speaker will wonder whether we as a nation are still capable of that kind of sacrifice. Then some veterans shoot rifles (blanks), somebody from the band plays Taps, and another high school kid, hidden like a ghost in the cemetery, plays them over again.

My grandma used to insist that we go, even though, as I remember, my parents didn't always feel like it on a sunny holiday morning. Grandma had a way of making everybody feel guilty if we didn't.

The reason was clear: her only brother was killed by a "one-pounder" in World War I. When those speakers talked about the supreme sacrifice, they were talking about her brother. A huge hole was left gaping in her heart when Edgar never came back from the killing fields of France.

Millions of soldiers died in World War I, more millions in World War II. Nobody wanted to die, of course, but all of them knew there was a cause more important than their individual lives, a cause worth dying for, worth giving "the supreme sacrifice."

Grandma's brother's sacrifice was huge—he gave his life for his country. But the Catechism says no created thing can pay the "supreme sacrifice" for all of our sin. No heroic soldiers, no freedom fighters, no human being, no creatures on earth can do that job. It's going to take someone that's much greater, much bigger.

The job that must be done to release you and me and my grandma and Uncle Edgar and every other human being from our darkness, that job requires someone more powerful than all creatures. That job requires nothing less than true God.

Thank you for the lives of the saints, Lord. Thank you for the lives of heroes, men and women who died because they were protecting other human beings. Thank you most of all for the gift of a God who became human, who came to live with us for a time, and then died so that we might live. Amen.

19

No Mere Mortal

Q&A 16

. . . but a sinner could never pay for others.

For Christ died for sins once for all, the righteous for the unrighteous, to bring you to God.

—1 Peter 3:18

Let's be blunt. The Catechism is arguing here that we're all going to hell—and hell's not some seamy Internet site either.

The only way out for any of us is if someone comes between our sin and God Almighty's justice. We need a lawyer, a go-between, a mediator. We need something or someone to take the biggest hit of all just for us, and we've already seen that that something or someone has to be much more than a hundred utterly selfless canaries or even an entire regiment of war heroes.

No ordinary human being is going to save us from the place no human being wants to go. Not even some extraordinary man or woman can do what's required. All of us, after all, have this condition called sin. If you think you don't have it—if you think you're without sin—you're only fooling yourself, the Bible says. We're all affected, so none of us can do the job.

Only someone like God can do the job, the Catechism says. Only someone bigger than life.

Ah, someone like, say, Superman—faster than a speeding bullet, able to leap tall buildings in a single bound? Superman can hear through walls, see through cement, even lift gravel trucks as if they were Tonka toys.

But even Superman has this problem with Kryptonite, right? One whiff and he's a wuss, Popeye without spinach. There are no real superheroes, no matter what Hollywood says. We're all alone here on earth, and we need something a whole lot greater than we are to deliver us from the impossible burden of our sin.

What we need is someone divine, someone holy. Banishing the darkness of our sin requires a light so bright it utterly wipes out the darkness.

The undeniable truth is that only God can save us. What we need is a Savior.

If we had all the money in the world, Lord, we'd try to buy our way out of darkness. But even that wouldn't be enough. You sent your Son for us—that's the truth. Please don't let us ever simply forget that it's your love that makes each of us sing. Thank you, Jesus. Amen.

20

Perfectly Stupendous

Q&A 18

. . . truly human and truly righteous.

Since the children have flesh and blood, [Christ] too shared in their humanity so that by his death he might destroy him who holds the power of death—that is, the devil. . . .

—Hebrews 2:14

All of this makes perfect sense, doesn't it? We can't save ourselves because we're human. So this mammoth job of saving us requires someone who is more than human, someone who is divine. That's clear. OK, who do we know who's divine? Well, Christ, of course.

If you've been brought up knowing the whole story, like me, the logic here is a piece of cake. Like basic arithmetic, it all adds up to (drum roll) Jesus Christ. Yawn.

Now hold on. Joe and Flo are sweethearts. They can't be apart from each other. It's sickening. When they're together, they're like leeches, stuck to each other's faces.

Finally—my goodness, finally—they get married. Now, everyone thinks, maybe they'll melt together like a sloppy sundae. You won't see Joe and Flo anymore, you'll just see FloJoe.

But that's not what happens. Joe and Flo get married, and they stop smooching each other in public. They sit on opposite sides of the car. Suddenly, you can live with them again.

Two people can't literally be one, despite what the marriage vows say. The closest lovers still think separate thoughts, breathe independently, and go to the bathroom at different times. Two humans just can't be one, no matter how deeply in love they are.

Now think of this. How can a God—a being beyond time and space, someone who knew your great-great-great-great-grandparents as well as you—how can such a God be a hicupping, nose-blowing, putty-bellied man?

Did you ever hear of a person who was half chicken? How about half fern? Humans are humans, right? You can't mix a human being with an organ-pipe cactus or a Rhesus monkey. It's impossible.

Well, so is the man/God Jesus Christ. You may have heard of him since you were knee high, but if you don't think of him as the most astounding miracle, then you really don't know him. He's human like us—and he's God. Both at once.

There's nobody like him and never has been. And, get this, he loves us.

Lord Jesus, what you did is perfectly astounding—coming to this world from a whole lot better place, then suffering rejection and pain, all for us. You were and are our only Savior. You loved us and you love us still. Our thanks for what you've done is our obedient lives. In your own name, Amen.

Breaking Up the Ice Jam

Q&A 18

Who is this mediator? Our Lord Jesus Christ.

For there is one God and one mediator between God and men, the man Christ Jesus.

—1 Timothy 2:5

I'm about to tell you a story you may not believe, but it comes from one of my students, and it's true.

Once there were two sisters. They were in their seventies, both of them widows. They lived in the same town.

Something of a rivalry existed between them because, well, they were different. One day, Sister One went to the other's house for tea, only to discover Sister Two gone. When she didn't return and didn't return (she was at the doctor or something and didn't get in right away), Sister One looked around Sister Two's house and started to clean. Seemed to her like a perfectly natural thing to do; she loved to clean. Unlike Sister Two.

When Sister Two came home, she threw a fit. She said things she shouldn't have (that happens sometimes). She read her sister's cleanliness as a criticism of her lack of housework, and she threw Sister One out like a spotted old mattress.

They didn't see each other for a while, and when they did, they didn't say a thing. A year passed—nothing but stony silence. Another year, and it became impossible for them to speak to each other because an ice jam of anger, resentment, and pride had formed between them. Another year, and another, and another. Here's the unbelievable part: these two sisters didn't talk for ten years.

Then one of the sisters died. And that's the saddest part of this otherwise almost funny story.

What those two sisters needed, more than anything, was someone to set them both down together. They needed someone to come between. They needed someone who would break the ice that had jammed up between them.

Ours was a similar dilemma. We sinned. God's judgment—God's justice—wasn't about to bend; so an ice jam of stony silence grew between us and the law of the Lord. Nothing was going to change.

And then, miraculously, there was a mediator, someone like us and—impossibly—like God too. Someone to come between, heal the division, bring us back into God's love.

"Who is this mediator?" the Catechism asks. "Our Lord Jesus Christ."

He stepped between. He blew away the ice jam. He did the job we couldn't.

He gave us the victory. Praise his name.

Because of your coming into this world for us, Lord, we have peace. Because of your taking our part, we can love. Because of your stepping in, our lives are filled with joy. Thank you for being our mediator. In your name, Amen.

22

Fundamentals

Q&A 19

How do you come to know this? The holy gospel tells me.

But these are written that you may believe that Jesus is the Christ, the Son of God, and that by believing you may have life in his name.

—John 20:31

Excuse my prejudice, but I'm an ex-football lineman. The truth is, when it comes to the gridiron, the skill players, the backs and the receivers, get all the glory. In football, the grunts get in mean crouches every time they approach the trenches, then hammer each other relentlessly for the entire game. Here's the way it goes: "26, 44, 46—hut," and just like that the meat men lunge into each other, trying to clear some daylight for those fancy-pants running backs.

Linemen usually are big and ugly, not sleek and quick. But without them, even the most lightning-quick tailback wouldn't gain a yard. That's because the fundamentals of football are blocking and tackling. Defensively, if you can't throw off a block or bury a shoulder into a ball carrier, the opposition is going to walk all over you.

Break the whole game down to its essentials, and that's what it's all about. Anybody who's ever played football knows that what happens in practice every day is drill after drill after drill. In what? You guessed it, the fundamentals.

Fundamentals are the key to any sport. If she can't dribble the ball up the field, the fastest girl on the team will ride the bench. If a kid can't bump a serve up to the setter, she won't play. If he can't handle the puck, he'd better try figure skating.

Fundamentals are what it all boils down to. Fundamentals are where everything begins. Fundamentals are bedrock.

So what do you think are the "fundamentals" of our Christian faith? What's the bottom line?

The answer is clear. If you want the fundamentals, says the Catechism, read the book. What really matters about faith is there already in Genesis, at creation—God's love and care for this whole world he fashioned out of nothing at all.

What really matters is there in the lives of Abraham and David, of Jeremiah and Ezekiel. Just pay attention to their stories, listen to what they say. They'll spell out the fundamentals.

What really matters is there in the bloody sacrifices of the Israelites (imagine getting blood all over you at church!). What really matters is there in the love behind the bloody sacrifice of God's own Son for our sin.

Want the fundamentals of the Christian faith? the Catechism asks.

Read the book. All you really need to know to win is there.

Thank you for the fundamentals of faith, Lord. Thank you for telling us the good news of salvation in the pages of your Word. It's all there. Amen.

23

Good News, Bad News

Q&A 20

Are all saved through Christ? No.

But small is the gate and narrow the road that leads to life, and only a few find it.

—Matthew 7:14

There's a kid down the block—I think his name is Aaron. I don't know much about him, but I know he's not a Christian. Nice kid, really. I used to walk home with him from school once in a while. Never said much, but once when I told him about my young people's group, he said he'd never been to church in his life. "My parents believe this God stuff is just a bunch of hooey," he said. "So do I."

Monica, a girl in one of my classes, always deliberately takes the opposite side in discussions from everybody else. One day we were talking about the novel *Brave New World,* and someone said that freedom included religion. Monica piped up, "Yeah, sure, and freedom *not* to have any religion too—like me."

Nobu Tanaka has more electronics in his room than anybody I know. There's an odd little shelf in their house, a God-shelf, our preacher called it. It's got all sorts of statues and stuff Nobu's family brought along from Japan.

I know this man at the store—Khalil. I know he gets time off from work every day to pray. But not to God—to Allah. Khalil is a devout Muslim, one of a growing number in North America.

Let's backtrack a minute here. Nobody can erase their own sin. That job requires no one other than the most unique person of all time—Jesus Christ.

The good news is that Jesus Christ has the power to make us—and all the people who believe on him—forever right with God.

The bad news is that not everyone will believe. Not everyone will be made right with God. Not everyone will gain eternal life.

Let's suppose that Khalil, Nobu, Monica, and Aaron do not believe in Jesus. They—and all others who have said "no" to Jesus—aren't going to be saved by the power of Jesus' blood.

The brutal truth is that I won't be saved—and neither will you—if I turn down Jesus as my Savior from sin. "Small is the gate and narrow the road that leads to life," the Bible says. Not everyone will find that road.

Jesus Christ is the only way. You know a Monica? Then you know your calling, too. We've got to tell the story.

Lord, you are the only road to salvation. By your grace help us to walk down that road. May our lives sing your praise. May everything we do witness to the world about your love. Help us to spread the good news to those who do not yet believe. Amen.

24

Tough Love

Q&A 20

Are all saved through Christ? No.

Whoever believes in the Son has eternal life, but whoever rejects the Son will not see life, for God's wrath remains on him.

—John 3:36

Sometime after 11:00 A.M. on the morning of April 21, 1999, two guys named Dylan Klebold and Erik Harris, armed to the teeth and dressed in military fatigues, walked into a high school in the Denver suburb of Littleton, Colorado, a place called Columbine.

I'm sure you know the rest of the story. By the time they raised their guns to their own heads, Dylan and Erik had killed thirteen of their classmates at Columbine High School.

You've probably also heard the story of Cassie Bernall, one of the kids who died. Whether the story is true or not is the subject of some debate, but it goes like this. When Dylan and Erik pointed their guns at her, they asked her if she believed in God. When Cassie said yes, they blew her away.

Some of you may remember another story about Columbine. Not long after the tragedy, people began to build a memorial near the high school. Thirteen crosses went up one night, and soon tons of flowers and other mementos made the place look like London after the death of Princess Di.

Then someone else put two other crosses up to symbolize the tragedy of the two murderers. Almost immediately, those crosses were jerked down. Most people didn't want to extend any sympathy to the cold-blooded killers.

That's understandable. Think of Erik and Dylan standing there pointing their semi-automatic rifles at Cassie Bernall. It's easy to hate those two guys, easy to make them demonic. It's almost sweet to think that right now those two are getting their reward for what they did.

Sometimes believers can take some joy in the fact that some people won't be saved, that Hitler is roasting in hell, for instance. It's even comforting to know that the evil oppressors of this world eventually get a taste of their own medicine. But remember Christ's dying words, "Forgive them, for they know not what they do."

Even though only some human beings will be saved, no believers should ever smile about the fact that some—even their persecutors—are going to hell. Another person's misery should never be our joy.

Vengeance is mine, the Lord says. Not ours.

Keep us from hate, Lord, even when it seems so natural. Keep us from pulling up our noses, from thinking we're better, from throwing people away. Keep us in your love, but keep us forever loving, as you are. That's tough, but help us, Lord, each day of our lives. Amen.

25

The Lessons of History

Q&A 20

Are all saved through Christ just as all were lost through Adam? No. Only those are saved who by true faith . . .

For God so loved the world that he gave his one and only Son, that whoever believes in him shall not perish but have eternal life.

—John 3:16

I've got this little vial on my shelf shaped like a tiny bottle of milk of magnesia. It's a relic. The label says it came from Greenwold's Drug Store in Grand Rapids, Michigan. Some long-dead druggist, maybe a century ago, once typed "Oil of Citron" across that label and sold it to my grandfather (I'm told), who likely used it to keep mosquitoes off himself and his kids. The label is so faded you have to look closely to see it.

I keep the bottle because it's a memento of my grandfather. It's old and really kind of cute, and no, I don't use what's left in it to keep off mosquitoes.

The Heidelberg Catechism has a history just as this little vial of oil of citron has a history. If you look closely, you can see it.

The whole discussion about "true faith" is a good example. One of the things that made Reformation leaders really upset about the Roman Catholic Church was their belief that the church and its priests stood between God and humanity. What the reformers preached was the necessity of people knowing God themselves, rather than just accepting the God delivered up to them by the church. That's why they wanted to read the Bible on their own. The reformers didn't want anybody running interference.

Question 20 was a radical question in its time because it made very clear that salvation comes only to those *individuals* who have true faith. Salvation isn't a gift from a priest but a gift from the Holy Spirit to *each* of us.

Question 21—What is true faith?—was and still is a biggie because it defines something really radical, the idea that people aren't saved by holy water or a papal blessing, but by the Holy Spirit who comes into their *individual* hearts.

What's the big deal, you say? For one thing, that kind of belief in the individual actually changed the world. Most of you reading this are living in some form of democracy, where *individuals* have a great deal to say about what happens in their lives.

But more importantly, no church worker or program is ever going to save you or me or the guy with the poodle down the street. Salvation belongs to the Lord.

If you believe that, the Catechism says, then you have "true faith."

Only you can save us, Lord. Only you can bless us forever with life and love. Only you are our Redeemer. Only you are our God. It's easy to say but sometimes hard to believe. Thank you for being our Lord, our God, and our Savior. In your Son's name, Amen.

26

Grafting

Q&A 20

Only those are saved who by true faith are grafted into Christ.

I am the vine; you are the branches. If a man remains in me and I in him, he will bear much fruit.

—John 15:5

We have an odd tree next door. Actually, in the neighborhood we live in, an old neighborhood, there are tons and tons of trees; but the one next door, maybe because it's so odd, is the one I seem to notice more than any other.

It's a maple, one of those maples with really broad leaves. It's probably twenty-five or thirty years old, so it's not full-grown yet, not half as big as our lindens just down the block. In fact, I don't think you'd even notice the tree if it weren't for one unusual feature.

About three-quarters of the leaves on that tree are perfectly dark green, as you'd expect. But the remaining one-quarter or so are variegated leaves that are almost yellow. Every fall that tree pulls color stunts that are just wonderful. It's like a joke, really.

I don't know whether someone grafted in a foreign branch when that tree was just a kid, long ago, or whether the tree itself is some genetic mutant. But I like it.

If you've ever worked in a greenhouse, you know what *grafting* is about. Let's say you want a bush with a really nice color, but you want it to grow better roots than it does on its own. Simple. Just take a small cutting from the pretty one, fuse it to the one with the good roots, lock up the graft with a rubber band, bury the joint in warm, moist soil, and let it grow for awhile, a year maybe. What you get—as if by magic—is a plant not unlike our neighbor's quirky tree—a little of this and a little of that.

When we say that believers are "grafted" into Christ, we mean that the real bush, the real vine, the real roots of our being saved are, of course, Jesus Christ. He's the tree, we're the branches that have been grafted in. In a way, we are the flowers of Christ. We're beautiful because we're planted deeply and eternally into his beauty.

The Bible teaches that not everyone is saved—only those who are made beautiful by being planted in nothing less than Jesus Christ.

None of us are original either. We're all grafts. Only Christ is the root. But to those who are in him, there's nothing better than the bountiful, beautiful life he gives.

Lord, every bit of who we are is bound up tight and growing because of your love. You are our root. You are what we live in and what we live for. You are our everything, Lord. You're our whole story. Thank you for letting us grow in you. Amen.

Head Knowledge

Q&A 21

True faith is not only a knowledge and conviction . . .

Now faith is being sure of what we hope for and certain of what we do not see.

—Hebrews 11:1

When your grandparents were kids, lots of teachers believed that reciting things—saying them from memory, "by heart"—was the way to learn. Ask your grandparents to recite a poem some time, or some passage of Scripture, or even Shakespeare. Lots of grandmas and grandpas can do it, because people used to think that "recitation," or memory work, was important.

Today, most teachers think it's not worth the hassle. And it is a hassle, especially if, like me, you're not good at reciting. Take learning the German language, for instance. I used to sit down with vocabulary words on little flash cards and try to smash them into my head by saying them over and over and over. The next day we'd have a quiz, and I'd be lucky to get a C. When it came to memorization, I seemed to have a learning disability. Still do.

But I do know Q&A 21—"What is true faith?" I had to learn it by heart. It wasn't easy, but today I'm happy I went through all the trouble of learning it. If you get a chance, take a look at this famous Q&A that so many people have learned before you. You may even want to learn it—and Q&A 1, another biggie—by heart.

My grandmother—she's been dead for twenty-five years—learned the entire Heidelberg Catechism in Dutch, even though she didn't understand the Dutch language. Some people in church thought the Heidelberg Catechism couldn't be understood in English, I guess. So she didn't learn it in the language she spoke, but the language of her church. You could say that she didn't learn the Catechism by heart, she learned it by head. She knew every word, but didn't have a clue what it meant.

Faith, the Catechism says, is more than head knowledge. Some people know absolutely everything there is to know about Christianity. Some people know everything there is to know about the historical Jesus. But head knowledge alone isn't faith.

We can know the Heidelberg Catechism. We can know the gospel. We can know all the books of the Bible. But that doesn't mean we have faith.

True faith is more than head knowledge. It's a whole lot more than that.

No matter how much sense all of this makes, no matter how well we know it in our heads, no matter how much we know about Paul and Barnabas, no matter how much we can recite—if we don't know all of that to be the truth in our hearts, it means nothing, Lord. Come into our lives and make us know, inside and out, that you love us, forever and forever. Amen.

28

No-Brain Faith

Q&A 21

True faith is not only a knowledge and conviction . . .

Now this is eternal life: that they may know you, the only true God, and Jesus Christ, whom you have sent.

—John 17:3

Not so long ago I read a story about a man who had tons of problems with drugs and alcohol. He'd gone through multiple divorces and had enough emotional problems for a file as thick as a phone book.

But then he learned that truth isn't something you can find in a bottle, and that joy isn't something you can smoke or snort. He got saved from his own horrors, and today he's living a whole new life, born again, as it were, by his new and precious faith.

You think it was Jesus Christ who saved him? Wrong.

He claimed he'd found meaning in a system of belief that existed on earth long before Christianity, something thousands and thousands of years old—ancient pagan rituals.

I'm not making this up. To read the article, you'd think that this guy had experienced a real Christian conversion. He had turned away from his old, messed-up life of sin and turned toward something he thought was a lot better. He was, he said, genuinely happy.

The Catechism says true faith is not *only* a knowledge and a conviction, but it doesn't mean it's *not* a knowledge and a conviction. It's that—and more. Yesterday, I tried to make it very clear that true faith was more than head knowledge. I'm not taking that back; but I am saying that true faith requires some knowledge.

You've got to be able to recognize the difference between Jesus Christ and ancient pagan rituals. Not everything that makes you feel good is Jesus Christ. In fact, having Jesus Christ in your life can be downright uncomfortable.

Look, it's kind of scary, but some conversions may well be phony baloney. Jesus Christ, on the other hand, is very real. His birth was in a barn. His death actually happened. So did his resurrection.

True faith is not only a sure knowledge, but it is partly that. We have to know Jesus Christ. We have to know what the Bible says is true. You can't be a Christian if you know nothing of the truth of the King of Creation, the Savior of humankind, and the Spirit that convicts us.

You can't have a no-brain faith.

Lord Jesus, help us know you—really know you—better and better throughout our lives. Thank you for the joy you bring us, and help us learn more and more about your love. Help us grow from nine to ninety. Thank you for things like the Catechism that help us know you better. Amen.

What Is Truth?

Q&A 21

. . . that everything that God reveals in his Word is true . . .

Sanctify them by the truth; your word is truth.

—John 17:17

I believe the Bible tells the whole truth. How about you?

Sure, you say—of course. The Catechism says it: "True faith is . . . a knowledge and conviction that everything God reveals in his Word is true. . . ."

It's just that simple.

Maybe you've heard the word *fundamentalism.* Then again, maybe not. Wars (not bloody wars, but wars nonetheless) have been fought about fundamentalism. Fundamentalists are people who take the Bible to be literally true—every word means exactly what it says.

This little phrase of the answer to the question about true faith is really a minefield. You don't even have to step off the path to blow yourself up.

When Pilate asked Jesus, "What is truth?" he wasn't just whistling Dixie. If you think that knowing exactly what the truth is, is simple, you're wrong. It isn't.

But that doesn't mean we can't know the truth at all. What, really, is the truth of the Bible? What does the Bible teach us that is absolutely true?

The Catechism says "everything." But if we really believe everything the Bible says is true, then why do women cut their hair? After all, the Bible says they shouldn't. The truth about "the truth" is that not every last word and phrase, not every allusion or story is literally and forever true. One of the toughest parts about living as a Christian is separating what is eternally and forever true from what isn't.

I'm about to step into that minefield. If I get blown up as I write this sentence, you'll know why.

Some things that are fundamental about the Bible, that are forever true, you already know: Through Adam we all sinned—and sin. Because we sin, we wander, trying to find our way through a host of wildernesses. *But* there's a Savior—a God/man who came to this earth, told us the good news, was crucified, and laid in a burial vault. But then—miracle of miracles—he walked out as if he had never left the land of the living.

That's the truth. The TRUTH (upper case) is our sin and Christ's redemption. The truth is our eternal life in him. True faith is a knowledge and conviction that through his blood we are saved forever.

That's what's fundamental. That's the truth. That's the forever-truth.

Thank you for the truth, Lord. Thank you for helping us get the whole truth from your Word. Thank you coming into this world, carrying all of our sin. Thank you for dying for us. Thank you for rising again and taking us with you forever and ever. Amen.

30

The Leap of Faith

Q&A 21

True faith is . . . also a deep-rooted assurance. . . .

Yet [Abraham] did not waver through unbelief regarding the promise of God, but was strengthened in his faith and gave glory to God, being fully persuaded that God had power to do what he had promised.

—Romans 4:20–21

You and your family are riding down the highway. In front of you is one massive semi hauling along some rig for gouging the earth in an iron mine. What's holding the thing on the trailer is—well, you're not sure what.

Now, who's to say the guy who chained that monster down wasn't half asleep or daydreaming? Face it, that monster rolls off when you're behind it and your whole family is history.

People don't think about such things very often. We take for granted that the monster machine won't roll off the trailer when you and the eighteen-wheeler are both doing seventy miles an hour.

Often enough, we live by faith. We assume that the meat we pick up at the grocery store isn't swarming with *e coli* bacteria. We have faith that the sandals we buy won't give out after one day at school. We really do live by faith.

Think about this: You weren't there when someone chained that monster machine down, just like you weren't there at Golgotha or the empty tomb.

Nobody can conclusively prove that Jesus Christ died for our sins. Nobody—not even a dream-team lawyer—can convince people that they need a Savior or even that there is a Savior. You can't explain Jesus Christ like you can lightning or computer chips.

So you've got to believe that the guy who tied down that monster machine did his job. You've got to be absolutely assured that what we've been talking about since you opened this book is true.

That's a jump, right? That's the great leap of faith.

We need the kind of deep-rooted assurance we have that tomorrow, after the darkness of night, the whole earth will turn once again toward the sun and the light will return. We don't even think about that. Yet we all have this assurance that tomorrow morning will dawn. No doubt about it.

The Catechism says that true faith is the blessed assurance that everything God reveals in the Scriptures is dead-on truth. True faith is conviction.

I'm sure about that.

Strengthen our convictions, Lord. Where there are people who wonder, give them answers. Where there are people who aren't sure, give them conviction. Help us to believe without worry or doubt or fear that everything you tell us is true. Remove our doubt and help us to see. Amen.

The Gift

Q&A 21

. . . created in me by the Holy Spirit through the gospel . . .

"But what about you?" he asked. "Who do you say I am?" Simon Peter answered, "You are the Christ, the Son of the living God." Jesus replied, "Blessed are you, Simon son of Jonah, for this was not revealed to you by man, but by my Father in heaven.

—Matthew 16:15–17

Some Christians think of unbelievers as consumer targets for spiritual sales. Some count the number of people they've saved as if those people were war scalps. It's true that no believer can deny the importance of telling others the good news of salvation. Christians who don't share their joy must not have much of it themselves. Evangelism is not only a responsibility, it's as natural to believers as breathing.

But when we start to think that we are saving people, we're dead wrong.

Billy Graham has ministered to millions during his long career as an evangelist. By way of his worldwide preaching, countless people have come to know the Lord. But Reverend Graham would never say that he saves people. Neither do you. Neither do I. Nobody *(no body)* saves people.

True faith, says the Catechism, is "created in me by the Holy Spirit through the gospel." That's right. Faith is a gift, the greatest gift you could ever get for any Christmas, for all the Christmases of your life. It is a gift so huge it's beyond all measuring.

Human beings don't change other human beings' hearts. We can spell out salvation in a tract, in a cartoon, in a three-hour TV special, in a movie with a cast of thousands. We can preach it forever, show it daily, wear it on our face like a ceaseless smile. But our best efforts won't do a thing if the Spirit—as in Holy Spirit—doesn't work in our lives.

Take the human heart: full of sin, full of itself, full of what we want, what we need, what we think is good for us. Then turn that human heart around, make it mindful of its own weakness and assured of its need of a Savior. Then take the human will and wrestle it to the floor so that it comes to understand that it can't do diddly without the Lord God Almighty. That's a huge job, so big nobody can do it—except the Lord, through the Holy Spirit.

Faith is a gift. It's not something we grow like body hair, nor something we can develop, like a cross-over dribble. It's something we're given.

Faith is created in us by the Holy Spirit.

Thank you for engineering something astounding in our hearts, Lord. Thank you for pulling off a stunt that's almost unbelievable. Thank you for giving us faith. Thank you for convincing us of our need for you. In Jesus' glorious name, Amen.

32

Sheer Grace

Q&A 21

. . . out of sheer grace earned for us by Christ . . .

For it is by grace you have been saved, through faith—and this not from yourselves, it is the gift of God—not by works, so that no one can boast.

—Ephesians 2:8–9

It's preposterous. It's plains nuts. It's sheer lunacy.

This student in my class wrote a story about a paraplegic kid who became a baseball pitcher of some renown in a club league. I figured it was made up, fiction. After all, I was teaching a class on fiction.

It's my job to critique those stories, to make sure that the writer creates "believable" characters. Now while I spent a few innings pitching myself in my day, I spent most of my college baseball career as a catcher. I know that what makes a chucker is legs. You've got to push off the rubber to get the weight of your body up into your hand and onto the ball. Pitchers run for spring training because the legs are key.

It's sheer lunacy, I told my student. No paraplegic is going to be a good pitcher.

Wrong, she said. I know. I was there. My criticism, she could have said, was sheer nonsense.

Sheer, according to my dictionary, means "unqualified" or "utter," as in "sheer courage." I told my student the idea of a pitcher who was paraplegic was utter, unqualified nonsense. But I was wrong. She was right. It's happened before.

Let's just stay with that word *sheer* for a moment. The Catechism says that our forgiveness is something we receive out of "sheer grace." In other words, "That's it; nothing else." We get saved for eternity out of "sheer grace," unqualified, unadulterated, unsullied. Just grace, nothing more.

We might think that if we do everything right—treat others kindly, smile a lot at Mom and Dad, sing lots of praise songs, never pick on our bratty little brother or sister, never cuss, never miss church—then we "get" salvation.

Dead, dead wrong. We "get" salvation by "sheer—that is, unqualified—grace." The Bible puts it this way: "For it is by grace you have been saved, through faith—and this not from yourselves, it is the gift of God." That's a verse worth learning by heart.

Grace, like faith itself, is a gift. We don't earn it by brownie points or perfect church school attendance.

God's grace has nothing to do with the strength in our legs or arms or shoulders, because sheer grace—and nothing else—makes us all eternal champions, no matter what our problems.

That's it—grace alone. Sheer grace.

Lord God Almighty, thank you for what you've done for us for eternity, something we've not earned, your gift. In Jesus' name, Amen.

At-one (ment)

Q&A 21

. . . my sins forgiven . . .
been made forever right
. . . been granted salvation.

And by that will, we have been made holy through the sacrifice of the body of Jesus Christ once for all.

—Hebrews 10:10

Once upon a time, it surprised me to realize that words have histories. I don't know why I was surprised; after all, nobody in, say, 1865, would have used the word *jetliner* because the truth is, there weren't any.

The computer has introduced countless words into the English language: *download, e-mail, Internet, motherboard, cursor*—you can easily add to the list. It has also rejuvenated some others that had almost disappeared to many of us: *icon,* for instance, a word you might not otherwise have encountered for years and years and years, but everyone knows today.

A whole ton of the words people ordinarily use when they talk about the Christian faith migrated into the English language years ago from Latin, by way of the French. Words like *sanctification, justification, communion*—whether or not you know what they mean—come to our language by way of English history.

A word like *sanctification* is really important. But for most of us, learning what it means is somewhat difficult because it's a word we just don't use every day. When was the last time you used *sanctify* in a sentence?

But one of those kinds of Latin words is really beautifully descriptive and so it's easy to learn. That word is *atonement.* OK, I know we don't use that word every day either. But the two root words that make up *atonement* are words we do use all the time: *at* and *one.*

Atonement is nothing more or less than the act of making things *at one.* Our "atonement" therefore is, very simply, God making us "at one" with him.

I say this because the end of question 21 is chock-full of joy. True faith, it says, isn't only a knowledge, it's a conviction, created by the Holy Spirit, that from nothing more or less than grace itself—here's the knockout punch—I am forgiven and given eternal life. I'm paraphrasing, of course, but you get the idea.

Truth faith is our assurance that we are *at one* with God. God has taken us out of our loneliness and sin, picked us up lovingly, brought us to him, and made us "at one" with him. All the high walls that sin has set between us and God have been broken down. We are "at one" with our Lord.

There's no greater gift.

In our prayers, in our Bible reading, in our rides to school and our rides back, in everything we do, Lord, bring us ever closer to you. Thank you for our atonement, for your love bringing us home to you. Bring us even closer every day. Amen.

34

More Than Just a Warm Heart

Q&A 22

What then must a Christian believe?

Always be prepared to give an answer to everyone who asks you the reason for the hope that you have.

—1 Peter 3:15

I just finished reading a horrifying book, *Fair, Clear, and Terrible,* the story of a group of believers a century ago who lived in the state of Maine at a place they called Shiloh.

The book isn't scary because the Christians were killed by some ferocious monster. It's scary because it's about Christian believers who pushed things way too far. The leader was a man named Frank Weston Sandford, a man who had great faith. About that there's no question.

What bound the people of Shiloh together were some powerful strategies for living. For instance, they all carried out jobs in the settlement, but few ever made any money. They believed God would provide for all their needs, if only they had true faith.

Mr. Sandford spent most of his days in prayer. Often, at a moment's notice, the whole community would respond to the tolling bell and spend hours in prayer, trying to discover sin in themselves and each other and to get rid of it, like a bad cold.

Eventually Sandford, in my opinion, went wacky. He began to think of himself as Elijah, and then as a present-day David. Nonetheless people jumped when he told them to, and thought of his word as something close to Scripture.

But the whole community went poof! Today there's no Shiloh. Sandford and his followers wanted to be the very best Christians on the face of the earth. But the dream fizzled like some third-rate sky rocket.

The Catechism has been looking at "true faith" (Q&A 21). The next question could have been, "How does it feel to have true faith?" Instead, the question is, "*What* must a Christian believe?" True faith, it says, starts with content, with a body of knowledge. We need to know *what* we believe.

Peter says the same thing in different words: Always be ready, he advises, to explain your hope in Jesus, your beliefs, to someone who asks.

Take a look at the history of Christianity and you'll find a number of Frank Sandfords. Many of them look for all the world like marvelous Christians. But the Catechism reminds us that Christianity isn't just a warm heart. Truth faith is faith *in* something.

In the readings that follow, we'll begin to see exactly what that something is.

Keep us humble, Lord. Keep us thoughtful. Keep us from believing that we know it all. Keep us committed to truth but ever capable of love. Amen.

The Whole Thing

Q&A 22

What then must a Christian believe?
Everything God promises us in the gospel.

All Scripture is God-breathed and is useful for teaching, rebuking, correcting and training in righteousness. . . .

—2 Timothy 3:16

I know people who think that the Ten Commandments should never be read in church. Why? Because they believe that our world is completely different than the world the Israelites knew before Christ. Back then, they say, people lived under the law: You've got to do this, you've got to do that. Today we live by grace, not by a bunch of laws.

In the Old Testament, for example, people lived by the slogan "a tooth for a tooth." But in the New Testament, Jesus taught forgiveness: "Father, forgive them for they know not what they do." Today it's a whole new world.

That sounds good, but if it results in throwing out much of the Old Testament, it's a pretty weak argument. Jesus himself said that he came not to abolish the law and the prophets, but to fulfill them (Matt. 5:17). And Paul claimed that *all* Scripture is God-breathed (inspired), not just some of it (2 Tim. 3:16).

During World War II, some Christians were active in the resistance movement in occupied Europe. For years, scholars have attempted to figure out why some believers risked their lives to save Jews while others looked the other way. Some researchers claim that the believers who took the Old Testament—the story of the Israelites—seriously were often those who risked their necks for Jewish people. They rescued Jews because they knew that Jews were God's people too; they knew it because they believed the Old Testament.

The Catechism gives a very simple answer to the question "What must a Christian believe?"

"Everything God promises us in the gospel," it says. We know from other questions and answers that by *gospel* the Catechism means the whole Bible, not just the first four books of the New Testament, which we usually call gospels.

"So what's the big deal?" you say.

The Bible is the Holy Bible. You can't just toss half of it down the chute. The whole thing fits together like a great story. Already from the beginning it talks about God, and God's love, care, and rule. Part of God's rule is the gift of Jesus, God's Son, who died for us.

It all fits together. Just listen to Handel's *Messiah* sometime.

Here's where our knowledge of faith and belief begins—with the Holy Bible.

For years, people have called believers people of the Book—with a capital B. Because we are.

Thank you for your Word, Lord. May we always stay close to the Book and its gospel of love. Amen.

Discuss—But Don't Fight!

Q&A 22

What then must a Christian believe?
Everything God promises us in the gospel.

Do not put out the Spirit's fire; do not treat prophecies with contempt. Test everything. Hold on to the good. Avoid every kind of evil.

—1 Thessalonians 5:19–22

As I write this today, the Southern Baptists, meeting in Orlando, Florida, are discussing a ruling that declares women should not be preachers.

That's odd, because the Southern Baptists already have a whole bunch of practicing women preachers. Nonetheless, a study committee determined that what the Scripture says about women should extend to the world of the church. Today they'll vote. Tomorrow women preachers in that large denomination may well be told they should stop preaching because it's not a biblical practice.

I probably don't have to tell you that church people argue a lot about what they believe. I once thought that the denomination I'm a part of was the absolute best at blasting each other. Then I wrote a book for a broadcast ministry and interviewed people from a variety of Christian backgrounds. I quickly discovered that members of my church aren't the only ones to whale away at each other. Everybody does, often in the name of Jesus. Go figure.

The Catechism says we are to believe "everything God promises in the gospel." That sounds easy, right? After all, don't we all believe in Jesus as our Savior and Lord? What could be clearer?

Sorry. It's not always that clear or easy.

Lots of Christians used to believe that God loved slavery. They were dead wrong.

Everything we need to know is in the gospel, but that doesn't mean everything we need to know is as clear as a mountain stream. It certainly doesn't mean that the church has been dead-on right for the last millennium or two. We know it hasn't.

We have to continue to discuss these issues in a gentle way that doesn't divide the church. "Test everything," says the apostle Paul. "Hold on to the good. Avoid every kind of evil."

Living the Christian life doesn't mean leaving your brain at the door when you enter the church. It means continuing to think about what a Christian must believe and practice.

Living by faith means trusting God always, more than anything else, even our own best ideas.

Dear Lord, keep your people from quarreling endlessly, as we have so often in the past. Keep us open to each other, keep us loving. Forgive us, today and always, when we fight. Help us to love as you do. In Jesus' name, Amen.

A Creed Beyond Doubt

Q&A 22

. . . a creed beyond doubt, and confessed throughout the world.

"I pray . . . that all [believers] may be one, Father. . . ."
—John 17:20–21

In A.D. 403, Huan Hsuan, emperor of Eastern Chin, a segment of what we now know as China, posed a question to a leading monk named Hui-yüan: Should a monk bow before the king? At that time, half the entire world was Buddhist. Hui-yüan told him that the spiritual lives of monks removes them from any obligation to bow to the monarch. The emperor said OK.

In Africa, the Kingdom of Ghana had achieved a high level of civilization, including advanced metal working and a widespread trading network.

In Central America, the Mayans had developed a system of writing with which they recorded astronomy, religion, and history. They developed a calendar more accurate than any other used around the world.

In A.D. 495, Clovis I, King of the Franks, then a pagan, was losing a battle against a rival Germanic tribe when he called on the Christian God for assistance. The Franks won the battle, and Clovis and his entire army were baptized.

All these things were happening in the world about sixteen hundred years ago at the time the Apostles' Creed was first being repeated throughout the Christian world.

It's difficult for North Americans, bombarded as we are with the here and now, to imagine that real people were alive and kicking that long ago. It's difficult to imagine that, like us, they worried about food and shelter and work. Like us, they prayed to God.

Just think of this as we go through the Apostles' Creed, as we are about to do. Remember that we'll be discussing words and ideas that Christians around the world have been saying for more than sixteen hundred years.

For several centuries it was simply assumed that the creed was, in fact, written by the twelve apostles. Each of the apostles, the story went, contributed one part of the creed. Although that's not what really happened, the creed does indeed express the faith of the twelve apostles and of the early Christian church.

When you say the Apostles' Creed, remember that Christians of every tribe, every nation, every headgear and footwear, every color of eyes and every shape of nose, every language and culture, are saying it with you, just as they have for almost two thousand years.

Just think of that. And praise God.

You have gathered people from every tribe and nation, from every street corner, from every acre of rural cropland. Thank you for making us all one through the gift of faith. Amen.

38

It's Simple—and It Isn't

Q&A 24

How are these articles [of the Apostles' Creed] divided? Into three parts. . . .

Believe in the Lord Jesus and you will be saved. . . .

—Acts 16:31

Let's summarize.

See Martha Pringle, that fat lady, walking into church? My goodness, don't you wish she'd lose a hundred pounds? And look at that huge bag she's got for a dress. Why doesn't she get a life?

Our minds and hearts veer off on bad paths. We make fun of some people and hurt others, and we want the best for ourselves. Sin is as much a part of us as the shape of our fingernails or the size of our feet.

Why do I always mock people? Last Sunday I sat right behind Martha, and I saw her cry when she sang "Amazing Grace." She may not be glamorous but she's a lot better person than I am. I'm sick of being me.

We want to be more than we are, but we can't, not by ourselves.

How can I not feel grubby for what I think about Martha Pringle and Emily Martin and Travis Blanchard? And what I say too. Jesus, help me.

We need a Savior.

That seems so simple. I ask Christ to come into my heart and just like that I'm a whole new work of art? That's all? It's too simple.

Yes and no. It is that simple and it isn't. There are two right answers here. Yes, becoming part of the family of God is very elementary. It's just a matter of believing. "Believe in the Lord Jesus and you will be saved," says our Scripture verse for today.

But the whole truth isn't that easy. What the Catechism is going to explain is the truth about being a Christian. Everything you ever wanted to know about faith.

We should never forget that we're talking about God here, the Being who knows every star and every planet, every mind and every heart, every hair on your head. We're talking about a Being far too complex for us to understand but—wonder of wonders—a Being who loves us. That much we know.

Want to know a good rule of thumb, something to live by? Try this. "I know God is real, but I sure don't know everything."

"How are these articles divided?" asks the Catechism. "Into three parts . . ."

It's just that simple—and it's not. There's always more, because God is not us—God is God.

Don't ever forget it.

Awesome God, the way to you is simple and clear. We know that. Yet you are far beyond our understanding. Help us to learn as much about you as we can. And to always believe in you. Amen.

Into Three Parts

Q&A 24

How are these articles divided? Into three parts: God the Father and our creation; God the Son and our deliverance; God the Holy Spirit and our sanctification.

In the beginning God created the heavens and the earth.

—Genesis 1:1

For God so loved the world that he gave us his one and only Son . . .

—John 3:16

But when he, the Spirit of truth, comes, he will guide you into all truth.

—John 16:13

It's easy to become a believer in God. All you've got to do is ask.

But understanding what being in God's family requires takes a lot more than a lifetime. If your grandfather or grandmother is a Christian, just ask one of them. Say, "Grandma, do you know everything about God?"

My guess is she'll laugh. Not at you, at the silliness of the question.

So let's start learning "the truth."

God is God, right? But God acts in a variety of ways, which is to say that God does a whole lot of things.

First off, God created the world. In the most incredible magic show ever staged, God Almighty turned light into darkness, whisked sea back from land, fashioned a dolphin, then made a human being—every last inch, from hair follicles to sciatic nerve to pinkie. Poof! Just like that, God made the first human being.

The Apostles' Creed talks about our God as Creator, epic-maker, showman, artist par excellence (think of the leopard), architect (picture the Canadian Rockies or the Grand Canyon), and comic (ever see a millipede?). Our amazing God takes our breath away.

But that's not the whole story. That God who made us loves us so much that he gave up his one and only Son for our deliverance. The Apostles' Creed also tells us about God the deliverer, who graciously gave us life. Bless God's name.

And there's more. Once that boulder before the grave was rolled away as if it were Styrofoam, once Jesus arose and ascended to his throne, he didn't leave us behind. He sent us the Holy Spirit to give us the strength and courage and vision we need.

The truth is, the Bible says, God has acted in three distinct ways since the beginning of earthly time: God created us, God delivered us, God sanctified us.

That's what we know. It's all we know, but it's enough to send one huge chill up your spine.

Thank you, Lord, for creating the world so beautiful that it takes our breath away. Thank you for your Son, who died for us. And thank you for your love that sends us out into the world you loved, singing your song. Amen.

The Trinity

Q&A 25

. . . three distinct persons are one, true, eternal God.

And I will ask the Father, and he will give you another Counselor to be with you forever—the Spirit of truth. The world cannot accept him, because it neither sees him nor knows him. But you know him, for he lives with you and will be in you.

—John 14:16–17

If I drive about ten miles west into the Iowa countryside, then take a left to an old cemetery, what I see out west is a sky as wide as forever, a huge blue quilt over the brilliant greens of the prairie, nothing but forever land and sky.

Just sitting there makes me think about the immensity of God. At the old cemetery I can't help but think about how small we are and how huge God is.

* * *

When I was a kid, my favorite verse was Matthew 11:28: "Come unto me all you who are weary and burdened, and I will give you rest."

I wish I knew why I found that verse so great. Christ says if we're tired and overworked, if we've got too much sadness or pain or hurt, he'll handle it personally. Something about that I liked—I still do.

* * *

If we were to ask any ten Joes or Ritas along the street what they think of Matthew 11:28, chances are some would shrug their shoulders. But some might smile, as if these words tasted like the sweetest chocolate in the world.

Like I said, I'm not sure why I liked that verse so much when I was a kid. But I do know this—I found those words comforting because something was working in me to find it so.

* * *

The word *trinity* doesn't even appear in the Bible. Yet Christians for all times have known that God functions in different ways.

I know God the Father is *above* me. I feel God's immensity in the broad prairie landscape.

I know Jesus Christ is *for* me because I believe that passage in Matthew. I know all who trust God will find rest in God.

And I know what Jesus says in Matthew is absolutely true because the Holy Spirit is in me, convincing me of God's own truth.

God the Father is *above* me, Jesus is working *for* me, and the Holy Spirit is working *in* me.

That's not three Gods—it's one God in three persons.

Thank you for being our Father, Lord. Thank you for being our Savior. And thank you too for being the Spirit that lives in us, even today. Thank you for being one God in three persons. Amen.

41

So Big

Q&A 26

. . . who out of nothing created heaven and earth and everything in them . . .

"This is what the Lord *says—your Redeemer, who formed you in the womb: I am the* Lord*, who has made all things, who alone stretched out the heavens, who spread out the earth by myself. . . .*

—Isaiah 44:24

If I want to buy milk, I walk three blocks. Bananas are five blocks away. Church is three blocks. Work is five minutes. If I started at one end of town and walked all the way to the other side, it would take less than an hour. Sioux Center is not a big place.

Last year I set my feet down in two mega-cities far, far away. São Paulo, Brazil, a huge industrial and financial center, is the largest city in South America and one of the largest cities in the world. Eighteen million people live in the greater metropolitan area. It took forever to drive from one end to the other; I don't want to guess how long it would take to walk.

Two months later I visited Tokyo, a jumble of skyscrapers and the political, cultural, and economic capital of Japan. Thirty million people live in Tokyo or somewhere close, and trains bring residents everywhere. Ride those trains and you feel like a sardine. If you want to observe a sea of Japanese people, visit the train stations at rush hour. The busiest station hosts three million people every day, as many people as live in my home state of Iowa. It would take a week to hike across greater Tokyo.

This morning I'm sitting in my basement typing these words. My lawn has to be mowed; I'll get at it this afternoon, now that the sun is shining. Tomorrow someone from work will be leaving, and there will be a party. Sunday is church.

From my basement the world can seem very, very small. It's almost impossible for me to imagine that, as I'm sitting here, Tokyo and Sao Pãolo even exist. But they do. People are moving, working, eating, laughing, and dying.

The world is a gargantuan place, isn't it?

God made it—the whole thing. And God watches it all. Isn't that amazing? Sao Pãulo and Tokyo, New York and Toronto. Australia and Africa, and 2 billion people in China! Shucks, Sioux Center is just a speck of dust.

But get this. God Almighty knows it all, sees it all, watches over the whole unimaginable business. God Almighty sees me here in the basement, and you wherever you are. Can you believe that?

God is the I am, the always, the Creator of everything. Praise God!

Bless the Lord, O my soul. Bless the Lord—and all that is within me, bless his holy name. For he has done great things. Amen.

42

Awesome

Q&A 26

That the eternal Father of our Lord Jesus Christ . . . is my God and Father . . .

Praise the Lord, O my soul. O Lord my God, you are very great; you are clothed with splendor and majesty.

—Psalm 104:1

Did you know that *she* snakes are bigger than *he* snakes? Or that apple blossoms are 87 percent sugar? Or that a man's skin is thicker than a woman's?

Or how about this? Penguins seem fearless. They'll walk right up to anything at all. Do they feel fear? Sure, they do. They're just horribly nearsighted.

Hawks have the finest vision of any bird on earth. Elephants drink fifty gallons of water a day.

Get a Texas horned toad riled, and it can squirt blood from the corners of its eyes. There are definite weight limits for flying birds—about thirty-five pounds is tops. A turkey or swan tips the scales heavier than that; that's why they stay on the ground.

Nobody really knows exactly how many islands make up the Philippines. A bullfrog closes its eyes when it jumps. Caterpillars eat only at night. If your canary has a temperature of 108 degrees, don't sweat it—most birds do.

You're lucky you were born human. Had you been a giraffe, you'd have dropped almost five feet, because giraffe moms give birth standing up. Girl babies—human ones—smile more than boy babies. Go figure.

Sad to say, some elephants have flat feet. A goat considers poison ivy a delicacy. Common earthworms are 72 percent protein and just 1 percent fat. If you were to go on an earthworm diet, you'd definitely lose weight—but then some people would prefer to stay plump.

Men often forget their change at the grocery counter; women never do—so says a long-time checkout person. Termites often get as old as fifty years (must be something about chewing on wood).

This zaniness, this madness, this astonishing world we live in was concocted by a single incomprehensible being, God Almighty. We can never, ever completely know this God.

But here's something we can know beyond a shadow of a doubt. The God who made all the stuff I've listed above and so much more loves us. This totally unimaginable dynamo of the whole huge universe actually cares for you and me.

God loves us. Isn't that something!

When we start to think too much about ourselves, Lord, use penguins to remind us of your glory. Don't let us stew about our problems. Charm us with daffodils. Enchant us with pelicans. Remind us of your glory in everything we see and smell and touch. You alone are God. Amen.

The Old, Old Story

Q&A 26

That the eternal Father of our Lord Jesus Christ . . . is my God and Father because of Christ his son.

How great is the love the Father has lavished on us, that we should be called children of God!

—1 John 3:1

In all the history of humankind there are really no more than a half dozen stories—from the tales swapped around a campfire to the thousands you'll find between hard covers at Barnes and Noble.

Take, for example, the love triangle. Maria and Kristine go to war over Jose. Both would like each other assassinated because Jose is, well, to die for. Heard that one before? Turn on the tube tonight, and you'll find another like it.

Here's a variation. Maria's already got Jose, but her father thinks Jose's tattoos make him an animal. Her father puts up a cement wall around the house to keep Maria locked up. Maria sneaks out. Her father is livid—he can barely speak.

Maria/Jose/Maria's dad is a variation on the love triangle. Three characters, love at the center. A variation on the theme.

Here's another variation. Two sweethearts are trapped on a huge ocean liner that's about to sink because it slammed into an iceberg. (See it?—Two lovers and an iceberg.) The guy dies selflessly, letting his darling live. That one made gadzillions a few years ago. You may have seen the movie.

Even though we know those story lines like the backs of our hands, we can't get enough of them.

Know something? The Bible is a story too. It's the story of God's love for people. Just like the other stories, you may have heard this one a thousand times. In fact, you've read it again on the pages of this book. In a way, it's another love triangle, but this one is unlike any story in history. What I'm about to tell you isn't going to come as a surprise, even though it would be nice if it would.

God made us. We sinned. God got totally mad. But God loved us so much God's own Son willingly came to die for us, and today we really are God's children.

If you think about this, the idea will last even longer than an all-day sucker. The creator of the universe—-the God who knows every star's luminosity, every planet's path, every John and Jane's main pain—that creator-God gave up his Son so we would become God's children again. And this awesome God wants us to call him "Father."

It's an old story, but trust me, it's going to take more than a lifetime to really comprehend. In fact, it's going to take eternity. God is our Father.

For right now, all we can do is praise God.

Lord, don't let us ever think of your story as old. Bless us with eyes that see it in everything around us, with ears that hear it fresh in the song of a lark. Amen.

44

What Do You Need?

Q&A 26

I trust [God] so much that I do not doubt he will provide whatever I need for body and soul. . . .

Cast your cares on the Lord *and he will sustain you. . . .*

—Psalm 55:22

God will provide whatever I need. That's a wonderful promise. But it's something we need to think about.

It's very possible to read that wrong.

A friend of mine lost her fiancé in the Nazi concentration camp called Dachau. She's not really exactly sure how he died; the Nazis didn't do autopsies. He wasn't lined up against a wall and shot or herded into a shower that emitted poison gas. Some friends of his—fellow prisoners—were there when he died. What killed him, perhaps, was starvation.

It's important to know that because he was a Christian, this man—whose name was Hein—decided early in the war to fight the Nazis, even though they'd already conquered his native Holland. So Hein and my friend—his girlfriend—decided to hide Jews, and thereby risked their own necks. He lost. He died.

Imagine Hein in his last days at Dachau. You think he didn't pray? You think he didn't ask God to save his life so that he could marry his sweetheart after the war? You think he didn't beg God for strength to see him through the misery?

He must have.

But he died.

Does that mean God's promise to provide everything I need for body and soul is phoney baloney?

No. The fact is, we don't always know what we need. I think we "need" a new car. You might think you "need" to lose ten pounds. My son thinks he "needs" a new computer.

Look, some things happen in life that will be mysteries until eternity. Hein's death and the unspeakable horror of concentration camps may well be among them. But we can still be sure of this: God will provide us what we need.

Those who watched Hein die claimed he died strong in his faith. Maybe that's what God knew he needed.

The truth is, we don't always know ourselves that well. God does. God knows our needs better than we do. Remember? God is God. The promise is not that we get what we want, but that we receive what God knows we need. There may well be a difference.

We do know God will always be there for us. That's a promise. That's a real comfort.

Lord, give us what we need today. Provide for us as only you can because you know what we need even better than we do. Give us this day our daily bread. Amen.

Mourning to Gladness

Q&A 26

He will turn to my good whatever adversity he sends me in this sad world. . . .

And we know that in all things God works for the good of those who love him, who have been called according to his purpose.

—Romans 8:28

There's a passage in Jeremiah that really lights me up. As you may know, much of what you'll find in the major and minor prophets is a slugfest of woe. But in the thirtieth chapter, Jeremiah begins to see a vision of the restoration of Israel, its return to righteousness. And when he does, the bleak visions are blown away.

The passage goes like this: "Then maidens will dance and be glad, young men and old as well. I will turn their mourning into gladness; I will give them comfort and joy instead of sorrow" (31:13).

Now that's a vision.

Last week, two kids who just graduated from high school were riding their motorcycles around town. Who knows why exactly, but suddenly one of them slammed into a steel pole. He was killed instantly.

Barely a month out of high school. Dead in a split second.

I didn't know him or his parents. I do know his grandparents, but in a small town like mine, the unforeseen death of any young person is as deafening as a scream in a closed room. Today, a week later, a Nike sweatband hangs from the white cross that's been placed at the spot where he died, and already there's a ton of mementos beneath it.

Maybe it's because I'm getting old, but sometimes I don't think I can take tragedies like that as well as I used to. Even though I don't know the family, I imagine their horror—the phone call, the news shattering their home. What I really can't stand thinking about is how they'll get up this morning, a week later, and feel their son's frightful absence. I can't imagine that pain.

This isn't the time to read today's Scripture passage about God working for our good in all circumstances to that grieving family. But God promises to do it. God Almighty, maker of heaven and earth, our Father, will turn our mourning into joy.

That's a promise you can take to the bank. When trouble hits, that's the bottom line. That's the gospel truth. Despite our hurt, our doubt, our anger, our grief, our Father will help us stand and sing for joy.

Believe it.

Somewhere, maybe not that far away, there are people crying right now, Lord. They weep through a hole in their heart left there by the death of someone they loved. Cover up that hole with your love, Lord. Wipe away their tears. Turn their mourning into dancing. In the name of Jesus, we ask this. Amen.

Breathtaking

Q&A 26

He is able to do this because he is almighty God; he desires to do this because he is a faithful Father.

Is anything too hard for the LORD?

—Genesis 18:14

Here's where I was—800 meters above sea level, 6 million meters north of the equator, 1 million meters west of the West Edmonton Mall. For geography classes, I was at 54.210 N latitude, 126.350 W longitude. Go ahead, figure it out.

I went cross-country skiing high in the Rockies of British Columbia where the tracks we made in the snow were the only ones I saw.

What happened was this. After about an hour, we came to a spot the others knew, the edge of a bluff that took my breath away. Nothing but snowy mountains like huge shoulders lined up as far as you could see, all of it spread with virgin timber—a huge landscape of deep brown, pure white, and dark green running for miles in three directions, all of it crowned with deep azure of a perfect sky.

"Wow!" I said. "What's out there?"

They shrugged their shoulders. "Moose, maybe," they said.

It was a colossal view.

Now I don't doubt for a moment that had I been there with people who weren't believers, had we suddenly come out from between the aspens and stumbled on this beautiful view, even they might have said something remarkably religious. Sheer unadulterated beauty can take your breath away and make you feel infinitesimal. Five hundred square miles of rugged Rocky Mountain beauty will make anyone swear there's a God.

You want to know the truth? Lots and lots and lots of people believe in God. Billions of them. There are, you know, foxhole believers—people suddenly thrust into life-and-death situations, people who have nowhere else to turn than up. They pray or die.

Really, it's tough being an atheist. The vast majority of the world's people believe in a god. Sometimes you just have to.

The mind-blowing surprise of question and answer 26 is not that there is a God, a Creator of the universe.

No, the real bang of this whole answer is the final line. This awesome God not only "can" protect us, love us, keep us in the palm of his hand—he "wants" to.

Few people really doubt that God exists. But as God's children, we know and feel more. We know that nothing is impossible for our God. And we believe that this same God loves us enough to want to be our dad.

Now that takes my breath away.

Dear God, thank you that you are not only able *to provide for us, but that you* want *to. Amen.*

Providence

Q&A 27

Providence is the almighty and ever present power of God by which he upholds, as with his hand, heaven and earth. . . .

The God who made the world and everything in it is the Lord of heaven and earth. . . . And he is not served by human hands, as if he needed anything, because he himself gives all men life and breath and everything else.

—Acts 17:24–25

In 1633, Roger Williams, a preacher in Salem, Massachusetts, demanded that all the churches in New England split from the Anglican Church. What's more, he claimed that the whole Massachusetts government was bogus. The king, he said, had no power to grant land because he didn't own it; the natives did.

Then he dropped a real bomb. King Charles I, he said, was the next thing to the Antichrist—not a sweet thing to say about your king in those days.

He was called before the Massachusetts General Court and apologized, but on April 30, 1635, he was summoned again and charged with preaching that the government had no right to punish violations of the first four commandments. To the Massachusetts government, Roger Williams was a sharp pain in the you-know-what.

What makes his story unique is that all the famous bigwig preachers of his time considered him, well, "a godly minister." So the courts commissioned those preachers to try to get Williams to reconsider some of his off-the-wall views. They failed.

On October 9, 1635, Williams was convicted of being the pain he was. In the words of the officials, Williams was "venting new and dangerous opinions against the authority of magistrates" and was booted from the Massachusetts Bay colony.

In April 1636, Williams and a few of his buddies took a long hike to a spot he was to call Providence. Today Providence, Rhode Island, is a city of about 175,000 in the smallest state in the United States.

Sioux Center, the town where I live, gets its name from the fact that it is in the center of Sioux County, Iowa. Very exciting. In the Midwest, many villages are named after railroad men who stopped the engine long enough to name a town.

But Providence, Rhode Island, is named after a Christian doctrine, a doctrine Williams knew and experienced, the idea that in every moment of our lives—no matter how much pain or tribulation—God is with us, around us, within us.

Take out a globe and spin it for hours. From my point of view, you won't find a more beautiful name than Providence.

Dear Lord, thank you for being at the wheel of our lives. Thank you for watching over us, for caring, for loving. Thank you for being there always. Amen.

48

God and the Weather Channel

Q&A 27

. . . leaf and blade, rain and drought, fruitful and lean years . . . all things, in fact, come to us not by chance but from his fatherly hand.

Do you know how God controls the clouds and makes his lightning flash?

—Job 37:15

You know, I think the weather channel makes God seem less real.

Imagine yourself out here on the plains one hundred years ago. No radio, no TV, no Internet. What you know about the weather is what you've learned from your grandparents, who have been watching the sky every day for most of their lives.

You walk out to the barn, spot thunderheads rising like fists in the west, and start to worry. Later, as you are sitting on your milking stool beside Daisy, thunder rattles the barn windows. It's a bad storm, but you don't know much more than that.

Back then, if you were a believer, you'd probably sit on that stool and ask for God's protection for you and your crops. Today, you'd turn on the weather channel.

My in-laws were married in the late 1940s. Like a lot of Iowa boys, my father-in-law wanted to farm, so he and his new bride moved to a farm adjacent to his father's land. That first summer they planted corn and wheat, nurtured the young crops the way good farmers did back then, and watched it all grow.

One night, as if out of nowhere, a hailstorm came and turned a lush green field into a carnage of broken shafts. It was too late to replant, so my father-in-law had to put his dream of farming on hold. Some mechanic in town offered him a job. It was several years before he could try his hand at full-time farming again.

Even then, fifty years ago, a storm probably seemed more like an act of God than it does today. If we knew nothing about atmospheric conditions, humidity and dew points, convection and rotation in cloud formations, a storm would be much more mysterious, don't you think? It's mystery that humbles us and makes us believe that some unknown power rules our lives. Doppler radar makes it all understandable. But it tends to keep God in church, not in the clouds.

Providence, the Catechism says, is the sure belief that God is in the church *and* in the clouds *and* in every last corner of our lives. We worship the God of "every leaf and blade," the God who controls "rain and drought, fruitful and lean years."

Providence is the firm assurance that not one thing goes on without God's knowledge. Nothing. Not a single thing. This whole world belongs to God. Even the storms, even the weather channel are in God's hands.

That's providence. That's how big God is.

Lord our Lord, how majestic is your name in all the earth! Our world belongs to you. Keep us in your hand. Amen.

An Intrusive God

Q&A 27

. . . health and sickness, prosperity and poverty—all things, in fact, come to us not by chance but from his fatherly hand.

O L*ORD*, *you have searched me and you know me. . . . You discern my going out and my lying down. . . . Before a word is on my tongue you know it completely, O* L*ORD*. *You hem me in—behind and before; you have laid your hand upon me.*

—Psalm 139:1, 3–5

The doctor said he needed to cut open my back, find this little broken-off chunk of disk, and slice it out like a sliver. He said he's done this surgery hundreds of times, never had a patient with any complications, and always brought, thereby, immediate relief. Stress on the word *immediate.*

That doctor is a smart cookie, but he lied.

Two weeks later, I was still in pain, swallowing pills as if they were water and I was a shipwrecked sailor.

A friend visited. "Jim," she says, "healing takes time. That surgery was intrusive."

Intrusive is not a word I use every day. What she means is that the good doctor's scalpel poked at my sciatic nerve, which is not especially fond of sharp objects. You could say that stupid nerve thinks of the scalpel, and the doctor, and the surgery as intrusive. And it's telling me so, two and three and four weeks later.

One meaning of *intrusive* is something that comes in "without permission or welcome." That's what my sciatic nerve thought. Another meaning, is, quite simply, something that "is thrust in." That works too.

Sometimes God can be intrusive. Listen to Psalm 139: "O Lord, you have searched me and you know me." How's that for intrusive? "You discern my going out and my lying down." Almost scary. "Before a word is on my tongue you know it completely." Long before they march across this screen in front of me, God knows the words I'm typing. God "hems me in—behind and before."

Providence means God is with us all the time, always—and yes, that can be scary. But it's also a great comfort. No matter what sickness or pain or poverty we suffer, or how much good health and prosperity we enjoy, God will always be there. No matter what we do, where we go, what we think, or what we say, God is there.

That's what providence means. It's intrusive, but it's wonderful.

By the way, my back is healing nicely.

At times we'd rather not know that you know everything going on in us. At times—and forgive us for those—we wish your eyes didn't fall on us. Like Adam and Eve, we'd rather hide. Thank you for forgiving us, and thank you for always being there. Amen.

50

Despair

Q&A 27

. . . all things, in fact, come to us not by chance but from his fatherly hand.

Then Job replied to the Lord, "I know that you can do all things; no plan of yours can be thwarted. . . . Surely I spoke of things I did not understand. . . .

—Job 42:1–3

I keep thinking about the young high school graduate who was killed on his motorcycle a week ago in a senseless accident. If you think for a while about a death that seems so meaningless, you can almost fall into despair. Right now, his parents and friends have to be feeling something huge and dark and empty. How could God let this happen? they must be wondering. I thought God loved us.

Let's assume something kind of weird. Let's assume that way back before the accident I had some kind of *X-Files* ability to see the future. One night I saw the whole accident, the funeral and everything. But I didn't tell the young man's father, even though we used to play volleyball in the same league.

Then let's assume that today, a few days after the funeral, I meet the young man's dad and apologize for not telling him what I knew back then before the accident.

"Look," I say, "twenty years ago, I knew what was going to happen." I drop my eyes. "I'm sorry, I really am. Had I told you, you could have avoided all that grief. You could have decided not to have your son."

He'd probably look at me as if I weren't around when brains were passed out. "You think we'd choose not to have him?" he'd say. "You think his mother and I don't treasure every minute we had with him?" Then he'd stare off into space. "It hurts horribly that's he's gone," he'd say. "But I wouldn't trade our life with him for anything."

I'm not sure anyone should give those grieving parents the promise of the Catechism: "all things come to us . . . from his fatherly hand." It's impossible to see the death of your child as coming from God's hand. Like Job, that Old Testament character who suffered so much, they might eventually come to say that it was simply in God's plan and beyond their understanding.

At the same time, however, I'm pretty sure this boy's mom and dad would never, ever wish they hadn't bundled him up and taken him home from the hospital and watched him grow into manhood. My guess is, though the darkness of their grief is thick and awful, their memories of his life bring the light of joy.

Providence is the abiding faith that, in all things, our lives belong to the Lord.

In the pitch darkness of our lives, Lord, in the worst of times, remind us that this is your world and that we are yours. Our lives are in your hands, Lord. Thank you for being our Father. Amen.

Hitting Bottom

Q&A 28

. . . nothing will separate us from his love.

For I am convinced that neither death nor life, neither angels nor demons, neither the present nor the future, nor any powers, neither height nor depth, nor anything else in all creation, will be able to separate us from the love of God that is in Christ Jesus our Lord.

—Romans 8:38–39

It's possible that everything I've been saying about providence will seem boring until you look out at the world someday and see nothing but darkness.

I once met a man who told me the Heidelberg Catechism meant less than nothing to him until he had to admit he was an alcoholic. Then he went to Alcoholics Anonymous, an organization that helps alcoholics and their families.

The man looked at the twelve steps that recovering alcoholics need to take. The first step was to admit that he was powerless over alcohol and that his life was unmanageable. The second was to believe that a Power greater than himself could restore him to sanity.

When he read those steps on the wall at that first AA meeting, this man said he saw the Heidelberg Catechism. First, we recognize sin; second, we acknowledge the power of the Lord. That's the pattern of the Catechism we've been through so far.

That night, for the first time, the man said, the Catechism made sense. He'd heard it throughout his life, but not until he'd hit bottom did it ring true.

You may never have hit bottom. You may never have been so low that looking up seemed downright impossible. You may never have been smacked in the face so hard that you didn't want to go back into the world, ever.

But, sorry as I am to say it, you probably will some time or other. It's true. Bad things happen, and just about everybody gets a chunk somewhere along the line.

The shocking beauty of the doctrine of providence is that even when things go entirely against us, we can be dead-on sure that God will be there with us. Nothing in all creation can ever separate us from God's love.

The bad news is that ugliness will catch up with all of us sometime in our lives. But the good news is that when it does, we won't be alone. Our God will be there.

Don't ever forget who that God is. We're talking about the God of the dolphin and dinosaur, of Saturn and Mars. We're talking about the God of the universe—your God, your Father.

God loves you. God will be there. That's the best news of all.

Lord, when we hit bottom in our lives, when the tough, tough times come, help us to believe your promise that you'll always be there. Because you will be. In Jesus' name, Amen.

Sovereignty

Q&A 28

. . . without his will they can neither move nor be moved.

Are not two sparrows sold for a penny? Yet not one of them will fall to the ground apart from the will of your Father.

—Matthew 10:29

When I was a kid, sometimes the neighbor boy and I would start to whack each other with plastic sand shovels or Wiffle ball bats. OK, I'm not proud of it. When we did, he'd hightail it back toward his house, then turn around suddenly and point at his feet. "You stay away from here now," he'd shout, his bottom lip curled like a wrestler. "This my property, see, and you can't cross this line."

I didn't cross that line. I figured his mother was watching, listening in, probably by a mike hidden beneath his shirt. Not only that, I figured she was just waiting for me to cross that line. The moment I did, she'd be after me wielding a Louisville Slugger.

The neighbor kid was staking out the imaginary line our respective lawn mowers never crossed, because on his property he was sovereign.

Countries today have sovereignty. United States sheriffs can't take a hike into Mexico to grab criminals. Neither can Canadian Mounties turn on their red lights and stream across the border to hunt down theirs.

When we say that God is *sovereign,* we're acknowledging that God has a kingdom too. The only difference is that God's kingdom knows no boundaries. My neighbor's property was just as much God's kingdom as the lot where our house stood. God doesn't hit the brakes at national borders. God's sovereignty extends everywhere.

Everywhere. Think of it. From Cape Town to the Cape of Good Hope, from the icy Arctic to the icy Antarctic, from Thailand to Tanzania, from Sioux Center to Sao Pãolo—it's all God's. God rules. His kingdom spreads from shore to shore and then some, because it covers the oceans too. It's everywhere.

This is God's world. "All creatures are so completely in his hand that without his will they can neither move nor be moved." Even the sparrows can't make a move without God's will.

God rules. He calls the shots. He's at the controls of the whole world, because our whole wide world belongs to him.

I don't know another thought that is quite so comforting. Our sovereign God reigns. It's all God's property, every last inch of it.

Jonah found nowhere to hide, Lord, and we can't run from your presence either. You reign everywhere. Your love beams radiantly in every corner of the neighborhood, in every township, in every country on earth. It's all yours. For thine is the kingdom and power and the glory, Amen.

Savior

Q&A 29

Why is the Son of God called "Jesus," meaning "savior?" Because he saves us from our sins.

She will give birth to a son, and you are to give him the name Jesus, because he will save his people from their sins.

—Matthew 1:21

Once, years ago, a little girl was hit on a bicycle right in front of our house. There was some blood. She wasn't badly hurt and life went on, but something really interesting happened later that night. Two old men, our neighbors, came out with buckets of water and washed her blood off the road, even though the blood was in front of our house, not theirs.

You may think I'm being silly, but I really believe those two old men had a higher reverence for life than I did at that point in my life. The idea of allowing human blood to sit in a wet vermilion pool just off our curb was something they just couldn't let happen.

They wouldn't have come over to clean up a spilled Pepsi or a melted fudge bar. Those old men couldn't stand the idea of human blood there on the street, and that's why I believe they felt the symbolic power of blood more deeply than I did.

It's sad but true that most of us probably don't feel the sheer power of what we're talking about today: Christ saves us from our sins. We've heard it so often. Listen: we're "washed in the blood of the lamb."

Yawn.

For many of us, that line has as much power as "Have a nice day." If we've heard it once, we've heard it a thousand times.

Stop and listen. We—you and me—were pigpen filthy, but now we're clean as fresh sheets. Fact is, we're even cleaner, perfectly clean, spotless, purified like something out of the lab. You know how we got that way? We took a bath.

OK so far? We were dirty. We took a bath.

Here's the kicker. We were bathed in blood, Christ's own blood. Think of a bathtub full of blood, the kind my neighbors wouldn't let sit beside our curb. Christ's blood was shed so that we'd be lily white, like nothing we ever were before. Think of yourself in that bath.

We are washed in Christ's blood.

Even if you've heard it a thousand times before, this time just think about it for a moment. Because right now we're at the very heart of the gospel. Jesus Christ is our Savior.

Think about it, and then thank him—today and for the rest of your life.

There is power, Lord, wonder-working power in the precious blood of Jesus. That blood has made us clean, washed away our sin, saved us. Thank you for your Son, who died that we might live forever with you in your glory. Amen.

54

No Other Name

Q&A 29

Salvation cannot be found in anyone else; it is futile to look for any salvation elsewhere.

"Salvation is found in no one else, for there is no other name under heaven given to men by which we must be saved."

—Acts 4:12

Everybody—yes, everybody—says this accomplishment is going to change our world. It's as big a deal as the invention of the wheel.

We're talking genome sequencing here. Within the DNA there are an estimated 50,000 or more genes. These genes determine the color of our eyes and hair, the shape of our fingernails, and whether or not we can touch our noses with our tongues or wiggle our ears.

Our genes also go a long way toward determining how well our bodies function. Flawed or missing genes, for instance, can cause disease. Scientists think that by looking at this whole genetic map—the arrangement of all of our genes—we might be able tell whether or not we'll ever get cancer, for instance, or, years down the road, Alzheimer's disease.

For that reason, mapping the entire human genome is seen as one of history's great scientific milestones, the biological equivalent of landing on the moon.

But now the real work begins. "We've been racing down white water in a narrow channel trying to get the sequencing done," said Dr. Francis Collins, head of the National Human Genome Research Institute. "Now we're opening into the ocean where the research possibilities and the effects on medicine are almost limitless. There is a very long list of things that we can now do, all of which will greatly benefit medicine," said Collins.

Researchers now will concentrate on finding disease-causing genes and developing ways of treating those genes. In other words, a time will come when human beings will be treated for cancer before they even have cancer—that is, before they have symptoms. The possibilities are limitless. That's why this genetic mapping is such a big deal.

But guess what? No genetic map will save us from our sins. No neurosurgeon will ever bring us eternal happiness. No lab research will make us at-one-d with God.

We call Jesus "Savior," the Catechism says, because he saves us from our sins.

Nothing else does. No genome sequencing, no genetic therapy, no miraculous scientific event. Only Jesus.

Lord, thank you for giving us the wisdom of science and medicine. Thank you for allowing us to discover things that benefit all of humankind. Help us use what we learn to your honor and glory. Amen.

The Real Thing

Q&A 30

. . . those who look for their salvation and security in saints . . .

Jesus answered, "I am the way and the truth and the life. No man comes to the Father except through me."

—John 14:6

When I was just out of college, the principal of the high school where I taught was a very strong Roman Catholic. He was also my best friend. It was obvious to me that we disagreed about some things about faith, but it was just as obvious to me that we worshiped the very same God.

Here's one of the most memorable things he ever told me: "When I go to Mass, Jim," he said, really emotionally, "I taste God." Wow.

Like all Roman Catholics, he believed that when he participated in the Lord's Supper, he was actually eating Jesus' flesh and drinking his blood. The bread and the wine, to him, weren't symbols; they were the real thing.

Sometimes people call Roman Catholics "sacramentalists" because what's absolutely central to their understanding of being a Christian are the sacraments—participating in Mass and taking communion. Sermons matter to Catholics, but sacraments matter more.

In many Protestant churches the pulpit stands up front between the baptismal font and the communion table. Long ago, Protestant theologians determined that God's Word read and preached would be central to the new Protestant church. Sacraments matter, they believed, but God's Word matters more.

Keep in mind that the writers of the Heidelberg Catechism were dyed-in-the-wool Protestants, and sometimes Roman Catholics were their sworn enemies.

Q&A 30 isn't wrong. Those who look to anyone—saint or sinner—other than Jesus Christ for their salvation and security are going to end up unhappy. Human beings are saved eternally only by the sacrifice of Jesus Christ. "No one comes to the Father except through me," Jesus said.

While Protestants still disagree with Roman Catholics on significant interpretations of Scripture, today Roman Catholics and Protestants are much better friends than they were five hundred years ago. And that's a blessing.

You'll have a hard time finding any Roman Catholics who disagree with the main point: We're all sinners, and our salvation comes from the Lord. If you think Mohammed or Buddha or Zeus or St. Francis or St. Benedict can offer salvation or give you lasting security, you're going to be sorry.

The truth is, there's only one Jesus, only one Savior. He's the real thing.

Lord, help us never to be arrogant, never to think that we've got truth by the tail and nobody else knows anything. Give us the heart and mind to know you better day by day. More than that, give us the ability to love. In the name of the one who loved more than any, Amen.

Messiah

Q&A 31

Why is he called "Christ," meaning "anointed"?

"But what about you?" [Jesus] asked. "Who do you say I am?" Simon Peter answered, "You are the Christ, the Son of the living God."

—Matthew 16:15–16

Call me old-fashioned. The fact is, I dislike the trend these days of people introducing themselves by their first name only, as if the world were a jumble of Jeffs and Judys. We're not just our first names, not at all.

Here's what I mean. Yesterday, the local hockey team named a new coach named Dave Siciliano. In case you don't know it, that name is 100 percent Italian. Siciliano is as Italian as Schaap is Dutch.

One of my old friends is named Buchholz—a perfectly good German name. Just outside of Sioux Center you can find an old cemetery filled with stones of people named Gustafson and Nielson—people of Scandinavian descent.

At one time people were named by their occupation. The German name *Zimmerman,* for instance, means "builder." In the small town where I live, the biggest construction family was named *De Stigter,* a Dutch name that means "the builder."

If we were to meet Jesus somewhere on the other side of the block, he might introduce himself as just "Jesus" too. But more likely he would have called himself "Jesus of Galilee." When we talk about Jesus today, we often use two names: Jesus Christ. Both have significance.

We've already said that *Jesus* means "Savior." *Christ* is not a personal name like Schaap, but an official name, like, for instance, Rosetta Bates, Judge of the Circuit Court or Lionel Hollins, Mayor.

Christ means "anointed," the Greek word for the Hebrew *Messiah,* the God-appointed one who was long-looked-forward-to. Many Orthodox Jews today still look for the Messiah prophesied in the Old Testament, the "Son of David" who was appointed by God to bring the whole nation of Israel back to glory.

For two thousand years the Christian church has believed that the Messiah has come, and his name is Jesus, Savior. For two thousand years we've believed that Jesus the Messiah is reigning now and will reign forever because he is the God-anointed one, the Son of David.

When we call Jesus "Christ," as Peter did in today's Scripture passage, we're confessing to the world that this Jesus, our Savior, is now and forever the Messiah. Praise his name.

Thank you, Father, for giving us your Son. Thank you that he came to the home of a carpenter, that he hung out with fisherman and was buddies with tax collectors. But most of all, thank you for making him Christ, the anointed one, the Messiah. Amen.

Lunatic Prophets

Q&A 31

[Christ] . . . has been anointed . . . to be our chief prophet and teacher. . . .

"For Moses said, 'The Lord your God will raise up for you a prophet like me from among your own people; you must listen to everything he tells you.'"

—Acts 3:22

Prophets suffer from a lousy image. Think of John the Baptist. Sure, everyone likes him today because he paved the way for Jesus, but if you'd been around in New Testament times, you'd have thought him a lunatic.

Imagine this, for instance. You and your mother are spending a perfectly sunny morning at the market in downtown Beth-Shemesh, when suddenly, out of nowhere, a bearded madman dressed in old camel's hair comes down the street, munching locusts and swallowing them with a mouthful of wild honey.

What's worse, he's shouting at you: "Repent, for the kingdom of heaven is near." Get a life, you think, I've got a soccer game this afternoon.

Now think of a modern-day prophet—Martin Luther King, Jr. You may not believe this, but many white folks thought that King was a dangerous madman for working toward racial equality. I know. I was there. White people I admired thought of him as one warped madman.

The Bible says Christ is our prophet. Strictly speaking, a *prophet* is one who speaks for God. That, of course, is exactly what Christ did and does every time we read his Word. He's a prophet, the Catechism says, because he "reveals to us the secret counsel and will of God." That sounds something like James Bond, but it isn't.

The "secret counsel and will of God" is nothing more or less than the formula for what the Catechism calls "our deliverance." In other words, Jesus the prophet tells us how we are saved. It's that simple. You might say that everything we've talked about in this whole book so far is explained in Christ. We know it because we know him, our prophet.

So is Christ the prophet a lunatic too? Sure, in a way. If you don't believe him, then you'd likely consider Christ the prophet, Christ the weirdo.

But if you do know him, then you understand that Christ's lunacy is our salvation; his zaniness is love; his wacko religion is our eternal joy.

If Christ is one strange bird, then give me wings. If Christ is a weirdo, then call me a lunatic.

How about you?

Sometimes when we think being a Christian isn't so tough, remind us, Lord, of how off-the-wall it really is. Remind us that those who follow him don't follow Hollywood or Wall Street. Remind us of love, faith, sacrifice—values the world finds odd. In the name of Christ our Messiah, Amen.

58

In Our Place

Q&A 31

[Christ] has been . . . anointed . . . to be . . . our only high priest who has set us free by the one sacrifice of his body. . . .

But God demonstrates his love for us in this: While we were still sinners, Christ died for us.

—Romans 5:8

Hermy was nobody's favorite. He had stringy hair and wore third-rate clothes. He smelled when you got close enough.

When he punched Randy Manson, the principal never really considered that there might be two sides to the story. You see, Hermy had been in trouble before. "One more incident," she said, "and you're history at Lincoln School."

Seeing Hermy get the boot would suit Randy Manson just fine. So one day after school, he put a live chicken in Hermy's locker and laughed as he thought of the mess the bird would make.

The next day Hermy came to school and flipped open his locker. Out sprang the chicken, scaring him half to death. Randy Manson stood there watching as if to say, go ahead and do something about it. Hermy started swinging.

Jamie Peters saw the whole thing. Hermy got hauled to the principal's office and everybody knew he was on his way out. But Jamie knew there was more to the story, so he went to talk to the principal about Hermy.

Hermy stayed at Lincoln.

That night, Randy Manson went after Jamie because Randy found himself in major trouble. Jamie came out of it bloodied—but happy he'd done the right thing.

Jesus Christ is our priest. Most Protestants don't know that word very well, except to say that Roman Catholics have them. But the Catechism says Christ is a *priest* because of the "one sacrifice of his body."

In a way, Jamie Peters acted as a priest. He took Hermy's side because it was the right thing to do even though he knew he was going to take a hit from Randy. He got whacked for the sake of the truth, and he saved Hermy from getting booted.

I'm not saying Jamie is like Jesus. But you get the idea, right?

Jesus Christ is our priest because he gave himself as a sacrifice for us. He stands between God and Hermy and Jamie and Randy and all of us, like the best lawyer in the world. His argument for our salvation is nothing less than his blood.

Christ is our priest, our sacrifice. He stood in for us. He got himself bloodied, suffered for us. He actually took our place. He is our Messiah.

We thank you, Lord, for sending your Son to do what we couldn't, to suffer in ways we should have, to die so we might live. Thank you for the sacrifice of Jesus Christ, our Lord. In his name, Amen.

The Lion and the Lamb

Q&A 31

[Christ] has been . . . anointed . . . to be . . . our eternal king. . . .

"See, your king comes to you, gentle, and riding on a donkey. . . ."

—Matthew 21:5

We may not know much about priests, but most of us are even more clueless about kings. After all, you weren't around during the reign of King George, the portly despot who sent the redcoats over to keep the colonies British. Maybe you've seen the movie *Patriot,* starring Mel Gibson. If so, you'll understand why so many of the colonists turned into "patriots" who thought that the very idea of a king was something worth spitting on.

The ultimate enemy during the War of Independence was the crown, the monarchy, the king of England. George was the nasty guy whose redcoats turned peaceful farms into killing fields.

So when the Catechism says Christ is our King, most of us south of the Canadian border don't know what to make of it. If anything, we tend to see kings as mean-spirited tyrants.

Christ is our eternal King, the Catechism says, because he "governs by his Word and Spirit" and he "guards us and keeps us in the freedom he has won for us."

Christ is our King because he rules. It's that simple. By way of what he says and what we see around us (his Word), and by way of his Holy Spirit (sent for us at Pentecost), he rules.

Like a good ruler, Christ watches out for us. Keeping us "in the freedom he has won for us" doesn't mean he keeps us in the freedom we now enjoy in the States and in Canada. It means that he keeps us free from the huge burden of our sin. He rules and he guards. He's a King—not a despot, not a tyrant, but a loving King, someone who rules by love.

Now hold on. There's a twist here that will knock your socks off. Christ is the King, the Lion, right? He rules over the whole jungle of our world. He rules.

But he rules like a lamb: by sacrifice, by meekness, by love. This lion is a lamb.

Never in human history have we had a King, a Lion, who was a Lamb. The boss of everything, yet the servant of everyone.

Long live the King—the Lion who is a Lamb. He rules!

King of creation, be king of our lives. Rule us with your love. Bless us with your peace so we may rule all our affairs with love and grace. Amen.

By Faith Alone

Q&A 32

But why are you called a Christian? Because by faith I am a member of Christ. . . .

For it is by grace you have been saved, through faith—and this not from yourselves, it is the gift of God. . . .

—Ephesians 2:8

Valleyfair, a big amusement park, is promoting its new ride this summer—a beast called "Power Tower," a mechanical giant that takes riders up 250 feet. Not good for people with easy nosebleeds. Once you're up there, guess what? You go down. Real fast. But then you go up 250 feet again before coming back down.

Figure this. Your friends Abdul and Rita take their trip on the Power Tower. They tell you that you haven't lived until you've had your own "extreme scream." "It's incredible," Rita says. "I thought I was going to die."

That night you just might bring up the possibility of your own family trotting off to Valleyfair. "Everybody's talking about it, Mom," you say.

The Christian life, you'll discover, has its big rides too. There are moments you'll experience your own wonderful kind of "extreme scream," moments when you feel God's presence so intensely it seems that God's heart is beating in your chest.

Maybe you've already had some great spiritual adventure—a service trip, a weekend retreat, a bonfire testimony, something that took you way, way up.

We want other people to experience the great thrills of our lives, whether they come from amusement parks or weekend retreats. The problem is, Christianity is more than a thrill, and what thrills us might not move our buddies off the couch, because God comes to us, each one of us, in different ways. God claims some people through the deaths of friends, some through tearful bonfire testimonies, others through slapping paint on the walls of downtown missions.

Question and answer 32 has to be one of the most important parts of the whole Catechism: Why are you called a Christian? The answers begins like this: "Because by faith I am a member. . . ."

It's not because I go to the right church or the right school; it's not because of the way I braid my hair or what it says on my T-shirt. No WWJD bracelet is ever going to save anybody.

Human beings are called Christians because they belong to Christ by faith. Because they believe. We are Christians by faith, not by what we do, what we experience, or how we dress. We are believers because we believe. It's that simple and that wonderful. It's called grace.

You're here, Lord. You listen or we wouldn't be saying what we are. Thank you for giving us the gift of faith. Please give those who don't know about you the assurance that you are here and will be forever. In Christ's name, Amen.

You're a Prophet

Q&A 32

I am anointed to confess his name. . . .

"Whoever acknowledges me before men, I will also acknowledge him before my Father in heaven."

—Matthew 10:32

Prophets suffer from a lousy image. Think of John the Baptist. Sure, everyone likes him today because he paved the way for Jesus; but if you'd been around in the New Testament times, you'd have thought him one strange bird. Most prophets seem like lunatics.

Hold on. You've read that before. There must be some mistake. We've already been through all that stuff about locusts and camels. Just go back a few readings.

You're right—I did say all of that before. We've been looking at what it means that Christ is anointed to be our prophet, priest, and king.

Guess what? We're on the same trail in Q&A 32. Only now we're talking about us. The question is, "Why are *we* called Christian?" *Christ,* as we've seen, means "anointed." So if we're followers of Christ, then we too are anointed.

Big deal. Nobody poured any oil over my head. What on earth does *anointed* mean?

Three words—*prophet, priest,* and *king.* We're all three.

Listen to the Catechism: We're prophets because we are "anointed to confess his name." Jesus said, "Whoever acknowledges me before men, I will also acknowledge him before my Father in heaven" (Matt. 10:32).

Prophets aren't always nice; they say things other people don't want to hear. Lots of people don't want a thing to do with Jesus Christ. They don't want people saying that Jesus Christ is our only means of eternal life. They don't like people saying that Christ makes claims on their lives.

Now I'm a Christian, and I happen to believe that abortion is wrong. I know some Christians don't believe that, but quite frankly, I think they're wrong. Yesterday, the United States Supreme Court determined that partial-birth abortion is legal. I think the five judges who made up the majority are dead wrong too.

Christians are called to be prophets. That's not always easy because we can be dead wrong ourselves. The moment I start thinking that God and I always think the same, I stop being a Christian, because God is God, and I'm only an old guy with a bad back.

No matter. Part of our calling as Christians is to confess God's name. Not just confess that we believe, but even shape our world. That makes us prophets, wouldn't you say?

Sometimes even lunatics.

Lord, help us to get off our knees and out into the world. Give us wisdom so we can help with the problems the world faces. Give us a voice that will be heard even in the wilderness of sin. In Christ's name, Amen.

You're a Priest

Q&A 32

I am anointed . . . to present myself to him as a living sacrifice of thanks. . . .

I urge you . . . to offer your bodies as living sacrifices, holy and pleasing to God. . . .

—Romans 12:1

Who ever said this was going to be a piece of cake?

You think being a Christian is a nice, fun thing? Oh sure, it's got its thrills. Hang around with a bunch of believers, and you sometimes feel as if you're part of a big, sweet family. You sing the right songs and sometimes the whole world glows.

Then you come across this gem: "I present myself to him as a living sacrifice."

Now hold on here, you say. I want to play soccer. When I get out of school, I want to be a computer programmer, a doctor, a bricklayer, a dairy farmer. I want to swap stocks and make big bucks, then retire to a Mexican villa. I want to dance, to sing, to write screenplays, to shoot movies, to be a star.

I want to live. That's the bottom line.

Now read it again: "I present myself to him as a living sacrifice."

Ouch.

But I want to invent a cure for cancer. I want to be a youth pastor—I'll play guitar and be everybody's friend. I want to be Prime Minister. I want to be a lawyer. I want to teach school.

"I present myself to him as a living sacrifice."

I've got a date. I'm going to the prom with this gorgeous girl. You can't believe how much I'm looking forward to volleyball. I'm going to letter in three sports. The city is finally putting up a ramp for skaters. Friday night I get the car for the first time.

"I present myself to him as a living sacrifice."

If you think this is a piece of cake, then read the fine print. Sometimes—even often—Christianity means denial. *Denial* is not a nice word. Nobody will ever sell Mountain Dew or a new pick-up with a word like denial. Our whole economic system rests on the assumption that you'll never deny yourself anything. Buy, buy, buy—if you don't have the money, just go into debt with a credit card.

"I present myself to him as a living sacrifice."

Our role as priests, like Christ's, is to sacrifice, to give up something of ourselves for something bigger. For him. For Christ who loves us, who sacrificed himself for us, who died that we might live, who gave that we might get. We're Christians because we give of ourselves.

"I present myself to him as a living sacrifice."

It's not natural for us to think about giving up stuff, Lord. Sacrifice isn't something we do well. Come into our hearts and teach us to give up ourselves, as Jesus did, for others. Teach us about sacrifice. Amen.

You're a King—Now

Q&A 32

I am anointed . . . to strive with a good conscience against sin and the devil in this life. . . .

Put on the full armor of God so that you can take your stand against the devil's schemes.

—Ephesians 6:11

In February of 1692, Betty Parris, the daughter of the Reverend Samuel Parris, of Salem, Massachusetts, got sick—oddly sick. She seemed to fall into fits. Sometimes she drew herself into a ball because of sharp pain and sometimes she seemed to be burning up. It was very strange. Her parents didn't know what to make of it.

Some of her friends became similarly afflicted. Ann Putnam, Mercy Lewis, and Mary Walcott did odd things like scream and hide under furniture and beds. The local doctor had no clue about what was going on, so he suggested the problems might be supernatural. Maybe the devil was doing it.

That conclusion wasn't strange. Cotton Mather, a very important Massachusetts preacher, had recently written accounts of young women, demon-afflicted, whose behavior was as unexplainable as the Salem girls'. Most people believed that the devil worked best on children anyway. Two and two makes four: The devil, they believed, was alive and well in Salem.

Maybe you know the story of the Salem witchcraft trials. It's one of the ugliest moments in Christian history, because eventually nineteen men and women, all accused by the girls and convicted of witchcraft, were carted to Gallows Hill and hung until they died. Hundreds of others faced accusations of witchcraft, until finally the hysteria subsided in Massachusetts.

The Catechism says our job as Christians is "to strive with a good conscience against sin and the devil." And Paul tells us to "take our stand against the devil's schemes." That's exactly what the good Puritans of Salem thought they were doing, but they were dead wrong.

Believers in Jesus Christ are prophets when we profess his name. We are priests when we sacrifice, like Jesus himself, for God's kingdom. And we are kings when we go to war against "sin and the devil."

But we'd better know what we're doing. Twenty people died in Salem because good people thought they were fighting the devil, when he was using them.

We are kings now because we rule over sin and the devil. But don't ever think you know everything.

We may be lions for Christ our King, but, like him, we're also lambs, ruling by service, ruling by love—not by the noose.

Give us the courage to stand up for our beliefs, Lord. But just as clearly, give us the wisdom to know what to believe about our world. When we're wrong, help us see it. Give us the courage of a lion and the spirit of a lamb. Make us more like Jesus. Amen.

You're a King—Forever

Q&A 32

. . . and afterward to reign with Christ over all creation for all eternity.

If we endure, we will also reign with him.

—2 Timothy 2:12

"Time is but the stream I go a-fishing in."

The guy who said that was something of an odd duck. He hiked to the edge of a pond where no one lived, nailed together a shack with open windows for birds and squirrels, grew a few vegetables, and hung out all by himself for two years while writing a book.

Lots of folks thought he'd lost his marbles. At best, they figured, he was an introvert, a loner.

The line about time and fishing comes from his famous book *Walden,* which was also the name of the pond where he nailed up his shack. His name, as you know if you've already taken American lit, was Henry David Thoreau, and he lived during the middle of the nineteenth century in New England.

I teach literature, and almost every year I have my students read big chunks of *Walden.* Sometimes I ask them on a test, "What does Thoreau mean when he says, 'Time is but the stream I go a-fishing in'?"

Some students get it, some don't.

Want to hear something really strange? There is no such thing as time. It doesn't really exist. What's real about life is eternity—foreverness. God's life is forever. God is the I AM, the eternally present. God was long before we were, and God will be long after we're pushing daisies—if you know what I mean.

There's no time to God. In God's world there are no watches, no bank clocks. He's given us time because it helps us schedule our lives. Time is a kind of gift. At noon we eat.

But God doesn't have a thing to do with time. God doesn't say, "Oh, my goodness, I should have been in Iowa ten minutes ago." God's always there, always here, always everywhere.

God is the I AM.

The Catechism suggests that we reign as kings here below when we fight sin and the devil. But it also makes very clear that we are kings with Christ "for all eternity."

Thoreau wasn't wrong. Time, for him, was just the place he picked up a perch now and then. Time didn't rule his life. He may have been a bit strange, but he wasn't wrong about the importance of time and eternity.

Eternity is forever. And we'll reign with him. That's a promise.

When we don't have any time, Lord, remind us that time isn't much more than the stream in which we go fishing. Eternity is forever. Thank you for promising us a place in a world that is forever. Help us remember forever. In Jesus' name, Amen.

Begotten

Q&A 33

Christ alone is the eternal, natural Son of God.

For God so loved the world, that he gave his one and only Son. . . .

—John 3:16

Begotten is one of those words we use only when we're talking about faith. Try to imagine ever using that word outside of the Apostles' Creed. I can't.

A true story. A couple I know adopted a child. She grew up, became an adult herself, and was planning to be married.

Suddenly, as if out of nowhere, her birth mother showed up in her life. She contacted her daughter and said she wanted to meet her. She said she'd be at a certain motel in Chicago, and she begged her daughter—the young woman she'd given birth to—to come and meet her.

Just for a minute, put yourself in the position of the girl's adoptive mother. For all the young woman's life, she'd been there for her. Her adoptive mother had changed her diapers, picked up her room, listened to her hurts, and taken more than her share of angry barbs. In other words, the adoptive mother had been her *mother,* except, of course, for the actual birth.

So the two of them, the girl and her adoptive mother, went to the motel where the birth mother said she would be waiting. They got into an elevator, went to the seventh floor, got out, and started walking down the hall toward the room.

Now the adoptive mother didn't know whether it was her place anymore to be there, she told me, so she started to back off. Her daughter kept walking, Mom falling farther and farther behind.

Suddenly her daughter turned back. "Mom," she said, "what's the deal?" And then she said, "You will always be Mom, you know—always."

Just then, that mom really felt like *Mom,* if you know what I mean.

We're all adopted. In the kingdom of our Lord Jesus Christ, there's only one *begotten* Son, only one *begotten* child.

If you've attended Sunday school all your life, you've likely thought of yourself as God's child. And you are. But remember, God Almighty has only one *begotten* child. And that, of course, is Jesus Christ, our Savior. He's the one, after all, who died for us so we could be God's children.

The Catechism says it's worth remembering that "Christ alone is the eternal, natural Son of God." Today it's God Almighty who turns to us and says, "What's the deal, you guys? Come on along. You'll always be my children, you know."

Think of it that way, because that's what God says and that's what God's done.

Thank you for adopting us as your children. Thank you for sending your Son to die so that we could be forever family members. Thank you, Lord, for loving us so much that you gave your only begotten Son. In his name, Amen.

Belonging

Q&A 34

He . . . has bought us, body and soul, to be his very own.

You are not your own; you were bought at a price.
—1 Corinthians 6:19–20

This week my wife and I celebrated our twenty-eighth anniversary. Well, maybe *celebrate* isn't a good word—we exchanged cards, not much of a celebration. But next week we're going to really celebrate by spending a weekend in New Orleans.

I suppose it's possible to say that I "belong" to my wife. She doesn't own me. She didn't pay a dime to get me. But we're married, we've sworn before God that we will be there for each other for the rest of our lives. In a way, I belong to her.

I belong to my parents too. Long after I grew up and stopped living by their rules, they continued to love me and worry about me. In a way, I guess, I still belong to my mom and dad. I'm sure they'd say that I'm among their most cherished possessions.

And I belong to the English department of the college where I teach, because the English department owns a good deal of my time. I'm under contract, so after a fashion, I belong to them.

It's not easy for me to say I belong to anyone. In just a few days, it will be the Fourth of July, and if the celebration is about anything, it's about freedom, the fact that I don't belong to anyone. In the United States and Canada, not many people enjoy saying they belong to someone else.

In case you haven't noticed, the Catechism has been defining Christ, and today it examines Jesus' title as "Lord." Five hundred years ago it wasn't tough to define Christ as Lord. To millions of ordinary people, a lord was a master, a ruler, a fact of life. Today, we bristle just to think of someone owning us, of belonging like a slave to someone else.

Bristle not, believers. Jesus Christ, our Lord, owns us. We belong to him. With his blood, he bought us, and now we are his. And guess what? He has set us free.

That's why we can say, "Jesus, we are yours now and forever. You bought us. You are our Lord."

I don't care what you say, that's comfort.

Today I belong to Jesus; Jesus belongs to me. Not just for the years of our lives, but for eternity. Thank you, Lord, that we belong to you. Amen.

Jesus Gives a Quiz

Q&A 34

He . . . has bought us, body and soul, to be his very own.

Having loved his own who were in the world, [Jesus] now showed them the full extent of his love. . . . [He] began to wash the disciples' feet.

—John 13:1, 5

Sometimes Christ's disciples called him "teacher." If you listen closely to Jesus' own words, you get the sense that being around him meant always being ready to take a quiz. For instance, this foot-washing thing.

The gospel of John says it happened just before Passover. Judas has already been plotting and scheming, and Jesus knows it, of course. But all the disciples are assembled. Without a word of explanation, Jesus unwinds himself from his robe, pulls a towel around himself, pours water into this big bowl, and starts washing the disciples' feet.

Nobody says a thing. They're all struck dumb.

Except Peter, who generally doesn't take anything sitting down. "No way," he says. "Jesus, I'm not letting you touch my feet."

"Unless I wash you," Christ says, "you have no part with me." It's almost as if he's got to do this foot-washing thing, or the whole ministry is on the rocks.

"If that's true," Peter says, "then don't stop at my feet. Bathe the whole business."

Sounds like Peter, doesn't it? He's always pushing.

Jesus finishes. Even Judas's feet get washed. Then Jesus gives the quiz. He wrings out the towel, wraps himself back up, stands, and says, "Do you get it? Do you understand what I'm up to here?"

There's the quiz. Give me an essay right now on what this means, Jesus says.

What would you answer?

I think it has something to do with Jesus Christ being Lord, with the Lion being the Lamb.

Jesus Christ is Lord because we are his. He bought us with his blood. He paid for us with his suffering. We are free because he paid our price. Now we are his.

But this Lord to whom we belong, this God-man who's done it all for us, washes our feet, deals in corns and bunions and athlete's foot. This Lord stoops to conquer.

He takes the dustiest, dirtiest, stinkiest part of us in his hands and cleans it all up. He gets down on his knees and does our dirty work because this Lord of our life does his job, oddly enough, as the lowliest servant.

This King is a slave. This Lion is the Lamb of God. He is Lord.

Blessed Lord, you got down on your knees for your disciples, and you hung from a cross for us. Help us show you love by getting down on our knees, by giving every bit of who we are so that your name may be glorified. Amen.

Born in a Barn

Q&A 35

. . . conceived by the Holy Spirit and born of the Virgin Mary.

The angel answered, "The Holy Spirit will come upon you, and the power of the Most High will overshadow you. So the holy one to be born will be called the Son of God."

—Luke 1:35

This whole gospel story is one magnificent epic of silliness. Lions are lambs and kings are slaves. The God of all the stars and planets, of Tokyo, São Paulo, and Sioux Center, the great I AM, the ever-present who knows no such thing as time or space—that God pulled on a tuxedo fashioned of human skin.

I'm telling you, this gospel story is just plain hard to believe.

The King of the universe, the Redeemer of the world gets born in a bed of straw meant for an ox and a mule. Joseph didn't check into the Marriott; he barely got a roof over his head. Jesus Christ—Wonderful Counselor, Everlasting Father, Prince of Peace—was born in a barn.

It's almost enough to make you laugh.

Jesus Christ turns absolutely everything on its head. Nothing's the same.

Most of you will always remember Y2K even though it really fizzled. You'll remember because those two letters and a digit came to be associated with the sweeping change of our calendar. Suddenly, the whole world shifted from a four-digit number that started with a one, to a four-digit number that began with a two.

A thousand years seems like more than forever. In North America, we have trouble enough learning a century of history. In much older civilizations like the Islamic world and the Orient, hundreds of years seem more memorable; but very few human beings really have a clue as to what exactly was going on a thousand years ago. A thousand years is a millennium. In fact, the word *millennium* has almost come to mean "forever."

I think it's wonderful that all this buzz was based on what happened in a barn. The entire world redigitized because once upon a time a woman who wasn't even married and had never had sex was visited by the Holy Spirit, became royally pregnant, traveled to an Israeli town named Bethlehem, couldn't get a room, and ended up having a baby in a barn.

I'm writing this in the year 2000. Isn't it wonderful that we've all come to pin that number to our walls and enter it into our computers, all because of a girl having a baby in a manger?

Incredible.

Forgive us for having trouble understanding that you could send your Son to walk in our shoes, to suffer and die so we might live. Sometimes it seems so extraordinarily huge that we can't get our minds around it. But we know it's true. Thank you. Amen.

Magnificat

Q&A 35

. . . from the flesh and blood of the virgin Mary . . .

And Mary said, My soul doth magnify the Lord, and my spirit hath rejoiced in God my Saviour.

—Luke 1:46–47, KJV

No wonder so many Christians make Mary into a saint. You've got to love her. She's not married but she's got a boyfriend. An angel visits with the most incredible news: She's going to have a baby. She says, "How? Me and Joseph, we never, you know . . ."

The angel chuckles. "The Holy Spirit will come upon you, and you'll be filled with his presence," the angel says. "You will carry the Son of God."

The most incredible interview in the history of humanity. And when it's over, Mary says, "May it be to me as you say." That's it—pure, unadulterated faith. She buys into the most outrageous revelation of all time without blinking an eye.

Once she visits her cousin Elizabeth, she's sure. Elizabeth, who's carrying John the Baptist, knows something big is happening because her little boy jumps inside her womb when he hears Mary's voice.

And then Mary sings. What a song! For years, Christians called it the Magnificat. "My soul doth magnify the Lord." That's the way it starts in the King James Version. You can read it in the long first chapter of Luke. "My soul doth magnify the Lord, and my spirit hath rejoiced in God my Saviour."

There isn't a dime's worth of arrogance in those opening lines. All glory, she says, be to God.

But she's in the song too. "For he hath regarded the low estate of his handmaiden," she says. "For behold, from henceforth all generations shall call me blessed."

I see her alone somewhere, sitting on a rock maybe, in sun, not shade—singing. It's a small voice; her eyes sweep the sky.

"For he that is mighty has done great things," she says. "Holy is his name."

The rest of the verses tell how God has been a constant presence to Israel, put down the mighty, scattered the proud, filled the hungry, spoken to Father Abraham. The Magnificat tells God's story and explains God's character. Mary speaks to God, this God who is her baby's father, this God who has conceived in her the Savior of humankind—musically, in reverence and in truth.

She worships, all by herself, in spirit and in truth.

I can understand why some people make her a saint. She is.

Bless us with faith like Mary's, Lord. Give us the kind of belief that doesn't falter or waver, even when we come to understand that you require things of us we wouldn't imagine. Help us to say, as she did, "My soul doth magnify the Lord." In Christ's name, Amen.

70

Away in a Manger

Q&A 36

How does the holy conception and birth of Christ benefit you?

God made him who had no sin to be sin for us, so that in him we might become the righteousness of God.

—2 Corinthians 5:21

I know places where you can get a fight brewing just by singing "Away in a Manger." I'm not kidding. Here's the crucial line from the second stanza: "The cattle are lowing/the baby awakes/but little Lord Jesus/no crying he makes."

And here is the big question: Did Jesus cry?

Crying is awful. If it's not a sin itself, it's a sign of sin. Surely Jesus didn't sin! He couldn't have cried. If he did, he wouldn't be God. If he wasn't God, then he couldn't be our Savior. You don't really believe, do you?

That's the argument, and it's already turned into a fight. Here's the other side:

Oh, ye of little brains. Babies can't talk, they can't write. So how do they communicate? They cry. Crying isn't sin; it's only the baby's way of communicating. Jesus Christ was human, and as a human he had to communicate. He didn't pop out of the womb and start to preach. Therefore, he had to cry. If he didn't, how could he be human? And if he wasn't human, he couldn't be our Savior. You don't really believe, do you?

We've got war.

Me, I side with those who argue for crying. But it's fair to say that none of us were there, and therefore nobody knows.

The argument itself is interesting. It draws a wide circle around the greatest mystery of all time: How can someone who is God be a person too? How can a human also be God? A dog is a dog; a cat is a cat; a human is a human; God is God. You don't shake and bake. God *and* man? That's very strange.

It is strange. If you try to understand it, you can't. We're human, not divine. We don't know everything. Some things are just mysteries. Christ was both God and man.

The Catechism says Christ's birth, his holy conception, makes a huge difference for us. Because he was man, he could suffer in our place. The apostle Paul puts it this way: "In him, we become the righteousness of God."

Because Jesus "had no sin" and was himself God, his death was enough. The greatest mystery of all is called the Incarnation. God—the I AM—pulled on a suit of human flesh.

Unbelievable—to all but the children of God.

May our lives be a song, Lord. May we give praise each of our days. For you sent your Son, the Prince of all eternity, to wear our clothes, to walk our streets, to eat our food, to die for us. Hallelujah, what a Savior. Amen.

Suffering and SUVs

Q&A 37

. . . that . . . he might set us free, body and soul, from eternal condemnation . . .

Therefore, there is now no condemnation for those who are in Christ Jesus. . . .

—Romans 8:1

I've got to be careful how I say this because my own kids drive one, but the proliferation of sport utility vehicles has got to rank as one of the greatest sales pitches of all time. As more and more people move out of rural areas and into cities, the automotive industry sells them SUVs because they'll all be going "off-road," as they say. Nonsense.

Ford advertises its SUVs with the phrase "outfitters," as if the company were offering canoe trips into the wilderness. Balderdash.

As the world continues to devour its limited supply of oil, the automotive industry creates a vehicle that drinks gas like a camel drinks water. Our blindness is as incredible as our ego.

But we buy.

Let's face it, marketing wizards are experts at selling the idea that life is fun. They promise our fantasies, then tell us we can buy on time and suffer no pain.

Their gospel is death. Nobody buys happiness. Trust me on this.

I much prefer the truth of an old Shaker hymn, "Consolation." In part, this is what it says: "Though through the desert I lead/for a path in the mountain ye pray/for strength in the hour of need,/I never will answer you, 'Nay.'" You'll notice the hymn doesn't question whether or not we'll suffer; it even admits the Lord will lead us through torrid deserts and seemingly impassable mountains.

Another stanza begins like this: "When tribulations oppress/when reverses and dangers await." It's not *if* tribulations come; it's *when* they come.

We know that Christ's suffering "set us free, body and soul," and that we will never be condemned if we are in Christ (Rom. 8:1). But don't make the mistake of thinking life is a Ford Ranger commercial. Sometimes we have to crawl through the desert of despair without an SUV.

When Christ shouldered our sin, he ended suffering—not now, but in the life to come. The Bible doesn't call this world a "vale of tears" for nothing. Still, those Shakers got it right. God also promises something for the here and now: "For strength in the hour of need,/I never will answer you, 'Nay.'"

God will be there. That's what Christ's suffering promises, for this world and the next.

Lord, forgive us when we believe that our comfort is in something we can buy: a new car, new clothes, a haircut. Forgive us when we trust in something or someone other than you. Bless us with true faith, real faith, the firm knowledge that you are our only comfort. Amen.

Then Is Now

Q&A 39

So that he . . . might be condemned . . . and so free us. . . .

"Do you want me to release the 'king of the Jews'?" They shouted back, "No, not him! Give us Barabbas!"

—John 18:39–40

What happened, happens. What went on back then, goes on now. History isn't dead at all; it's still happening. Same chapter and verse. The past is the present. The *then* is the *now.*

Jesus of Nazareth was brought before Pilate, the judge, the symbol of Roman justice and power. Now the Roman Empire wasn't some banana republic. The Roman system of justice became the pattern for Western democracy. Our courts still use their symbol—Lady Justice, blindfolded—because justice isn't justice if it isn't blind.

Imagine the scene: You've got Pilate, the symbol of Roman justice, declaring to everyone that he can't find a reason on earth to punish Jesus of Nazareth. He doesn't know what the guy has done wrong.

But the straight is made crooked by the crazed hatred of Jesus' own people. They want him dead. Worse, they want him crucified. So Pilate rips the blindfold off Lady Justice and gives in to the frenzy of the mob.

The innocent is pronounced guilty. Jesus didn't deserve to die. Even Pilate admitted it. But that screaming mob wanted him gone, so he was condemned.

Imagine Barabbas, a guy with a rap sheet as long as his hairy arm. He's cooling off in some dark cell somewhere, when suddenly a barrel-shaped guard opens the door.

Barabbas holds his hands up in front of his eyes and lets out some profanity.

"This is your lucky day, you jerk," the guard says. "You're getting a free ride."

"What's the joke?" Barabbas says, still squinting.

"This is one crazy world," the jailer says. "You're going free, and this Galilean, who's never raised a stick to a dog, is going up on a cross."

The innocent dies, the guilty go free.

In a way we're all like Barabbas, with rap sheets as long as the arms of a wide receiver. But along comes Jesus, who's perfectly innocent, and takes our punishment.

What happened, happens. What went on, goes on. By his stripes, we are healed. Pilate knew he couldn't lay a hand on Jesus, but the innocent suffered so the guilty go free.

That's the whole gospel. For Barabbas, that was Good Friday. For us, it was and forever shall be "Good Friday" too.

Even today, Lord, we are like Barabbas. You suffered so we might live. We'll never deserve that sacrifice. Just help us, today and always, to be thankful. In your Son's name, Amen.

73

Cursed and Crucified

Q&A 39

. . . since death by crucifixion was accursed by God.

Christ redeemed us from the curse of the law by becoming a curse for us, for it is written, "Cursed is everyone who is hung on a tree."

—Galatians 3:13

Nathaniel Hawthorne's novel *The House of Seven Gables* is all about the effects of a family curse. Here's some background: Judge Pyncheon will do anything to get Matthew Maule's property, but Maule won't sell. So the judge accuses Maule of witchcraft. Maule is convicted, but before he is hung he curses Pyncheon: "God will give you blood to drink and quench your greed for eternity."

Big deal, Pyncheon thinks. A curse is just so much hot air. He buys the property and invites his friends to a housewarming, which he never gets to enjoy because he dies mysteriously from a massive throat hemorrhage.

Nathaniel Hawthorne himself was a descendant of a judge who wrongly sentenced people to death because of allegations of witchcraft. Lots of people think Hawthorne was writing about a curse he felt very personally in that famous novel.

But let's face it. The Pyncheon-Maule thing seems like an *X-Files* story. Who'd believe it? Besides, it doesn't take a whole lot to get yourself cursed today. Cut someone off on the freeway and see what I mean. Some freeways are spillways of curses and obscene gestures. But then curses themselves really don't mean much, do they?

Not so fast. In the Old Testament, curses aren't just hot air.

Consider Deuteronomy 21:22–23: "If a man guilty of a capital offense is hung on a tree, you must not leave his body on the tree overnight. Be sure to bury him that same day, because anyone who is hung on a tree is under God's curse."

Jesus Christ died on a tree. He was, as the Old Testament claims, therefore "under God's curse," which is, of course, not at all hot air.

The Apostles' Creed specifically mentions that Jesus was crucified. Why, the Catechism asks, is it a big deal that Christ was crucified? The answer is simple. Jesus Christ was cursed, but not by Pilate nor by the Jews who wanted him hung. Jesus Christ was cursed—now take a deep breath, this is the big one—Jesus Christ was cursed by God.

The cross strapped on his shoulders was our sin, which did and does deserve God's curse. Nothing is more obscene than this: God's own Son is cursed with our sin.

Here's the good news: By doing that, God freed us to live in love with God forever. We should never take that lightly. God certainly didn't.

Your curse, Lord, was our blessing. Your death was our life. Your suffering is our eternal joy. In the busyness of all of our daily lives, don't let us forget how absolutely important you are to our lives. Amen.

A Cross and a Crooked Chunk of Cement

Q&A 40

Only the death of God's Son could pay for our sin.

"But you must not eat from the tree of the knowledge of good and evil, for when you eat of it, you will surely die."

—Genesis 2:17

I've told you before about the young person who was killed on a motorcycle on a road not far from where I live. Every time I go down that road, I can't help but see the cross his friends put up. His Nike visor is there, and flowers are strewn all over.

In a way, the memorial makes his death easier to take. It shows the love other kids had for him. That festooned cross is a symbol of how they feel.

But right beside it is something terrible: a crooked chunk of cement that once held the long pole of a streetlight. The concrete is tipped akimbo because the rider of the cycle hit that pole and was killed instantly.

Two memorials sit on that field of grass. One of them is a symbol of life, the life the young man has in the memory of his friends; the other is a symbol of hurt, pain, death.

Every last human being who ever lived, died. And unless Jesus returns soon, it doesn't appear that you or I are going to break that record.

Now let's go all the way back to the beginning. After fashioning the finest garden ever grown, God told its happy occupants there'd be no eating from one tree. "When you eat of it, you will surely die," God said.

Here's the divine trade-off. To stand in our place, God's Son had to suffer the full penalty we deserved.

The Apostles' Creed says Jesus was crucified and died. "Did he have to die?" asks the Catechism. The answer is yes.

Jesus Christ didn't only have to wear a crown of thorns or be innocently accused or be spit on by the mob. He didn't only have to hang from a cross. He had to die, because death was what we had coming: "When you eat of it, you will surely die."

That crooked chunk of concrete alongside the highway is a stinging reminder of death itself. It's awful. Thank God for the cross beside it.

That same cross stands next to our deaths and the deaths of every member of God's family. It's a reminder that only the death of God's Son could pay for our sin.

You had to go all the way, Lord. Being spit on wasn't enough, that crown of thorns wasn't enough, hanging on the cross wasn't enough. You had to die so we might live. May our lives be ever alive with your love. Amen.

Ghosts and Old Graves

Q&A 41

His burial testifies that he really died.

He was assigned a grave with the wicked, and with the rich in his death. . . .

—Isaiah 53:9

Just a few days ago in New Orleans, my wife and I toured a cemetery in the Garden District of that amazing city. I love old cemeteries, no matter what they look like or who hangs out there, but this one is unique to North America because the bodies, even today, are interred above ground. They aren't really buried at all; they're stacked in a sepulcher.

Now hold on to your lunch. These graves are, in a way, reusable. I'd seen that before in Europe, of course, but the idea still is, well, chilling to those of us who are more accustomed to thinking of the dead having their own little chunk of terra firma.

The cemetery we visited was, as I said, old. Unless they're kept up, old things fall into disrepair, right? So do old graves. At one site, the ground beneath an ancient tomb was broken up a bit, and, guess what? I saw human bones. Eerie.

One of New Orleans's many attractions is a tour of the city that documents its ghost stories. Burying people above ground in multiple-use tombs, it seems to me, is bound to increase the chance of people seeing ghosts and goblins.

That Jesus Christ died on the cross was, according to Scripture, undisputed. One of the Roman soldiers pierced his side, you remember, as if to prove the fact. And Jesus himself said, "It is finished."

But he was buried too, as if to finalize the whole horrible and humiliating experience, even though the burial was honorable and distinguished (an unused tomb, his body anointed with spices, the whole operation in the hands of friends and family). The Apostles' Creed makes a point of saying that Jesus "was buried." And the writers of the Catechism also want us to understand there was no question of Jesus Christ's having died.

"He was buried." His limp body was lifted into a tomb that was sealed. He definitely died.

End of story? Not quite. He died, was buried, but he came back to life.

Sounds like a ghost story, but it isn't.

Jesus Christ was buried, but he's alive—hallelujah! He was buried, but he's alive, so don't be scared. He was buried, but he's alive, so have no fear, now or ever.

He lives.

What language shall I borrow/to thank you, dearest Friend/for this, your dying sorrow,/your mercy without end?/Lord, make me yours forever/a loyal servant true,/and let me never, never/outlive my love for you. Amen.

Just the Beginning

Q&A 42

Death . . . is our entrance into eternal life.

"Where, O death, is your victory? Where, O death, is your sting?"

—1 Corinthians 15:55

A short, quiet woman named Flannery O'Connor is one of my all-time heroes. She's a writer who died quite a long time ago after turning out only a few books. She wrote about the rural American South, a region she colors with fascinating, sometimes weird characters. But the people she writes about aren't fascinating simply because they're weird; they're fascinating because, even in their weirdness, they're somehow like us.

She was not only a writer but also a Christian. "I see from the standpoint of Christian orthodoxy," she once wrote. "This means that for me the meaning of life is centered in our Redemption by Christ. . . . I don't think that this is a position that can be taken halfway or one that is particularly easy in these times to make transparent in fiction."

O'Connor knew it wasn't easy to write and be a Christian, but she stuck by her guns in everything she wrote.

Often she used violence in her stories. By the end of her short story "A Good Man Is Hard to Find," an entire family gets wiped out by a mass killer whose nickname is "the Misfit." Doesn't sound very inspiring, does it?

But O'Connor, who was a strong Roman Catholic, knew very well that "death is our entrance into eternal life." When Christian readers asked her why her stories had all that horrible violence in them, she told them that to Christians there are a lot more horrible things than dying.

She's absolutely right, of course, and the Catechism makes no bones about it either. Even though Christ died for us, we still have to physically die. It comes with the package. But our physical death isn't the end; it's just the beginning of one grand eternal life.

The old woman at the heart of "A Good Man Is Hard to Find" is scheming and arrogant. Yet, at the very moment of her death at the hands of "the Misfit," she sees very clearly that she is no better a person than the murderer. Having seen that, she is, for the first time in her life, ready to die, because she knows death is but an entrance to eternal life.

That's not an easy thing to learn. It took the old lady all the years of her earthly life. But now she's spending eternity with her Savior.

"O death, where is your victory? O death, where is your sting?"

Lord, it's hard not to think of death as the end of life, but for believers it's only the beginning. Thank you for giving us life after life, life after death. Thank you for our eternity with you. Amen.

No Scars

Q&A 43

Through Christ's death our old selves are crucified, put to death, and buried with him.

For we know that our old self was crucified with him so that the body of sin might be done away with, that we should no longer be slaves to sin. . . .

—Romans 6:6

When children in the seventeenth and eighteenth centuries went to school in New England, they had to learn their alphabet like little kids today, only they didn't have *Sesame Street* to help. Instead they used a book titled *The New England Primer,* which taught the ABCs with its own special twist.

For instance, for F, the kids learned this little rhyme: "The idle *Fool*/is whipped at school." Interesting. For C, "The *Cat* doth play/and after slay." Sweet, isn't it? How about this for T: "*Time* cuts down all/both great and small." Try to stick a smiley face on that one!

The most memorable little poem, however, is the one for A: "In *Adam's* fall/we sinned all." I doubt *Sesame Street* would ever say anything like that.

But you understand the idea behind the "Adam's fall" rhyme. When Adam took the fruit from Eve, who took it from the tree after listening to the snake's snow job, we all took a bite. OK, neither you nor I were there, but the representative of all humanity disobeyed, and all of us were affected. "In Adam's fall/we sinned all."

Christ is often called a kind of "second Adam." Like Adam, Christ was sinless and was tempted to sin; unlike Adam, he didn't fall. Christ also "represents" us in the same way Adam did.

Now here comes the tough part. When Jesus Christ died on the cross, so did we. "Our old self was crucified with Christ," Paul tells the Romans. And the Catechism repeats the idea: "Through Christ's death our old selves are crucified."

I have a little scar on my wrist where I jabbed myself with a screwdriver yesterday. It still hurts, but I've got no nail holes. I wasn't around Jerusalem in A.D. 33. I wasn't born for almost another 2000 years. How can I have been crucified?

"For as in Adam all die, so in Christ all will be made alive" (1 Cor. 15:22). When Jesus Christ toted our sin up on that cross, he was, Paul says, toting us too. Something of us died there, something vile, something blackened with sooty sin.

The miracle is I don't have scars. The miracle is that even though something of me died up there on the cross, somebody else suffered all the horror.

That's exactly what we call "the good news."

Thank you, Lord, for toting our sins up there with you. Thank you for taking our place. Thank you for wiping out all our darkness with the brilliance of your sacrifice. Thank you for being our Savior. Amen.

78

The Kingdom of the Dead

Q&A 44

Why does the creed add "He descended into hell"?

"My God, my God, why have you forsaken me?"

—Matthew 27:46

I won't kid you. Tons of people hold different opinions about this phrase from the Apostles' Creed. I know wonderful believers who won't say the line because they believe it doesn't convey the truth about Christ's life and death.

Their reasons are complex but understandable; they stem from their sense that "he descended into hell" gives the wrong impression: that Jesus Christ was actually in a place we know of as *hell.* I know, I know—that's exactly what the line says. But it isn't all that simple.

Historically, people used words like *Sheol* (Hebrew) and *Hades* (Greek) to mean a kind of temporary holding tank for the spirits of the recently dead. So, years ago, if I were a Jewish kid whose grandma had just died, I might say, "She's in *Sheol,*" meaning she's in a place where the spirits of the dead go. If I'd said that, I wouldn't necessarily mean she was suffering in what we consider "hell" today.

Many people much smarter than I am claim that the Apostles' Creed means here that Christ's own spirit descended to a place where all dead spirits go, a kind of "other" place.

The problem is, few Protestant Christians believe that idea anymore. Some Roman Catholic Christians still hold to various views about where the spirits of the dead go once the body is cold, but most Protestants believe, like the martyr Stephen, that we'll find ourselves in the most comforting spot in the universe, in the arms of God. "Lord Jesus," Stephen said, "receive my spirit" (Acts 7:59).

What's more, we have Christ's own words. "Father," he said on the cross, "into your hands I commit my spirit" (Luke 23:46). Note that Jesus mentioned his father's hands, not the kingdom of the dead.

Behind all this is the big question: what is *hell* anyway? Again, most theologians I respect would say that hell is a place where God doesn't ring any doorbells, where God's light doesn't shine. Hell is being really alone.

Did Jesus Christ suffer that separation? You bet. "My God, my God, why have you forsaken me?" he said. Hell means being completely forsaken by God; we know Jesus suffered that horrifying loneliness.

In that way, "he descended into hell" is absolutely true.

That's awful . . . but finally wonderful. Praise God.

We will never know how much you suffered, Lord, during the agony of the cross. All we know is that your suffering delivered us. May our lives celebrate you every day. In your name we pray, Amen.

Bad, Bad Places

Q&A 44

Christ . . . by suffering unspeakable anguish . . . has delivered me from the anguish and torment of hell.

He was cut off from the land of the living; for the transgression of my people he was stricken.

—Isaiah 53:8

June 5, 1944. England is in the middle of a tremendous pounding by German missiles and bombers, but something big is about to happen.

That night, General Dwight D. Eisenhower gave the order to start the largest invasion in military history, the invasion at Normandy. The result was a logistics nightmare that became known as D-Day, the invasion that eventually meant the end of the Nazi regime.

The objective? Invade deeply fortified, Nazi-occupied France with 150,000 troops and 1,500 tanks by way of 5,300 ships and landing craft, 12,000 airplanes, and 20,000 paratroopers.

When the English people saw the troops going into the English channel that night, they yelled, "Give 'em hell."

Sounds like swearing, and I suppose it is. People likely even meant it as swearing, in fact. But nobody in England or in those landing craft could have imagined the horror that would follow. In a matter of minutes, the beaches were full of dead troops. Thousands died in the time it takes for you to walk across the house.

What happened on those Normandy beaches was a kind of hell on earth. To get a sense of what it was like, watch *Saving Private Ryan* if you can.

I don't know if the Allies gave the Nazis hell, or if hell was simply the result. But if we can't stretch our minds around whatever it is that *hell* means, then just imagine those beaches at Normandy.

Here's the reason for all of our talk about hell. The Catechism says that Jesus Christ, at the very least, suffered the worst of our horrors. Nobody anywhere or anytime can say they've suffered things Jesus Christ didn't suffer. He was there at Normandy. He was there at Auschwitz. He endured the hell of AIDS in Africa, of earthquakes and famine in India, of a teen spraying a high school hall with gunfire in North America.

That's what we have to know. When we think no one understands, we're wrong. Jesus does. There isn't any horror any of us can suffer that's beyond his understanding, his love. He descended into hell.

For us.

Lord, we know that what you went through for us on the cross was worse than the very worst suffering we can imagine. Strengthen us with the firm conviction that no matter how much we suffer, no matter how bad our nightmares, you've been there. All praise to your name. Amen.

Winners

Q&A 45

How does Christ's resurrection benefit us? . . . He has overcome death, so that he might make us share in the righteousness he won for us by his death.

Jesus answered him, "I tell you the truth, today you will be with me in paradise."

—Luke 23:43

The big story on Golgotha the night of Jesus' crucifixion was—and forever shall be—the death of one God-man. But just for a moment think of those two men beside him. They might have known each other, but they were probably in the dark when it came to Jesus.

What do we know about these men the Bible calls "criminals"? There's no question about their being as guilty as the Lord Jesus Christ was innocent. We don't really know what they did, but it's altogether possible these men were rapists or murderers as well as thieves.

One of them has an incredible story, which begins when he tells the big-mouth beside him to shut up, to stop taunting Jesus. "Don't you understand?" he says. "We are punished justly, for we are getting what our deeds deserve. But this man has done nothing wrong." Then he said, "Jesus, remember me when you come into your kingdom" (Luke 23:41–42).

And just like that, Christ says the magic words: "Today you will be with me in paradise."

Think of the guy's rap sheet. Wrap your greatest fears into a single felon, if you like. Thief, rapist, drug dealer, murderer, and more.

Bang! in the twinkling of an eye it's all gone. All the evil, all the crime, all the ugliness. A mile-long rap sheet disappears in the swath of a Handi-wipe full of grace: "Today you will be with me in paradise."

Just like that, a miserable thief is washed clean. Just like that, we've got a real winner. Just like that, a saint has emerged like a butterfly from the cocoon of a real sinner.

When the Catechism says Christ's resurrection benefits us by making us share in his righteousness, you can't do better than to think of that miserable thief suddenly transformed into a saint. When Jesus comes into our lives, we get made new, inside out. We become righteous.

Sometimes in the twinkling of an eye. Sometimes at the moment of death. But always, whenever it happens, we get made new. That's what his resurrection does for us. We share in his righteousness. We aren't what we were. We're something else altogether.

We're made new. We're winners.

You've made us new, Lord, just as you carried away all the sins of the thief on the cross. You've given us new life, eternal life, joyous life with you. Thank you for making us winners. Amen.

Voted Off the Island

Q&A 45

We too are already now resurrected to a new life.

Therefore, if anyone is in Christ, he is a new creation; the old has gone, the new has come!

—2 Corinthians 5:17

Last year, the biggest television hit of the summer was a show called *Survivor.* For a while I was a sucker and watched along with everybody else. Just fewer than twenty men and women tried to set up a life on an otherwise uninhabited island. Here's the complication: Every other day or so, one of them has to leave. The winner—the one still there at the end—takes home a million clams—that's dollars, not the stuff you dig up from the beach.

A guy named Dirk, a dairy farmer, happened to be from my home state of Wisconsin. Now I happen to believe a Wisconsin dairy farmer can do no wrong, so I started pulling for him. You know what else? He was a Christian, an evangelical Christian. Dirk often read his Bible; in fact, he even witnessed to the others.

Sadly enough, Dirk went home early, without the million clams. He got himself voted off the island so quickly I wondered why he got the boot.

I'll let real *Survivor* fans argue about why Dirk got voted off the island. But his early retirement was really fascinating to me because the Bible never promises that all our problems will disappear if we love Jesus. In fact, most often it warns about troubles we can expect if we're really trying to live up to our name as Christians. Christ himself said he came with a sword—quite a confession from the Prince of Peace.

The Bible says (and the Catechism seconds) that Christ's resurrection benefits us by resurrecting us to a new life. But did you notice that we are "already now" resurrected to a new life? Because Jesus died and arose, we can begin living a new life. Not tomorrow, but today.

That's great! But it doesn't mean that everyone is going to like us.

What it means is that we'd be living a whole different life if we weren't saved. And not just on the outside, maybe not on the outside at all. We're changed inside. We've got a new life: new goals, new missions, new strategies, a whole new ballgame.

If we didn't have the Lord, we wouldn't look into the same future. We wouldn't act the same or be the same. We're believers, and that's a comfort.

Just don't ever think that being a Christian means you won't get voted off the island.

A new life not only comes from God, it belongs to God.

Lord, when we take different positions than people around us because we're sure you would, when we get kicked off the island for being Christians, shelter us in your arms. Keep us strong. In Jesus' name, Amen.

Humpty Dumpty and God

Q&A 45

Christ's resurrection is a guarantee of our glorious resurrection.

Now if we died with Christ, we believe that we will also live with him.

—Romans 6:8

I've been to funerals where the casket was closed. Sometimes that happens if the person who died was in a car accident or suffered some disfiguring death. But I've also been to funerals where the body *was* shown, even if what happened wasn't at all pretty. Once I attended the funeral of a man who'd died of AIDS. Seeing that body demonstrated clearly the horror of a disease that has already killed millions.

When planes explode in midair, they're torn into a thousand pieces—and so are the bodies of the passengers.

My great-uncle was killed at the end of World War I, the victim of a shell. His commanding officer said his body wasn't recognizable.

When I was a kid, I thought cremation was really wrong; after all, how would God ever reassemble a body that had been burned into dust?

When we recite the Apostles' Creed, we say that we believe Jesus rose again from the dead on the third day. The Catechism says that Christ's resurrection is wonderful for at least three reasons: First, it helps us become righteous; second, we begin a brand-new life; and third, we are guaranteed our own resurrection.

I certainly don't claim to know exactly what will happen at the end of time. It's fascinating, even scary, to think that suddenly each person in a graveyard will pop out of the ground like some jack-in-the-box puppet. Is that the way it will happen? Will I carry the scars I've always carried? Will bald guys have hair? Add your own questions to the list.

I guess we'll just have to wait and see exactly what happens. But here is our guarantee: Christ's resurrection means not only that we too will be resurrected, but also that our resurrection will be—and don't doubt this for a minute—glorious!

Nothing ghoulish about that. No terror. Only joy. Only blessedness. Believers all will be resurrected, no matter how they died. Christ's resurrection means our glorious resurrection.

Humpty Dumpty is only a children's story. We know for sure that God Almighty, Creator of heaven and earth, can put anything together, anything he wants.

And he wants us.

Thank you, Lord, for the promise that some day—maybe soon, maybe not—we'll be united again with those we love. Thank you for the assurance that we'll all live forever in you. What a great promise! Amen.

God's Headquarters

Q&A 46

What do you mean by saying, "He ascended to heaven?" That Christ . . . was lifted from the earth to heaven. . . .

This is what the Lord *says, "Heaven is my throne, and the earth is my footstool."*

—Isaiah 66:1

For a very short time in human history, God Almighty actually had an address. Although it changed quite often, he really did. When? While the Israelites wandered in the desert, God Almighty designated a meeting place where heaven touched earth. If some tourist had wanted to know where he could meet God, the Israelites could have simply pointed at the temple.

Of course, the temple was hardly a shopping mall. Who could go in and who couldn't was closely supervised. Even the high priests' comings and goings were strictly monitored.

Now if you think it must have been a tremendous blessing for people back then to know where to meet God, remember the Book of Exodus and how the Israelites couldn't stop grousing about everything under the sun. Just because people knew God's address didn't mean they found it any easier to obey God. We're sinners, all of us.

For years preachers in my church used to say, "God is in his holy temple" at the beginning of worship. It wasn't hard for me to think God lived in our church.

But that's not true. At least, God doesn't live *only* in a church. Remember the old story Christ told about giving care to the needy? "When I was sick," he tells the people, "you paid me a visit." The people look puzzled. "When were you sick?" they ask. "We don't remember that."

"If you did it to the least of these," Christ says, "you did it to me."

Christ isn't only in a church. He's God. He's all over the block all of the time.

The Apostles' Creed says Jesus "ascended to heaven." People once thought heaven was just above the clouds. Get up high enough and you can't miss it. Today we know that even if we travel millions of light years, we won't get to a sign that says, "Heaven." It's not just a galaxy or two farther than our best telescope can probe.

What do we know about heaven? This much for sure—it's the place where God rules. "Heaven is my throne, and the earth is my footstool," the Bible says in one of the funniest verses in the Old Testament (Isa. 66:1). Andrew Kuyvenhoven, author of a book on the Catechism, calls heaven "God's headquarters."

When Jesus ascended, he didn't go just beyond the sunset. He went to God's headquarters. And there, as we shall see, he rules.

Even though we can't find heaven on a map, Lord, we know you're there. We know you're in power, ruling our world from your headquarters. And we know we'll live with you someday. Thank you for giving us a place to live forever. In your Son's name, Amen.

History—and Old Baseball Gloves

Q&A 47

In his human nature Christ is not now on earth . . .

[Christ] must remain in heaven until the time comes for God to restore everything. . . .

—Acts 3:21

When baseball began, no one wore gloves. Slowly, however, gloves emerged. They were stringless and webless. Then someone strung leather between the fingers, and eventually somebody else sewed in a pouch between thumb and forefinger, probably somebody with a sore hand.

An expert could look at a hundred baseball gloves and know roughly when they were made. Old baseball gloves all bear some signs of their age.

So does the Heidelberg Catechism. Like an old stringless glove, it shows its own history in many places. None of these places is perhaps more revealing than questions 47 and 48.

At the time of the Reformation, there was a mega-debate about the bread and wine served at the Lord's Supper. The Roman Catholic Church had always maintained (and still does) that when someone "eats the bread and drinks the cup," that person is literally eating Christ's flesh and drinking his blood.

Some Reformers found that idea wrong. The writers of the Heidelberg Catechism couldn't have slept if they'd left the argument out.

The Catechism's real objective here is to argue that Christ can't be here, literally, in the bread and the wine because he ascended into heaven. That's why "in his human nature Christ is not now on earth." He's at God's headquarters, and he can't be both here and there.

Does that mean Jesus is not with us here on earth? Not at all. "In his divinity, majesty, grace, and Spirit he is not absent from us for a moment," says the Catechism. But physically present? No.

For hundreds of years, followers of John Calvin, a famous reformer, have said at communion, "Lift up your hearts." They've said it because they believe, as I do, that Jesus Christ is on high, at the right hand of God Almighty.

The next time you take communion, the thing to remember is this: Jesus Christ died for us so we may live.

That says it all.

Thank you for giving us reminders, Lord, of your love. Thank you for flowers, for spring, for mountain streams. And thank you for your sacraments. Thank you for giving us bread and wine to help us remember that you gave yourself. Amen.

Lifted Up in Prayer

Q&A 49

How does Christ's ascension to heaven benefit us? First, he pleads our cause in heaven. . . .

Christ Jesus . . . is at the right hand of God and is also interceding for us.

—Romans 8:34

Not a day passed without the teacher and the students praying really hard for Ashley's mother. Her cancer came out of nowhere, it seemed. One day her mother was in class helping kids one-on-one like she had once a week throughout the year; the next day she was in the hospital, tubes in her nose and all over her body.

She'd been feeling a little tired, Ashley told the kids, so she went to the doctor, who said she really ought to go to the hospital right away and get a whole battery of tests. He didn't like the constant pain she'd been having in her stomach. It had been there too long.

So she did. They did the tests, and the news was not good—cancer, lots of it. Every day after that, the whole class, some of them on their knees, prayed for Ashley's mother, not only because she was Ashley's mother but because they all knew her. She'd been in their class all year. They knew her, and now it looked as if she were going to die.

But she didn't. It was a long recovery, but she lived. Even came back to visit once or twice with her hair—or what there was of it—in a babushka.

One day Ashley raised her hand during devotions. "Sometimes," she said, "sometimes it seemed as if every one of you guys was in the hospital room with us—I mean it." She looked around at the walls and bit her lip a little. "My mom says it was as if we were lifted up in the arms of your prayers."

Maybe you know a story like that. Maybe you've heard or experienced what Ashley experienced: the blessed sense that a whole mountain of prayer is holding you up.

That has to be one of the greatest feelings a person can experience.

Now think of this. Christ's ascension means that "he is pleading our cause" with the Father. The apostle Paul says Jesus is "interceding" for us. He's on our side. He's in God's headquarters and he's on our team.

As wonderful as it is to feel all your friends behind you in the very worst of your problems, think how much better it is to know that Jesus Christ the Lord is the real captain of your prayer team.

Dear Lord, thank you for being the captain of our prayer team. Thank you for pleading our cause in heaven. Thank you for loving us even when we don't love ourselves. Thank you for being our God and Savior. Amen.

One of Us

Q&A 49

Second, we have our own flesh in heaven—a guarantee that Christ our head will take us, his members, to himself in heaven.

"In my Father's house are many rooms. . . . I am going there to prepare a place for you."

—John 14:2

- A bunch of years ago, my family and I were up on Table Mountain, a huge, flat rock that sits like a mammoth footstool far above Cape Town, South Africa. I don't remember how, but all of a sudden we ran into another American family. We talked like old friends. I suppose if we had met on the streets of Chicago, we wouldn't have looked at each other. But half a world away, because both families were American, we were suddenly friends.
- Lots of Canadian students attend the Iowa college where I teach. Some of them have told me they never thought of being "Canadian" until they came here to the States.
- Last weekend in New Orleans, a woman asked me, "That name of yours—what nationality is it?" I was proud to tell her, "I'm Dutch-American."
- In a whole gang of Christians, I often seem to feel most at home with others who belong to the denomination I do—Christian Reformed. Very strange, but true.

We have loyalties, a whole bundle of them, even though—unfortunately—they sometimes keep others away. The fact is, we identify with people who have similar experiences, a common homeland, or comparable beliefs.

One of the benefits we receive from Christ's ascension is that we have "our own flesh" in heaven. We can be eternally joyful because Christ, one of us, is at God's headquarters.

He identifies with us because he's had some real human experience. He's not from North America, doesn't associate with any denomination, and has no comparable ethnic background; but he was human. And that's what matters. We can take immense comfort in Christ's ascension, because he's one of us and he is at the Father's side.

One day we will join him there. He's preparing a place for us right now, says John. Someday we'll see Christ face-to-face in heaven.

He's there now, and he guarantees we'll be together in a place so beautiful you won't believe it.

"We have our own flesh in heaven—a guarantee that Christ our head will take us, his members, to himself in heaven."

Lord, it's comforting to know that in your headquarters there's someone who probably once stubbed his toe. Thank you that Jesus, our Savior and Lord, is preparing a place for us for the rest of eternity. Thank you, Jesus. Amen.

Chicken Little

Q&A 50

Why the next words: "and is seated at the right hand of God?" Christ ascended to heaven, there to show that he is head of his church, and that the Father rules all things through him.

And God placed all things under his feet and appointed him to be head over everything for the church, which is his body. . . .

—Ephesians 1:22–23

Chicken Little was a portly little bird who ran all over town yelling that the sky was falling. I don't even remember what he'd seen, but he became absolutely convinced that the whole world was coming apart at the upper seams. So he took it upon himself to tell the world. "The sky is falling! The sky is falling!" he screamed.

Ever feel like Chicken Little? I know I do. It's not hard at all to feel as if the rug is getting pulled out from under everything important. It's not hard to think that the wrong people are in charge. It's not hard to think that really bad people have it good and really good people have it bad.

One of my favorite old gospel hymns goes like this:

Tempted and tried, we're oft made to wonder
why it should be thus all day long,
while there are others living about us
never molested, though in the wrong.

Some bully makes the first string, and a kid everyone loves, a kid who works his tail off, gets cut.

You talk once in class, and bam! you're nailed with a detention. But your neighbor sounds like a talk show host, and your teacher looks the other way. Sometimes it just seems like the wrong person is in charge.

Now we'd be dead wrong if we believed God acts like that—just looking the other way or letting things fall apart.

The Apostles' Creed says Jesus is "seated at the right hand of God." And the Catechism says this means Jesus is the head of his church, and God is ruling all things through him. In other words, Jesus is running the whole show!

So if we believe what the Bible and the Apostles' Creed and the Catechism say about who's in charge . . . if we really believe that, then we shouldn't go running around like Chicken Little, warning people that everything is falling apart.

Christ is at the right hand of God, ruling his church—all believers. Ruling *all things.*

That's real comfort, even when the sky seems like it's falling.

Forgive us, Lord, for sometimes thinking that you're not in charge. Forgive us our fear. Forgive us our anger. Forgive us for our belief that the world's going to ruin. You're still in charge. Thank you for being King of creation. Amen.

A Thousand Years

Q&A 50

Why the next words: "and is seated at the right hand of God?" Christ ascended to heaven, there to show that he is the head of his church, and that the Father rules all things through him.

And I saw the souls of those who had been beheaded because of their testimony for Jesus. . . . They came to life and reigned with Christ a thousand years.

—Revelation 20:4

Believers who sing and pray together sometimes part company over a little phrase in today's Bible passage: "a thousand years" or *millennium.* Revelation 20:1–10, which you can check out for yourself, is really big in this discussion.

Here's the issue: Should we believe that "a thousand years" means exactly one thousand years, as in 1002 to 2002?

"Absolutely!" say Christians who take the Bible literally at this point. "One thousand years means exactly that." Other Christians disagree. They say that sometimes the Bible means things symbolically, not literally. For example, when Christ said to forgive people seventy times seven times, he wasn't really saying to stop forgiving them once you've done so 490 times (70 times 7).

In the same way, they say, "a thousand years" may mean something like a huge chunk of time rather than exactly one thousand years.

OK—here come the big words.

Pre-millennialists believe that "a thousand years" refers to the exact amount of time that Christ will rule the world from his throne in Jerusalem. A loud trumpet will sound, believers will join Christ in the air (an event called "the rapture"), but unbelievers will be left to suffer through seven years of terrible tribulation. Then Christ will return and will rule from a throne in Jerusalem for exactly a thousand years. After that, Satan will be destroyed in a final battle and all people will be judged.

Lots of Christians hold to this view.

Amillennialists think that "a thousand years" is a big chunk of time but not a literal thousand years. They don't believe in a "rapture" that removes believers from a world about to be plunged into seven years of suffering. They believe that Jesus *already* rules, that he is already king of his church, that God's kingdom won't only have a street address in Jerusalem but is already found in the hearts and minds of believers.

The Catechism supports that view when it says that Christ is "head of the church" and that the Father "rules all things through him." In other words, God and Christ are already on the throne, ruling minds and hearts and the world itself.

Here is the whole truth: Jesus rules—yesterday, today, tomorrow, and forever.

Lord God Almighty, you are on your throne. You rule, even today, over the powers of the world—kings and Presidents, mullahs and Prime Ministers. Thank you, Lord. Amen.

A Carry-Out Faith

Q&A 50

. . . that the Father rules all things through him.

Then Jesus came to them and said, "All authority in heaven and on earth has been given to me."

—Matthew 28:18

Sarah loves Christianity. Her new church really rocks. They've got this praise band that just won't quit, a youth group that goes white-water rafting twice a summer, and a youth pastor named Jeff who can pick a guitar like nobody's business.

Not long ago, Sarah's dad left her mom, so she's had plenty of ugliness in her life. When she gets to church, she gets this lift, this shot in the arm. It's absolutely wonderful. Sometimes she wishes every day were Sunday so she could feel as good as she does at church. It's the greatest thing.

In fact, lots of believers think of some spiritual experience as the high point of their lives. I once did a story on a young woman who told me that her cancer was absolutely the best thing that ever happened to her because it brought her closer to the Lord than she'd ever been. Sometimes even our lows become highs through the Lord Jesus Christ.

Faith can be so good that we want to stay there, like Sarah. We want to stay up, stay high. For some of us, Christianity is an incredible thrill. It makes us happy.

Day-to-day life, on the other hand, can be a chore. You've got to show up each day at school and work hard to get a good grade. At night there's homework to do, tables to clear, dishes to put away. Work means work, not happiness.

It's easy to see how faith can become something that leads us away from the work-a-day world. An old theologian, now dead, used to say that becoming a Christian means two conversions—one to God, and another back to the world.

That guy was on the money. I'm not saying Sarah is wrong. Thank God she loves her church. Thank God she can't wait to go back every Sunday. Thank God she's thanking God.

But her faith will grow when she learns to take it back into memorizing French, into finishing that research paper, into learning once more to love her father.

The Bible says that Jesus has been given *all* authority in heaven and on earth. And the Christ, at the right hand of God, rules all things—not just church, but home and homework, high school and college, basketball court and theater, auto shop and office.

Faith isn't faith until it's carried out of the church.

Help us carry our faith back into the world, Lord. Fill us with grace so that every bit of who we are shines with God's glory. Strengthen us for the tough task of being a Christian every day—every hour—of our lives. In Christ's name, Amen.

Puppies and Other Gifts

Q&A 51

Through his Holy Spirit he pours out his gifts from heaven. . . .

We have different gifts, according to the grace given us.

—Romans 12:6

Consider Kayla. She's five. She's skipping off to school, her backpack snugged up around her shoulders. Her mind is on what to name the puppy her mom brought home yesterday, and she's also thinking about that little house made of Popsicle sticks she started working on yesterday in kindergarten. She's got a great life.

Now consider Matlyn. She's seventeen. She's driving her beat-up Cavalier to school, but she knows it won't be long before she has to shell out big bucks for a brake job. She's in love—sort of. Sammy's a great-looking guy, but she doesn't trust him, even though her friends would think she was nuts to drop him. Today the list of who made the soccer team is going up; she's afraid she won't make it because there are a bunch of ninth-grade wonders all over the field. Last week, she had this paper due in English. It still isn't in. She's got a great life too, but it's got more shadowy corners.

The difference between Kayla and Matlyn is something called growing up. What does Kayla know about AIDS? Nothing. Kayla doesn't have a clue about boy problems either. Matlyn, on the other hand, has a worry list as long as a row of lockers.

When you become an adult, life gets more complex because the world gets much bigger. My own children are about to have their first baby. That sweet little blessing will change their world completely. That's what they're going to find out.

So how do we get along in a world where cars have bad brakes and weeds grow in the cracks of sidewalks? How do people live when life gets terrifyingly more complicated than kindergarten?

The Catechism says that Christ's being glorified today with the Father benefits us by the gifts he pours out to Matlyn and Kayla, to you and me, by way of his Spirit. What gifts? The gifts of the Spirit. The Bible talks about those in several places—Romans 12; 1 Corinthians 12; Ephesians 4—but the easiest way to summarize them is in three words: *faith, hope,* and *love.* You probably already know the greatest of these.

When life gets bigger and more tangled, when we graduate from kindergarten—as we must—then remember these gifts: faith in God, hope that all things will work together for our good, and love for God above all and our neighbors as ourselves. That's how to live.

Gifts. From Jesus. Because he rules.

Bless our faith, Lord, make it grow. Shine up our hope each day of our lives. Strengthen our love for others and for you. Thank you for the gifts of your Spirit. Amen.

On Patrol

Q&A 51

By his power he defends us and keeps us safe from all enemies.

My sheep listen to my voice; I know them, and they follow me. I give them eternal life, and they shall never perish; no one can snatch them out of my hand.

—John 10:27–28

Last week something really important happened, something many of you will remember for years. What? The fourth book in the Harry Potter series was published, *Harry Potter and the Goblet of Fire.*

J. K. Rowling's book hit stores at midnight on July 8, 2000. With prepublication sales, it sold three million copies in just a day or two. The publisher, Scholastic, plans to reprint two million more and another million later.

I'm thrilled. I like writing, I teach writing, and I like books. In the last decade, some people were afraid that computers would wrestle books out of the picture. So the success of Harry Potter makes me smile. Millions of kids are discovering the magic of reading. And that's good.

Some Christians think the Harry Potter books are dangerous. They think their kids might get interested in witchcraft and other magical stuff discussed in the books. I've told you before that Christians don't always agree with each other. They pray to the same God, but they don't always ask for the same things. We're different, and that's not all bad.

But when I read the Catechism, this is what I hear: Remember, Christ's in heaven, God's headquarters. "By his power," it says, "he defends us and keeps us safe from all enemies." I believe that. Christ himself is on patrol for us, 24/7, always.

Does that mean I can drive seventy in a forty-five zone? Does that mean I can surf the Net and read whatever I want? Of course not.

But God rules, remember. It's probably fair to say that most Christians love Christmas more than Ascension Day—after all, there are no presents under the tree in May. But the Catechism makes clear that Christ's ascension is very important. Because he rules. He's King. Today, the baby in the manger is King of the world.

He's in charge. Satan is alive and kicking, but God rules. We don't have to be afraid. We don't have to sit in the corner and chew off our fingernails. We don't have to worry endlessly—Christ is King. He's the Lord of our lives, and he rules every inch of this world.

So go ahead—read Harry Potter, if you haven't already. But always remember and always believe that God reigns, now and forever.

Help us not to be afraid, Lord. Help us to trust in you because we know you ascended and you rule. Although darkness is in us and around us, you are King of the universe. Amen.

Unimaginable

Q&A 52

I turn my eyes to the heavens. . .

When the Son of Man comes in his glory, and all the angels with him, he will sit on his throne in heavenly glory. All the nations will be gathered before him. . . .

—Matthew 25:31–32

Guess what? I'm going to be a grandpa. Our daughter called to tell us the news. It's true. We can't believe it.

In fact, it's really unimaginable. But then, so much about life is like that, don't you think? When my kids were tiny little people, it was impossible to think of them going to school. When they were grade school kids, it was impossible to think of them growing into high schoolers. When they were in college, it was impossible for me to think of them married.

Listen to this impossible story. Someday in the not-too-distant future you have a very good chance of selecting, from all the possible applicants in the whole wide world, one man or woman to be the husband or wife you will live with for the rest of your life.

In fact, someday most of you will be parents. Last night we were in the local hospital where a young mother was glowing like the evening sun, her brand-new baby in her arms, her family all around her. Impossible as this may seem, most of you will probably go on to become grandparents too. Like I'm going to be.

Look around you. Ten years down the line every face you see is going to look a whole lot different. Impossible to think about, isn't it?

Actually, the big changes ahead of you in life are not as impossible to imagine as Christ's second coming. After all, some of you have older brothers and sisters or uncles or aunts who graduated from high school or college, who settled into a career, who married, who have kids of their own. In other words, what seems impossible isn't really all that far-fetched, because we already recognize a pattern into which many of our lives will fall.

But nobody's ever seen a second coming. Nobody's ever witnessed anything close to what the Scripture promises. One day, the Apostles' Creed says, Christ will descend from heaven to judge the living and the dead. Unimaginable, isn't it?

Like air flight. Like television. Like people walking on the moon. Like cyberspace.

No. I take that back. Even bigger. More unimaginable.

Someday the totally unimaginable will not only be imagined—it will really happen. Jesus is coming again.

Believe it.

Lord, it's impossible for us to imagine, but someday the world as we know it will end and you will return. Help us not to forget this as we live out each day of our lives. Amen.

Faith and Sight

Q&A 52

I . . . confidently await . . .

Then Jesus told [Thomas], "Because you have seen me, you have believed; blessed are those who have not seen and yet have believed."

—John 20:29

Let's be perfectly honest. There's a lot we really don't know.

Did God actually make Mary conceive, or is that just some weird idea?

How do we know for sure that a bunch of Jesus' followers didn't spike the soldiers' drinks, push the stone away from the cave where Christ was buried, and then make up stories about his coming back? How do we really, really know what happened?

Who's to say a couple of guys didn't get together and make everything up? Every one of the gospel stories is a little different, right? Three of the four gospels don't even mention Jesus being born in a manger.

Joshua holds his hands up and the sun stands still? Give me a break. The sun stands still all the time. Who's trying to pull my leg here? If the earth stopped turning, even for a second, we'd have catastrophe all over the globe.

Moses raises his hands, and the Red Sea breaks in two like a frozen candy bar? Come on. The Israelites are hungry, so bread falls from the sky? I'm sure.

Fantasyland—that's what it is. The whole Bible is just a book of fantastic stories that people are stupid enough to believe.

And here's the last silliness: Someday he's returning. Some supersized trumpet will sound from Lapland to Las Vegas, from the top of the world to the bottom, and everyone everywhere at the same time will see Jesus riding down on the clouds. Believe that and you've got to be delusional.

Let's face it—the Bible offers a lot to swallow. Faith is really something of a miracle. Why do some people believe and others think the whole business is one huge myth?

All I know for sure is this: Faith is a gift from God. Thomas had it, but he saw Jesus in the flesh. Jesus said we're blessed if we believe without seeing him at all.

That takes confidence. But the Bible insists that someday our faith will be sight. What we only believe right now will someday be as real as the chair I'm sitting on.

Then everyone will know that once upon a time a baby was born in a stable. Every last pair of eyes will see Jesus Christ. They'll all know, beyond any doubt, that God Almighty was the baby's father.

Someday every knee shall bow because everyone will see. Everyone will know.

Lord, we know that one day you will be not only in our hearts and minds but also on our doorsteps. Help us not to be afraid of that day but to await your return confidently, knowing that you love us. Amen.

94

The Last Judgment

Q&A 52

I . . . confidently await as judge the very One who has already stood trial in my place before God and so has removed the whole curse from me.

For God did not send his Son into the world to condemn the world, but to save the world through him. Whoever believes in him is not condemned. . . .

—John 3:17–18

Frank C. Baker was a fine man. Those who knew him understood that sometimes he and his wife went through some major battles, and sometimes the house turned cold as ice. Nonetheless, Frank C. Baker was a fine man. A list of the people he helped would run as long as your arm.

Frank C. Baker had a secretary. Sometimes he'd tell her about his problems. She'd listen. Once or twice she hugged him because he felt so rotten. One day she hugged him, and he kissed her. Then she kissed him. In about a month they were sneaking out to a motel.

Want to know something else? Frank C. Baker was a pastor.

I'm making this up, but stories like this really do happen. Some of you have lived through them.

Frank C. Baker broke the commandment about adultery and his promise to his wife. He also broke the relationship he had with his kids and the people in his church. His secret sin was secret no more.

In a way, we're all Frank C. Bakers. All of us have secret sins of one kind or another. We all know something about ourselves nobody else does.

For centuries, the Last Judgment has sent shivers down the spines of Christians because it means a public airing of everything we've ever done. No more secrets. Of course, Jesus Christ knows it all already, but come Judgment Day, everything we've ever done gets plastered on the front page—everything. No question, that's scary.

Here's the good news. At the trial we'll all go through, the judge who hears about our sins is on our side. God sent him into the world not to condemn us but to save us (John 3:17–18). He suffered for us. He's been taking our part ever since. And when all our ugliness is on the evening news, he'll forgive us. That's a promise.

Should we be scared by the Last Judgment? Sure.

But here's our *comfort*—remember that word? The judge, Jesus Christ, loves us dearly.

Don't despair. He's on our side. He'll bring us home.

Certainly we all have sinned, Lord. Nobody would want everybody else to know how. Thank you for being our judge. It's wonderful to know that you will be with us to comfort and to bless. Clean up our hearts and lives, Lord. Make us ready for the coming of the Lord. Amen.

He Is Lord

Q&A 52

In all my distress and persecution . . .

At the name of Jesus every knee should bow . . . and every tongue confess that Jesus Christ is Lord.

—Philippians 2:10–11

Maybe 1 percent, at best, of the people reading this right now are persecuted. The vast majority of books like the one you're reading will be distributed in North America, where believing in Jesus Christ is no crime.

Oh, sure, public school students can't pray in class, and it's probably possible for people to be fired from a job for refusing to work on Sunday. But outright persecution for personal beliefs is something North Americans don't tolerate. Let's face it, the vast majority of Christians in North America today have it pretty good.

But for believers—like the writers of the Catechism—who suffer persecution any time or any place, thoughts of Judgment Day overflow with joy. They know they will be big-time winners, and their persecutors will be powerless against them.

The Catechism talks about our *distress,* something we all experience. Parents hassle us, boyfriends or girlfriends want out of a relationship, a beloved grandparent dies, we mess up—big time. But to the writers of the Catechism, *distress* was just another word for *persecution;* and you have to admit that there's not too much of that going on around town.

Maybe it's a good time to think about another whole scene on Judgment Day. Remember the song "He Is Lord"? It goes like this: "He is Lord, he is Lord,/he is risen from the dead/and he is Lord./Every knee shall bow,/every tongue confess/that Jesus Christ is Lord."

Every knee? *Every* tongue? Yes! Every Islamic cleric in the world, every Shintu priest, every head of state, every New Age guru, every homeless mother, everybody who eats hotdogs, every baby, every teenager, everybody ninety years old, every last human being—*not just believers*—will bend their knee and confess Jesus' name. What a picture!

Some won't be happy, but every knee shall bow. Everyone will know; every last shred of every last bit of unbelief will be torn away. All that will remain is what's enthroned before the eyes of the whole world: Jesus Christ is Lord.

When that day comes, there will be no doubt. He is Lord. He is risen from the dead, and he is Lord.

Lord Jesus, come quickly. Thank you for assuring us of our own salvation. Thank you that one day everyone will know that you are Lord. You reign. Yours is the honor and the glory forever. Amen.

Stones Rolled Away

Q&A 52

Me and all his chosen ones he will take along with him into the joy and the glory of heaven.

[God] will wipe every tear from their eyes. There will be no more death or mourning or crying or pain. . . .

—Revelation 21:4

Lori and Simone found each other sometime in grade six or so. They weren't from the same neighborhood exactly, but somewhere in middle school they sat beside each other, and, for the most part, never really parted again. They were both believers.

Almost daily each wore something of the other's clothes. They had this thing about laughing at exactly the same things. Sometimes one started a sentence and the other finished.

Lori was better at volleyball, but Simone was better in school. No matter. They were almost like a team.

One night on the way home from practice, Simone's mother was stopped at a red light. A drunk came through the intersection in a blaze, lost control to avoid a head-on, and slammed into the passenger side of the car, killing Simone instantly.

Simone, people said, didn't suffer at all. In a flash she was gone.

Lori suffered immensely. For more than a year, she was a loner. It was as if an entire chunk of the book of her life had been ripped out of the bindings. She quit volleyball. Most of the time she sat up in her room doing absolutely nothing. Hiding, maybe.

Like lots and lots of people, Lori has a stone in her heart, a weighty horror that makes her feel as if every morning, even before she gets out of bed, she's toting a hulking backpack. Look around sometime in church. There are lots of Loris.

And now listen to this. On the Day of the Lord, Lori's loss will be ended, her grief will be wiped out, her sadness deleted. On the Day of the Lord, the horror of death will no longer tower over her life like some gigantic, gloomy shadow. On the Day of the Lord, the stone in her heart will be rolled away.

On the Day of the Lord, every knee shall bow, every tongue confess that Jesus Christ is Lord. On the Day of the Lord, there will be no more tears. On the Day of the Lord, Jesus Christ will show sin and death the door forever.

On the Day of the Lord, Simone and Lori will have each other. But far more than that, they'll have joy that never ends.

My only comfort? In life and *in death* I belong to my faithful Savior, Jesus Christ.

Thank you for your promise that you are coming again to throw death and sin out of our lives forever and ever. Be with those who mourn. Give them—and all of us—the comfort of knowing that a time is coming when there will be no more tears. Amen.

The Holy Spirit

Q&A 53

What do you believe concerning "the Holy Spirit"?

But you will receive power when the Holy Spirit comes on you. . . .

—Acts 1:8

I think the scariest member of the Trinity is the Holy Spirit. Let me try to explain.

Last night at a big national political convention, some pop singer named Lee Greenwood got up after a speech and sang his song "I'm Proud to Be an American."

All the ingredients for a big thrill were already in place. Thousands of delegates, all decked out in red, white, and blue, had been treated the night before to a full dose of red-blooded patriotism by a handful of heroic World War II veterans. What's more, the speaker who preceded the song had brought the delegates to their feet time after time. The crowd was up, soaring like eagles.

When Mr. Greenwood sang, most of the delegates sang with him—many with their hands raised high into the air, eyes shut tightly, bodies swaying to the beat.

It reminded me of the kind of worship that's become really fashionable, believers high on the thrill of Jesus' love. Of course, the thrill at the convention was strictly patriotic, not spiritual.

One reason I say the Holy Spirit is "scary" is that we sometimes mistake the work of the Holy Spirit for sheer excitement in church. You can't blame us for that, I guess. Maybe church has been far too boring for far too long. But getting high on the Lord—if that's where it ends—isn't a whole lot different than getting high, period.

I say all of that because it's strange that in the whole Heidelberg Catechism, there's only one question about the Holy Spirit, the third person of the Trinity. Sure—I know the work of the Spirit is described in many other questions and answers. But only one question directly asks what we believe about the Holy Spirit. There must be lots of reasons for that. Maybe one is that it's kind of hard to pin down exactly when the Holy Spirit is at work. And that can be scary.

I could list a ton of examples: believers who thought they heard God's voice telling them to do this or that, believers who claimed the Holy Spirit had convinced them to build theme parks or utopian villages.

Who's to say, finally, they weren't right?

That's why we need to listen carefully to what the Bible says about the Holy Spirit. That's why we need to ask the Spirit to live in our hearts.

"Scary" or not, we can't be Christians without the Spirit.

Lord, thank you for the gift of the Holy Spirit to comfort and to bless us. Amen.

Head and Heart

Q&A 53

First, he, as well as the Father and the Son, is eternal God.

"But you know [the Spirit], for he lives with you and will be in you."

—John 14:17

In one of John Updike's novels, two totally different characters go to war. The first, an older guy, a professor of religion, knows biblical languages, and he knows the Bible inside out. He knows why each gospel tells different stories about Jesus. He understands why Baptists believe one thing and Roman Catholics another because he has made a career out of studying Christianity from apostolic times to today.

But get this—he doesn't believe a word of it.

His rival is a young computer buff who knows nothing about the history of faith and very little about the Bible or its great themes. What he knows for sure is what he feels in his heart: that Jesus is his Savior. He knows he is saved. Of that he's absolutely sure.

The old guy has head knowledge coming out of his ears. The young guy has heart knowledge that just won't quit. The computer geek is absolutely convicted; the religion prof doesn't believe anything. The two of them are, Updike suggests, two sides of a coin.

In the whole Catechism, this single question about the Holy Spirit starts with this affirmation: The Holy Spirit is eternal God. Period.

What we have to know in our heads—first off—is that the Holy Spirit isn't a sweet, touchy-feely moment. The Holy Spirit is not a plateful of delicious onion rings before a great dinner. The Holy Spirit isn't a smile. The Holy Spirit *is* God. Put that in the department marked "head knowledge." Know it.

But how can we come to really know that? Only through the Holy Spirit at work in our hearts. Only the Holy Spirit makes it clear. We know in our heads that the Holy Spirit is God because the Holy Spirit convicts us in our hearts.

The old man in Updike's book didn't have the Holy Spirit at work in his heart. His immense head knowledge wasn't enough. He needed heart knowledge, something only the Holy Spirit can give.

You need to know that the Holy Spirit is "eternal God"; but the only way you'll ever know that for sure is by way of the Holy Spirit's work in your heart.

Head by way of heart. That's the work of the Holy Spirit, eternal God.

Holy Spirit, work in my heart so that I will know beyond doubt that you are God. Amen.

A Personal Savior

Q&A 53

[The Holy Spirit] has been given to me personally. . . .

Do you not know that your body is a temple of the Holy Spirit, who is in you, whom you have received from God?

—1 Corinthians 6:19

Some people, me included, tend to get a little queasy when people continually call Jesus Christ their "personal Savior." To me it suggests that Jesus Christ is something like a credit card, always there in your billfold to use whenever you need a little cash. It's got your name on it; you can pull it out whenever you need it.

Calling Jesus "my personal Savior," in effect, makes him into something of a pet—a handsome thoroughbred maybe, but a pet nonetheless, something we could corral in our backyard.

You know as well as I do that Jesus Christ, who died for our sins, rose again, and ascended into heaven to rule over all the earth, is neither a credit card nor a thoroughbred. He's the King of the universe. But sometimes it seems we'd rather think of Jesus as ours, and ours alone, instead of as the Lord of every corner of all our lives.

But then I read the Catechism. It says the Holy Spirit "has been given to me *personally*." That word *personally* comes at the end like a clap of thunder, because it's the featured word.

Listen: The Holy Spirit isn't a wave of emotion that comes over a crowd at a spirited political rally; the Holy Spirit comes to us *personally*. In fact, the Holy Spirit operates in each of us as our *personal* Holy Spirit.

For me and you to know that the Holy Spirit is eternal God, the Holy Spirit has to convict us individually, up close, personally.

You may have heard the saying "God has no grandchildren." It's an odd line, but I think it's true. Your parents may be Christians, as mine are; your grandparents may be Christians, as mine were. In fact, some of your families may have been believers for hundreds of years.

Does that make you a believer? Nope. Faith isn't like the color of your hair or the size of your feet. We don't inherit it.

The Holy Spirit works in you personally. In me too. The Holy Spirit works in every believer.

The Spirit's not a fad, but a presence. Someone who's in us.

In me, in you. *Personally*.

Thank you, Lord, for giving me the Holy Spirit, for coming into my life and into my heart. Please send your Spirit into the hearts of those who don't yet know your comfort and blessing. Help me to show the joy of knowing, in my heart, that you are eternal God. Amen.

The Catholic Church

Q&A 54

. . . out of the entire human race . . .

By your blood you ransomed for God saints from every tribe and language and people and nation. . . .

—Revelation 5:9 NRSV

Mark and Jenni met on a church work trip. A medical ministry in Venezuela wanted a dormitory built for people who needed medical help, people who had to travel long distances to get to the clinic.

Mark and Jenni went to work on it along with about twenty other kids. It was unmercifully hot in Venezuela. The village where they lived had no cement trucks, so, like the slaves in Egypt, they had to mix concrete by hand.

Mark and Jenni had never worked harder in their lives. After three days, both wondered why they'd come. The mosquitoes were as big as SUVs; in fact, every insect was jumbo-sized. The food wasn't much either, and at night there was nothing to do.

On Sunday they went to church—all the kids did. The church building had no glass in its windows, just open air. The roof was caving in and ancient folding chairs stood on a dirt floor. No organ. No piano. The service lasted two hours.

But something happened at that service.

One of the men who had been working with them—his name was Jesus, a common name in that part of the world—stood up and took off his hat. Jesus said stuff they understood, even though he was speaking in Spanish. He pointed at them, at the place where they were working, at the paths people might take to the new dormitory, and he cried.

All around them the people started praying, so that soon every tongue in that place was praising God.

For Mark and Jenni, that moment changed the whole trip. For the first time they'd seen God's holy catholic church, the church universal. They'd seen God in Venezuela.

All of a sudden that strange line in the Apostles' Creed—I believe in a holy *catholic* church—took on new meaning.

Catholic, as I'm sure you know, means "universal." So when we say we believe in the holy *catholic* church, we are saying that we know the church of Jesus Christ is huge. We know that Christ gathers his own in every corner of the world.

Jesus Christ is everywhere. And so are those who follow him.

Lord Jesus, you have followers in every corner of the world. Help us to remember that millions of people from every tribe and nation are praying and singing and praising your name. Thank you that your church is big enough for all of us. Amen.

Harvest Time

Q&A 54

The Son of God . . . gathers, protects, and preserves. . . .

A farmer went out to sow his seed.
—Matthew 13:3

How many people have you saved? Think about it for a minute. How many people can you say you personally brought to Christ?

In some faith traditions, that's an important question. If you can't name even one—just one solitary human being—then maybe you ought to wonder about whether or not you are witnessing enough.

Sounds right, doesn't it? But really there's something goofy about that idea. Goofy because it implies that *we* bring people to Jesus. We don't.

The Catechism says "the Son of God" does three things: *gathers, protects,* and *preserves.* Did you notice who's doing the work here? Who's doing the gathering, protecting, and preserving? It's not us. It's the Son of God.

You may remember the parable of the sower. The sower went out and did his job, spreading the seed. Some fell on hard ground, some fell among thorns or rocks, and some fell on good ground. The sower spread the seed. That's all. He had nothing to do with which of those thousands of seeds sprouted. Nothing.

It's God who brings the harvest. God who works in people's hearts so that the seed of the gospel sprouts. God who gathers the holy catholic church.

Does that mean we should just sit back on our La-Z-Boys and watch Turner Classic Movies? Of course not. Even though God does everything, God wants us to preach the gospel. Remember Christ's last words before his ascension? A command: "Go into all the world and preach the gospel." He didn't say, "If you've got nothing to do, how about telling others about my love?" Nope, it was a command.

Today almost every church has some great idea about evangelism. We have so many people worrying about the "unchurched" and the "underchurched" that we get tired sometimes—we start to feel like the "overchurched." It's great when churches run a list of outreach programs as long as your arm—as long as they don't get the idea that they're the ones who are bringing people to Christ.

That work is done mysteriously. It takes place deep, deep within every single human being who comes to know the Lord.

The Catechism says Christ gathers, protects, and preserves. It's not the elders, the bishop, the pastor, or some other committee. It's not even the church.

Jesus Christ builds his holy catholic church in his way, in his time.

He is God. We are his people.

In all of our busyness, Lord, help us never to forget that we are not divine. Make us instruments of your peace, your love, your grace. All praise and glory be to your name. Amen.

Scowling in Church

Q&A 54

Of this community I am and always will be a living member.

I tell you that you are Peter, and on this rock I will build my church, and the gates of Hades will not overcome it.

—Matthew 16:18

I used to think that my church argued far too much, that our anger burned far hotter than our commitment. In a way, I still do. I wish we didn't beat each other up so often. I wish people—like me—didn't have to have their way all the time.

But I've come to believe my denomination isn't any different from others. Last year, for a book I was writing, I listened to the life stories of people from many different churches. One chapter of each of their stories seemed pretty much the same. "We used to go to this church, but then the pastor . . ." or "We attended that church but didn't like the worship. . . ."

No church I've ever attended is without sin. It's probably fair to say that where two or three gather to worship, eventually somebody's going to scowl at someone else.

The Catechism tells us that the holy catholic church is gathered, protected, and preserved by no less a power than the Son of God. Those who are so gathered, protected, and preserved, it says, are "chosen for eternal life" and "united in true faith." In the holy catholic church, the church of which you are a member, there is no squabbling. No one walks away, and no one has the wrong idea.

The holy catholic church, you see, is not made of brick and mortar. It doesn't have a street address, even though you can find it all over. It's not only Baptist or Christian Reformed or Lutheran or Roman Catholic. It's not only Reformed, Presbyterian, Methodist, or Assemblies of God. It's all of those, and more.

The holy catholic church exists wherever people *do* something in God's name: It's the place where they confess their faith, pray, speak for people who have no voice, bring God's truth to politics and art and farming, speak the truth in love.

Members of the holy catholic church work and pray in New York, New Guinea, New Iberia, New Holland, and Newfoundland. And you want to know what else? The holy catholic church will be there in the new heaven and the new earth. Even hell itself can't overcome the church, says Jesus.

That's a promise. The holy catholic church will last for eternity.

And get this: If you love Jesus, you're a member.

Lord, help us not to forget that you draw your people from every corner of the world. Thank you for making us members. Help us each to do your work in the world. Amen.

Better Than Bucks

Q&A 55

What do you understand by "the communion of saints"? First, that believers one and all, as members of this community, share in Christ and in all his treasures and gifts.

And now these three remain: faith, hope and love. But the greatest of these is love.

—1 Corinthians 13:13

I see the word *treasures* and I see the darkened galley of a ship full of colorful, swashbuckling pirates. Their hands and arms are thrust into overflowing chests of loot, each of those pirates running gold doubloons through his fingers, the whole heinous mess lit by jumpy torchlight. Their laughing crackles like wildfire. The treasures glow in those heavy chests.

Not too many Christians I know would like to be mistaken for pirates. In fact, take a dozen old monks and put them in the same ship with all that gold, and, try as I might, I just don't get the same kind of wicked glow.

But the Catechism says that believers share in Christ and in all his treasures and gifts. So it's really not that much of a stretch to imagine a whole cast of Christians sitting around, laughing, maybe even crackling like wildfire, thrilled with God's gifts and treasures.

God's gifts and treasures aren't exactly pirate chests overflowing with ancient doubloons. The Catechism certainly means more than money, because what we share as believers is far better than bucks. So what exactly are these gifts?

A good place to look for an answer is 1 Corinthians 13, Paul's famous passage on faith, hope, and love. Faith, let's remember, is a gift, not something we earn, not something we take on and pull off like a cap on a bad-hair day. And hope? Well, hope comes as a result of faith. Believers know there's more to life than what meets the eye.

Love, "the greatest of these," is *why* we have faith and hope: because God loves us. God's love is the gift that keeps on giving. Because of God's love, we have faith; because of faith, we have hope.

If believers have no faith, they're not believers. If the faithful have no hope, they're not faithful to God's promise. If those who hope for life in eternity with the Lord have no love, then they really don't give a toot about eternity.

What links believers are these three infinitely precious gold doubloons: faith, hope, and love. Those gifts sit in the center of our lives and glow with the radiance of the Holy Spirit. Go ahead, run your fingers through them.

Sometimes it's amazing to realize, Lord, how indebted to you we really are. Thank you for faith, thank you for hope, thank you for love. Amen.

Bowling Alone

Q&A 55

Each . . . should . . . use these gifts . . . readily and cheerfully for the service and enrichment of the other members.

If I have a faith that can move mountains, but have not love, I am nothing.

—1 Corinthians 13:2

In 1995, a man named Robert D. Putnam published a book titled *Bowling Alone: The Collapse and Revival of American Community.* I don't think he became an instant millionaire, but it's fair to say that the book stopped a whole lot of people in their tracks. Almost immediately he was invited to speak to the President, and after that he made the rounds on talk shows.

Putnam said something really big was changing in our culture, and he used bowling leagues to illustrate his point. People weren't joining teams anymore, he said, just as they weren't joining civic organizations, just as they weren't going out for big picnics with their friends. The whole culture, he said, was losing its interest in being with other people.

Why? One reason, certainly, is television, the one-eyed monster. People watch it much more than they ever have.

Two-career families and sheer busyness are other roadblocks to people getting together, said Putnam. He's right. My son, for instance, lives in a huge apartment complex near Burbank, California. Thousands of people live right next to each other, he says, but few of them know their neighbors.

Instead of bowling in leagues, Putnam said, people do almost everything by themselves. Our society is losing the glue that makes us a community. People don't care much about others.

The church simply can't be like that. The Apostles' Creed says the church is supposed to be a "communion of saints," a place of real love and concern for others. Believers have to be there for each other.

If you think about it, the whole idea makes sense. After all, believers have the great treasures of faith and hope and love. Each is a gift. Each comes from the Lord of heaven and earth. It makes no sense whatsoever to think that people who have been blessed like that should sit on those gifts.

Christ's real church—the holy catholic church, the communion of saints—makes it a habit to "be there" for each other and for others. Believers go the extra mile, hard as that sometimes is. Believers drive welcome wagons. Make sure there's cold water to go around. Do the work of the Lord, bringing love and faith and hope to a world of folks who sit alone behind the tube far too often, who are sometimes starved for companionship yet look passionately for love.

The church loves. That's the bottom line.

Lord, don't allow us to sit on what we've been given. Remind us that we're blessed beyond belief, and help us to share that love with others. Amen.

Forgive and Forget?

Q&A 56

What do you believe concerning the "forgiveness of sins?" In his grace God grants me the righteousness of Christ to free me forever from judgment.

I, even I, am he who blots out your transgressions . . . and remembers your sins no more.

—Isaiah 43:25

When I was two years old, my aunt was killed in a car accident. I don't remember the accident. For that matter, I don't remember my aunt. She used to play with me, I'm told, but of her I don't have even the faintest memory.

I do know she was on a date the night she was killed. I know who she was dating too. Years later, my parents told me.

It's fair to say that I'll never forget the man who was with her on the night she died. Even though I didn't know my aunt, even though I don't remember the accident, even though I never shed a tear about the whole incident, I do know who was with her, and I'll never forget it.

I don't blame him. I can't. My parents don't blame him either. Chances are, he may well blame himself, because in situations like that, good people tend to take the blame for things that went way, way wrong.

I suppose this capacity not to forget is something human. Maybe there are real saints walking around on earth who can totally forget the bad things that happened, but I don't know of any.

Oscar Hijeulos wrote a beautiful novel titled *Mr. Ives' Christmas,* a sad yet wonderful story about forgiveness. In it Mr. Ives, a very religious man, suffers the death of his son, who is murdered senselessly just outside a church and just before Christmas. Mr. Ives' faith nearly chokes on his own deep sorrow, but empowered by God, he learns to forgive the man who murdered his son. Mr. Ives forgives, but I don't think Mr. Ives ever forgets.

Only God forgives *and* forgets. Isn't that a miracle? Even though we sin by deed and by nature, when God forgives, God honestly even forgets. The Catechism says we live free from condemnation. It's gone. Forever. There's no trace of anything in God Almighty's memory. It's as if our sin never happened.

God will remember our sin no more (Isa. 43:25). God forgets our sin just as easily as I can delete this sentence forever from the screen in front of me. I can't forget like that. Only God can.

That's what we call "amazing grace."

Thank you, Lord, for sending your Son into the world so that every last bit of our sin can be completely deleted. Even if we can't forget, we know that you do. Thank you for forgiving our sins and freeing us forever. In Jesus' name, Amen.

Want a New Body?

Q&A 57

Even my very flesh . . . will be . . . made like Christ's glorious body.

The Lord Jesus Christ . . . by the power that enables him to bring everything under his control, will transform our lowly bodies so that they will be like his glorious body.

—Philippians 3:21

You may know about Christopher Reeve. He was a bona fide Hollywood star who played the role of Superman in the movie by the same name some years ago. In May 1995, Reeve was riding a horse named *Easter Express* in a cross-country event in Culpepper, Virginia. The horse threw him at a rail jump, and because his hands were tangled, he hit the ground head first. The impact fractured his spine. For the rest of his life he was confined to a wheelchair.

For a man who once played Superman, living as a paraplegic wasn't at all easy—which is not to say that it's easy for anyone. Reeve, who became a crusader for medical research for spinal-cord injuries after his accident, once told a reporter that he cried every single day for years after his injury. "To wake up and make that shift, you know," he said, "and to just say, 'This really sucks' . . . to really allow yourself the feeling of loss, even two years later . . . still needs to be acknowledged."

Once Reeve broke his leg during the regular physical therapy he did every day in an effort to regain the ability to walk.

I don't know if Christopher Reeve was a believer or not, so I'm not sure if he ever thought about what the Apostles' Creed describes as "the resurrection of the body." But I do know this: That promise from the Scriptures comforts me—the promise that someday, in eternity, all the believing Christopher Reeves in the world will walk right out of their wheelchairs as if they'd never sat there for a moment.

Not only that, they won't suffer broken legs when they dance before the throne. All those brittle bones will be changed in the twinkling of an eye. We'll all be supermen and superwomen, not because we're stronger or faster or equipped with sharper eyesight, but because all our bodies will be transformed into bodies that are as glorious as Christ's own.

The dead will arise, the lame walk, the deaf hear, the blind see. That's the power of the gospel.

I believe in the resurrection of the body.

Lord, comfort those whose bodies don't work as well as they should. Thank you for your promise that one day, in eternity, everyone will dance. Amen.

Whispers of Eternity

Q&A 58

Even as I already now experience in my heart the beginning of eternal joy . . .

"He prays to God and finds favor with him; he sees God's face and shouts for joy."

—Job 33:26

Last night on TV, I watched a huge Pentecostal rally led by a powerful preacher who had the whole crowd absolutely on fire. All over, people were waving their hands, speaking in tongues, and being struck, as they'd say, by the Spirit.

I don't think I'll ever experience the Lord in the way the people in that crowd did. For some reason, that doesn't really bother me. I don't long for a spiritual experience like the rally attended by those thousands in that huge church.

But neither would I tell them that what they experienced wasn't good or right or "Christian." God Almighty uses a huge arsenal to fight the devil, an arsenal that includes just about everything under the sun. I'm sure lots of believers who left that auditorium last night felt themselves strengthened in the Spirit and stronger in the Lord than they were when they walked in.

We all experience moments—and not necessarily in church—when we hear whispers of eternity, when we see and touch and know a little taste of the divine.

I've said this before, but I'll say it again. I could show you a place not far from where I'm sitting, a quiet place on the slope of a long hill where you can see almost forever. Whenever I take my writing students there, nobody says a word. God seems so close.

Here's another of those moments. Just a few weeks ago, I held a baby during a communion service. I'm going to be a grandpa soon, the Lord willing. I knew that before the service, but when I held that baby that morning, I just about fell apart. I can only describe that joy as a whisper of eternity.

For some of us watching Tiger Woods play golf is as close as we'll get to sheer perfection. For others music is the language of eternity. When I hear "Surely He Has Borne Our Griefs" from Handel's *Messiah*, my own flesh almost disappears.

Sometimes the worst of times can be the best of times. Cancer or unexpected death, for instance, brings people to their knees and thereby closer to God than they'd ever been.

The Apostles' Creed says we believe that we have "the life everlasting." According to the Catechism, we don't have to wait to get a taste of the joy of everlasting life—we *already* experience whispers of the magnificent joy of eternity.

Know what I mean?

Lord, thank you for life—for the good times and bad. Thanks for allowing us little whispers of the great joy we will know forever with you. Amen.

What No One Knows

Q&A 58

. . . perfect blessedness such as no eye has seen, no ear has heard, no human heart has ever imagined . . .

However, as it is written, "No eye has seen, no ear has heard, no mind has conceived what God has prepared for those who love him."

—1 Corinthians 2:9

Listen to this: "It's impossible to know what no one knows." The words themselves circle meaning like a dog chasing its own tail. But it makes sense: It's impossible to know what no one knows.

It's true, of course—try as we might, we can't know what can't be known. Which is not to say that all knowledge that is not known is unknowable. Fifty years ago or so a horrible, disfiguring disease called polio roamed freely throughout humankind. All over the world people caught it. Many died. Many were crippled. Nobody knew what to do. A cure, it seemed, was unknowable.

Along came teams of scientists headed by Jonas Salk and Albert Sabin. They picked virus samples of the disease, also called "infantile paralysis," out of a test tube and began immunization. Soon enough, what no one knew was known. People stopped dying from polio. Polio was toast.

The Catechism isn't really talking here about something discoverable. When it describes "perfect blessedness" as something "no eye has seen, no ear has heard, no human heart has ever imagined," it's talking about something so far from human experience that it can't even be dreamed up.

The fact is that those little whispers of eternity we sometimes hear and experience now are just that: whispers. A few weeks ago, Tiger Woods smacked a tree with a nine-iron. As perfect as he can be, sometimes he misses putts. That baby in my arms at the communion service? She could well have dirtied her diaper at just the moment I was blissfully imagining my own first grandchild. And Handel's *Messiah?* Sometimes even the best choirs mess up.

Eternity is unending blessedness, perfect perfection. To us mortals, eternity is beyond imagination. Take the most wonderful moment of your life so far and stretch it into forever. You can't. Nobody can.

Time to take stock. How does the fact of life everlasting comfort you? It promises something so great it's unimaginable. Try to get your mind around eternal joy. You can't. But believe it—what's to come will make the very best moments of our life into forever.

And more. And more. And more.

It's impossible to know what can't be known. Lost? Sure. So am I.

Just believe. Life forever with Jesus is just plain divine.

Thank you for your eternal promise, Lord, and thank you also for your promise of eternity. Help us never to forget that even the very best moments of our lives are just a little taste of what we'll enjoy someday with you. Amen.

So What?

Q&A 59

What good does it do you, however, to believe all this?

Whoever believes in the Son has eternal life. . . .

—John 3:36

Years ago, I was lecturing away on a writer named Henry David Thoreau. Sixty students sat in straight-back chairs, most of them pretty well convinced that an old guy who nailed together a clapboard house and lived by himself for two years was the kind of weirdo who wasn't worth their time. I could almost read their minds: "Give me the goods, Schaap. We don't care about him. What's going to be on the test?"

A student raised his hand. "So what?" he said when I called on him. "So what?"

Now, I happen to think reading Thoreau is a big deal. So I threw my chalk, kicked the wall, yelled and screamed, and tried to abuse the whole class into feeling the same way I did about Thoreau.

I don't know if many of those sixty students remember my tirade, but I do. And so does the person who asked the question. Today, twenty years later, he's my friend.

Any teacher worth his or her salt loves a question like that. I was no exception. It gave me the opportunity to go off like some Roman candle and spout what I thought was the truth about Thoreau.

That's why I love this question in the Catechism. We've just reviewed the entire Apostles' Creed, every last jot and tittle. At this point, the Catechism voices the question lots of us might be thinking: "Big deal—so what?"

Yeah, so what? The Apostles' Creed didn't get you out of doing that big paper that's due next week. It didn't get you a new set of wheels, and you probably still don't look that much like Leonardo DiCaprio or Jennifer Lopez. So where does all of this knowledge about faith get you finally?

The Catechism says that if you know it and believe it, then you're right with Christ. You're an heir of eternal salvation. That's it. No television appearances, no movie contracts, no new Mustang.

But—you already know this, don't you?—bucks disappear, beauty fades, snowmobiles rust. Eternity is forever. Eternity is always. Eternity never fades, spoils, rots, or blows away like so much dust.

What does faith promise in the end? Life everlasting with God Almighty.

No more. But no less.

And that's the "so what" of believing.

Lord, it's really hard sometimes to keep our eyes on you. There's so much really good stuff in the world, so much we want. Help us see that nothing is as important as your love. And help us to love others. Amen.

'Fess Up Time

Q&A 60

How are you right with God? Only by true faith in Jesus Christ.

God so loved the world . . . that whoever believes in him shall not perish. . . .

—John 3:16

Yesterday the Catechism asked, "So what?" We're almost halfway through, so maybe it's time for me to 'fess up. Why am I writing all of this stuff?

Easy. Because sometimes I wonder if too many believers today think that being happy or being good or feeling blessed is what faith is all about. I think there's more to it. Believing is terrific, but it's also important to know *what* you believe. The Catechism teaches us the content of our faith.

Let me try to explain. Just yesterday, the Roman Catholic Church issued a declaration rejecting what it called the growing feeling people have that all faiths are pretty much the same.

I admire the Roman Catholic Church for arguing that all kinds of faith aren't the same. Muslims aren't Jews, after all. Roman Catholics aren't Baptists. Mormons aren't Lutherans. Seventh Day Adventists aren't Reformed. I agree.

In their thirty-six-page declaration, the Roman Catholics claim that their church is the original and mother church, and that all other Christian fellowships "derive their efficacy from the very fullness of grace and truth entrusted to the Roman Catholic Church."

So what does *that* mean? The Roman Catholic Church doesn't say you have to be Catholic to be saved, but it does argue that other Christians can be saved *only* because other churches and denominations are like children of the Roman Catholic Church. Believers who are Reformed, for instance, can be saved even though they aren't Catholic, but only because Reformed churches were once connected to the Roman Catholic Church.

Now listen to the Catechism: How are you right with God?

Only by true faith in Jesus Christ.

That answer doesn't even mention the word *church*. That's because Reformers like Luther and Calvin were absolutely sure that the church couldn't give away or sell passes to eternity. A believer was "right with God" only by true faith, by believing—not because of the church itself. Churches don't save people; God does.

Why am I writing all this stuff? Because it's important for believers to know *what* they believe. I guess I'm a kid of the Reformation, because I believe we are right with God *only* by true faith, like it says in John 3:16.

That's important to know, don't you think?

Dear Lord, we know it's impossible to know everything about you. You are God, and we aren't. Help us grow daily in our faith. In Jesus' name, Amen.

"Nobody's Perfect"

Q&A 60

Even though my conscience accuses me of having grievously sinned against all God's commandments and of never having kept any of them, and even though I am still inclined toward all evil . . .

"Teacher," he declared, "all these [commandments] I have kept since I was a boy."
Jesus looked at him and loved him. "One thing you lack. . . . Go, sell everything you have and give to the poor. . . . Then come, follow me."

—Mark 10:20–21

Mr. Barriston looked over the history quizzes when he got home that night and discovered that only two of his students had perfect scores—Kelly and Mark. Odd, because they happened to sit beside each other. Mr. Barriston knew they weren't buddies, so they surely hadn't studied together. What's more, Mark didn't, on the average, average above the average, if you know what I mean. Perfect scores weren't something Mark made daily.

Kelly, on the other hand, was tops in everything she did in school, so it was no surprise to Mr. Barriston that she got all the right answers. But Mark? No way.

So the next day Mr. Barriston went to Mark privately just before break. "Mark," he said, "not that you couldn't do a ton better than you usually do, but I was shocked at the history quiz yesterday. You and Kelly were the only ones who got all the right answers."

Mark looked around, his eyes shifting. But he knew Barriston had him dead to rights, so he shrugged his shoulders and threw in the towel. "Yeah, OK, OK," he said. "I looked at her answers."

"How come?" Barriston asked.

"Hey—nobody's perfect," Mark said, with that funny little smile of his.

Mark's not wrong, of course. Even though it's no excuse, he's right when he says that nobody's perfect.

That's exactly what the Catechism says too in this Q&A. Nobody's perfect. It's a reminder of the old biblical idea that sin has got its hooks into all of us—you, me, Barriston, and everyone else under the sun.

Sin had a grip on the rich young man from the Bible too. He came to Jesus and told him that he was a regular at keeping the commandments. Ever since he was a boy, he said, he'd worked his tail off trying not to do anything wrong. Being good was a way of life with him.

"You're not doing one thing," Jesus told him. "Give away every cent of your money and follow me."

The Bible says that nice rich young man dropped his head then. He knew he couldn't do it. Belief starts right there—with the knowledge that we can't get it all right. We sin. Nobody's perfect. Not an excuse, a reality.

We need a Savior.

Lord, help us to know how much we need you. Please wash us whiter than snow. Amen.

112

At the Heart of Things

Q&A 60

. . . nevertheless . . .

We lived in malice and envy, being hated and hating one another. But when the kindness and love of God our Savior appeared, he saved us, not because of righteous things we had done, but because of his mercy.

—Titus 3:3–5

Just about everybody's heard of Romeo and Juliet, but William Shakespeare created lots of other memorable characters too. Take Hamlet.

Here's the play in a nutshell. The young prince Hamlet is approached by a ghost, who tells him that King Hamlet, his father, didn't just die—he was murdered. To find out if the ghost is telling the truth, Hamlet devises a plan. He quickly writes a play that will be performed by a traveling troupe of actors. In that play a king is murdered in the same way Hamlet believes his father was murdered.

Here's the plan. Hamlet will watch the supposed murderer—the king who took over his father's throne—and if the new king gets really itchy, Hamlet will know whether or not the ghost was right.

Maybe you can guess what happens. The moment the king sees the murder on stage, he gets into a snit. At that moment Hamlet knows King Claudius murdered his father.

All of that happens in Act III, the very center of the play. When King Claudius sees what's going on on stage, he gets to his feet—and so does everybody else, because when the king rises, so does every last one of his subjects. The little play is over because the place goes crazy. Hamlet knows Claudius is guilty. Claudius knows that somebody knows he's guilty. Now we got trouble in River City. Hamlet knows, but he's also in trouble.

Shakespeare had a thing about timing. Big, big moments, when the fortunes of the hero suddenly turn on a dime and fly off in another direction, often happen exactly halfway through the whole play. There's a kind of bull's-eye in many of Shakespeare's tragedies.

We're at the very heart of things in the Catechism too, almost exactly halfway through. In Q&A 60, we come to the very core of the most essential truth of the whole Catechism. It's a single word: *nevertheless.*

That little word comes right after a reminder that nobody's perfect. Then, *nevertheless*. Everything turns on that one word.

Nevertheless, God loves us.

That's the gospel. That's the good news from the very heart of the Bible.

Dear Lord, thank you for the greatest gift we'll ever receive—that you love us even when we don't deserve it. Teach us to carry our thanks into the world around us. Amen.

The Tower Experience

Q&A 60

All I need to do is to accept this gift of God with a believing heart.

For in the gospel a righteousness from God is revealed, a righteousness that is by faith from first to last, just as it is written: "The righteous will live by faith."

—Romans 1:17

Most people believe that the single act that started the Reformation was Martin Luther nailing ninety-five theses on the door of the Castle Church at Wittenberg, Germany. But those theses, or arguments, had to come from somewhere, and they did. They came from Luther's reading of the Bible and his experience.

Luther realized the truth about faith, historians say, sometime earlier, during what they call his "tower experience." Like other devoted believers of his day, Luther knew he was a sinner. No question there. He tried to rid himself of his sin by doing all kinds of unsavory things, like torturing himself. He must have been convinced that if believers bloodied their knees crawling up the church steps, they would realize how sinful they really were.

But no matter how bloody he made himself, he still felt rotten. Even though he did everything the church said was necessary to get righteous, he never felt clean.

What Luther struggled with, he said, was the justice of God. He got mad at God because he thought God's justice meant only God's punishment. He couldn't figure out why God would want people to feel so rotten.

Day and night he looked at Romans 1, ending with verse 17: "For in the gospel," Paul says, "righteousness from God is revealed, a righteousness that is by faith from first to last, just as it is written: 'The righteous will live by faith.'" From first to last, beginning to end, righteousness comes from God.

Boom. Lightning struck. Not real lightning, but a pure and powerful insight. Suddenly Luther saw a whole new meaning to those words. He'd been thinking that sinners create their own righteousness, but suddenly he realized that Paul was saying something completely different: Righteousness comes by faith. It's a gift. It's not something we earn by bloody knees or 24/7 torment. Righteousness is a gift.

That's exactly what the Catechism says: "All I need to do is to accept this gift of God with a believing heart." Nothing more, nothing less. Justification comes by faith, not by works. And that's how the Reformation began.

Only what you have done, Lord, can save my guilty soul. Only your sacrifice brings eternal joy. Set us free from the idea that we can do it, that we can be perfect. We can't. You are. Thank you for your love. Amen.

No Bragging

Q&A 61

It is not because of any value my faith has . . .

It is by grace you have been saved, through faith—and this not from yourselves, it is the gift of God—not by works, so that no one can boast.

—Ephesians 2:8–9

We just had something stinky happen at the school where I teach. Some student got an e-mail from someone he knew who claimed that Hollywood was about to put out a really ugly movie that lied about Jesus Christ. The e-mail said every Christian on the face of the earth should protest this movie.

As you may have guessed, there's no such movie. The whole story is bogus. Good Christian people get their dander up and write or call, only to find out that the whole story is one big lie. Three hundred names were at the bottom of that e-mail by the time I saw it.

To the world out there, that makes us Christians look truly dumb. Why do so many people fall for a hoax like this? Maybe because we want "evil" to be easy, something we can quickly squelch with a letter of protest.

Then again, maybe because signing such a list makes us feel good. Adding our name is a way of saying "See, I'm a Christian too." It's almost like signing our names to God's book of life. Putting our names on the line so that hundreds of other folks can read it almost gives that impression. Trouble is, only God can write in God's book. We know that. We can't write our names there even if we sign a thousand e-mails and pass them along. As we've been saying again and again, we can't do a single thing to earn our salvation. No believer ever wrote his or her name in God's book.

Funny thing about us humans—we'll do anything to get free stuff, except when it comes to salvation. Then we're begging, "Please, please, Lord, let me help pay the bill." I disliked the list of names at the end of that e-mail because it offered the people who signed something that tasted like salvation.

Don't be mistaken. We don't earn the love of God. God doesn't love us because we go on service trips and help poor people. Or because we don't spit or smoke or say bad words. Or because we're nice.

This question and answer won't let us get it wrong. God doesn't love us because we believe, because we have such cool faith. God loves us because God loves us. We are believers because even our faith is a gift from God. It's definitely not something to brag about.

"By faith alone"—that's the way Luther put it. And that's the way it is.

Lord, we owe everything to you. Even our faith is a gift from you. Thank you for loving us so much. In Jesus' name, Amen.

Un-American

Q&A 62

Even the very best we do in this life is imperfect and stained with sin.

All our righteous acts are like filthy rags. . . .

—Isaiah 64:6

Way back in the pages of this book, I think I told you that my dream of high jumping never made it over the bar. Even before I had back surgery, Michael Johnson never lost a minute's sleep worrying about me. I never was a sprinter. Coaches used to say that I ran too long in one spot.

Any dreams I might have had about working as a United Nations translator would have turned into useless babbling because I never was any good at memorizing languages.

My huge hands are way too big for factory jobs that require quick, flexible fingers.

Not long ago I sat beside a Green Bay Packer lineman on an airplane. I didn't tell him as much, but I don't think he'll ever make a gymnast.

People like to tell kids they should "dream high," because in America every child can be what he or she wants to be. A basic principle of American life seems to be that we can be anything we want to be. We can pull ourselves up by our own bootstraps. We can do it. Work hard and we'll get our dreams.

But let's face it. There was only one Einstein. Not every kid who can throw a football seventy yards is going to become a Brett Favre. My guess is there may be a million wanabee Oprahs.

Here's an idea that may sound awful but it's true: The Christian faith is kind of un-American. Here we are at the very heart of the Catechism, and all we get is question after question about what we *can't* do. We'd love to believe that God loves us because we're good people. We go to church without complaining. We try really hard to be nice to our brothers and sisters. If the neighbor needs her lawn mowed, we volunteer. We pray for other people when they're sick or lonely or grieving. We go on service projects with the youth group. Every day of the week, we try to do the right thing.

We do good. And that's great. That's the way it should be. Just remember, says the Catechism, the good we do can't make us right with God. Even our best acts, says the Bible, are like "filthy rags" when it comes to earning our salvation. Only Christ's work can buy us a ticket to eternity.

We don't like to hear it, but it's true.

Dear Lord, thank you for doing it all. If we had to rely on what we do or what we are, we'd be in trouble. Only in you do we find joy. Thank you for the gift of eternal life. In Jesus' name, Amen.

What Peter Earned

Q&A 63

This reward is not earned; it is a gift of grace.

Rejoice, and be glad, because great is your reward in heaven. . . .

—Matthew 5:12

It's not hard to understand why Jesus liked Peter. Of the twelve, it was Peter who could best light up a dark night. He was the guy who hopped out of the boat the minute Jesus suggested anyone could walk on water, the one-man army who whacked the ear off the palace guard.

Of course, he's also the one who said, "Who, me?" three times when the crowds asked him if he wasn't a follower of this rat named Jesus.

Brash Peter, never one to hold back. He's one of those mouthy guys who's dangerous just to be with, and sometimes, like us, he just doesn't get it.

A couple of readings back, we talked about the rich young man who claimed he'd followed every single commandment, he'd never broken a law. But when Jesus tells him to part with all his possessions, he slouches off, sad. Christ suggests he doesn't have a clue about faith.

Then, just like that, Peter lets fly. "We have left everything to follow you!" he says (Mark 10:28). You can almost hear him thinking, Now, what's coming to us as a result of all our sacrifice? He didn't really get the point about the rich young man and his possessions.

So Jesus patiently explains. When the final judgment comes, Jesus says, every last believer who, like the disciples, has left home to follow him will get back a hundred times more than they left. They will inherit eternal life.

There's your reward, Peter. That's what's coming to you. You wondered what you might earn—there it is.

Now here's a real problem. How on earth do we square what Jesus Christ says in Matthew 19 with the Catechism's many sermons about how we really do nothing to earn our salvation? Something is messed up here, right?

That's exactly what the Catechism asks in question 63. "Look," it says, "the Bible says there are rewards, so how can you say we don't earn anything?"

The answer isn't surprising: It's all a gift. When it comes right down to it, even the disciples' decision to leave everything and follow Jesus was a decision that God coached them into making.

It's all a gift. We have a will, but God owns it. We make decisions all right, but God Almighty makes them the right ones.

"The reward is not earned; it is a gift of grace."

We like to think of ourselves as pretty good people, Lord, but then we realize that you have made us what we are. You have given so that we can receive. Thank you, Jesus. Help us show that love in your world. Amen.

What God Does

Q&A 64

It is impossible for those grafted into Christ by true faith not to produce fruits of gratitude.

For we are God's workmanship, created in Christ Jesus to do good works. . . .

—Ephesians 2:10

A long time ago kids assumed they'd go into the line of work their parents did. Women back then didn't have many options; if you were female, you were almost certainly destined to become a mom and a homemaker.

Guys had only a few more choices. If your father was a farmer, everyone simply assumed that you would be a farmer too. If your father poured cement, you'd likely end up being a mason. For a long time in human history, people didn't really choose a profession. Work was something they inherited.

These days people change professions four times, on average, during their lives, according to the folks who study these things. So a mason might become a cop, a nurse might become a lawyer, a truck driver might become a real estate salesperson. Think about it—four times. Almost scary, isn't it?

The Lord God Almighty doesn't have just one job, of course. He runs the whole show, right down to the last little detail.

But when the apostle Paul talks about God's work, he talks about us. "*We* are God's workmanship," says Paul (Eph. 2:10). Great line, huh?

Masons pour driveways. Teachers teach kids how to add and subtract. Moms raise kids. Dairy farmers milk cows and help us along with our Wheaties. Writers write. People who sell insurance deliver customers from hail damage. Plumbers install toilets. Drywallers hang drywall.

And what does God do? We are God's workmanship. We are what God does.

If God made us and controls our lives, and if we can't earn our salvation on our own anyway, then why shouldn't we just party our way through life? That's what the Catechism asks in question 64.

The answer is simple. If we're grafted into Christ by true faith, then we will do good things because it's impossible for us to do otherwise. Put it this way: If we're God's workmanship, we will shine. After all, we are what God does. And God created us in Jesus Christ to do good works.

We are God's workmanship.

From birth to death, we're what God does.

Praise God.

Dear Lord, thank you for making us your workmanship. Thank you for forming us in our mother's womb, for shaping us throughout our lives, for helping us bring your love into the world. Remind us always that in everything we do, we belong to you. Amen.

How We Come to Faith

Q&A 65

Where then does . . . faith come from?

But God has revealed it to us by his Spirit.

—1 Corinthians 2:10

Just down the block live some kids who aren't believers—let's call them Eddie and Betty. Eddie and Betty are nice enough kids—I mean, they don't strangle cats or sell drugs to second-graders. They just don't believe in God.

On the other hand, you do. If you're reading this book right now, you likely have some belief about God.

So how come Eddie and Betty—two pretty ordinary kids—don't really believe in Jesus Christ at all, and how come you do?

Maybe you're thinking, I'm a believer because my parents are. Or I'm a believer because someone—a teacher, a pastor, a friend—brought me to Christ.

But suppose Eddie and Betty have heard the gospel too. They've visited the church down the block with their friends, gone to Sunday school, even watched gospel TV. But they still don't believe.

How come faith sticks to some people like Superglue? How come other people, even if they've been raised in a church, just stop going? How come you have faith and this nice kid you know doesn't?

Faith, says the Catechism, is the work of the Holy Spirit. I'll buy that. But, in a way, that doesn't answer the question. Let's put it this way: Why does it seem as if the Holy Spirit works like mad in your heart, but not at all in the hearts of Eddie and Betty?

Some questions don't have easy answers, and this is definitely one of them. Why some people shrug off God's love and others think it's the greatest gift of all isn't easy to understand.

Try this: Next time you're in a crowd, check out people's noses. See if you can find two exactly alike. You won't. Remember that the same God who gives each of us a unique nose also gives each of us a unique story. So don't ever think that the Holy Spirit has thrown in the towel on Eddie and Betty. The Holy Spirit works in a zillion different ways in human hearts. No two of us have the same nose or the same story.

Someday Eddie and Betty might just become loyal followers of Jesus Christ. Who knows—maybe the Lord God Almighty plans to use you—that's right, you—as the Superglue. It happens.

Blessed be the name of the Lord.

Lord, help us to tell others how great a gift you've given all your children. Help us to bring the good news in our neighborhood, in school, at work. In Jesus' name, Amen.

The Preaching of the Word

Q&A 65

The Holy Spirit produces [faith] in our hearts by the preaching of the holy gospel. . . .

And how can they hear without someone preaching to them?

—Romans 10:14

"Don't *preach* at me all the time!"

"Lannie is always trying to make me be like her. She ought to be a *preacher.*"

"You've got to live by example—walk your talk. *Preaching* won't get you anywhere."

Ever hear stuff like that? The fact is, preaching doesn't get good press. What all three of those comments share is a pretty negative view of preaching.

No wonder. When I say "preaching," what picture comes to mind? Some pointy-headed guy in a starched collar, jerking his finger in the air and trying to tell people how worthless they are?

These days, even preachers don't want to be preachers; they want to be pastors because *pastor* sounds like something soft and lovely from the grassy banks of Psalm 23.

But the Catechism uses the word *preaching.* You want to know why some people have faith? The Holy Spirit produces faith in our hearts by the preaching of the holy gospel. To understand that emphasis on preaching, you've got to go back half a millennium.

The centerpiece of the Roman Catholic Church was—and still is—the Mass, what most Protestants call communion or the Lord's Supper. Years ago, the Roman Catholic Church said the only way to God was by way of the sacrament, by way of taking Mass. Get this: *the only way.*

Protestants ("protestors") left the church because they thought there was more to faith than kneeling before a priest and receiving the sacrament. They wanted to read the Bible themselves. They wanted preachers to preach the Word, not just dole out the sacraments.

The Catechism is a Reformation document. The "preaching of the holy gospel," the Catechism says, is the means by which the Holy Spirit produces faith in us.

Is that right? I think so. Does that mean that the only way we get faith is by listening to a preacher hold forth from a pulpit? I doubt it.

After all, even pastors *preach,* right? In fact, now that I think about it, you're really listening to a sermon right now. And I'm not really a preacher. Wait a minute—am I? In a way, I guess.

What about you? Do you ever tell anybody else about God?

Are we all preachers?

Dear Lord, bless us with wisdom and courage and all kinds of street smarts so that we know how to bring the holy gospel, a gospel we know because your Spirit has planted it in our hearts. Help us to be your witnesses. In Jesus' name, Amen.

Are We All Preachers?

Q&A 65

The Holy Spirit produces [faith] in our hearts by the preaching of the holy gospel. . . .

For we do not preach ourselves, but Jesus Christ as Lord. . . .
—2 Corinthians 4:5

The Internet is a wonderful thing. I use it every day for lots of reasons, one of which is to get the news. But I've discovered that some sites give me one version of the news while others give me an entirely different version. If I read the daily news from some webmaster who believes that God only cares about white people, I'm going to get warped really fast, right?

Not all news is created equal. Not all information is perfectly reliable. And not all preachers preach the same gospel.

But are we all preachers? Yeah. Every last believer who knows that God is love will certainly take that love into the world. And that makes us preachers, doesn't it?

Well, sort of. More than twenty years ago, Jim Jones, a respected preacher, pulled his people together in Jonestown, New Guinea, because he was afraid his dreams were going down the tube. Then, he did something absolutely awful. Using his authority as a preacher, he told them all to drink Kool-Aid spiked with poison. Almost a thousand of his followers died in a mass suicide.

Jim Jones was a preacher. So is Billy Graham. But being preachers is about the only thing they had in common.

Are we all preachers? Well, yes. The Catechism says "the preaching of the holy gospel" is the means by which the Holy Spirit produces faith.

If what the Catechism says is true, then we've got to understand that the preaching of the holy gospel is really, really serious because it's the means by which the Holy Spirit works. If that preaching is wrong, it can lead to death, not life.

All of us are ministers of the faith. All of us spread the gospel. Faith really isn't that tough. It's a matter of believing. And as Jesus Christ himself made clear, even little kids do that well—often better than adults.

But faith is not mindless or blind. Jim Jones, in his anguished horror, forgot the truth of the holy gospel, the good news of salvation. The Holy Spirit didn't produce faith in that sermon of death. Jim Jones's preaching led to despair, not faith.

The Holy Spirit works through the preaching of the holy gospel. But just as we don't entrust the job of brain surgery to writers, we don't entrust the job of preaching to just anybody either—we want someone who can preach the truth of the holy gospel. Should we entrust our souls to anyone less?

Lord, thank you for preachers. Give them wisdom and insight and strength to bring us the truth of the holy gospel. And help us all to be ministers of your love. Amen.

On the Job

Q&A 65

The Holy Spirit produces [faith] in our hearts by the preaching of the holy gospel. . . .

Jesus answered, "I tell you the truth, no one can enter the kingdom of God unless he is born of water and the Spirit."

—John 3:5

Millions of Christians could tell you exactly when they first believed: "It happened at 3:15 on the way home from school on December 10, 2000." Each has a different story—maybe it happened in church or around a campfire or in a hospital. They may have been alone in their bedrooms, or in a car on a freeway, or in the middle of mountains so beautiful only God could have sculpted them. Many of these same millions could point to someone—a buddy, a neighbor, a preacher, a woman from work—who sat listening to their questions for hours. There are as many stories of conversion as there are noses.

Millions more Christians can't put a date on the day they first believed. But many of these same Christians recall a time when they didn't love Jesus. They talk about being gently nurtured in their faith by a Christian family. They might point to a mom or a dad whose Bible reading and prayer and daily example brought about the kind of peace and joy their kids wanted for themselves from the very beginning.

If we had the stories of every Christian in North America written on those little Post-it notes, we could plaster those stories across every billboard on the continent and not have a double.

Or picture this. On a long library shelf are hundreds of thick books containing the stories of every last Christian alive right now in the world. The shelf is huge. Pick out a book—say the one from Canada. In that book you see millions of little paragraphs in tiny type. Reading all those books and all those stories would take at least the rest of your life.

But no matter whose story, no matter where it happened, one ingredient is always the same. In every one of those millions of tales, the Holy Spirit was doing the job. Green hair, blue eyes, big nose, stubby fingernails, size 14 feet, a Barbie-doll figure or someone who's eaten far too much fudge—all of them share a fluttering movement some might not even have recognized. Somewhere in their heart of hearts, the Holy Spirit was busy bending, shaping, nurturing each and every believer toward faith.

It's all the Holy Spirit's work. When people come to the Lord, whether suddenly or gradually, you can bet the Holy Spirit was doing the job.

Blessed Spirit, you are my gracious Teacher and Friend. Live in me always. Keep my heart in the way of life eternal. Amen.

122

Eating and Drinking

Q&A 65

The Holy Spirit . . . confirms [faith] through our use of the holy sacraments.

And he took bread, gave thanks and broke it, and gave it to them, saying, "This is my body given for you. . . ."

—Luke 22:19

In some places in the world today, people go days—even weeks—without eating what most of us polish off at a single Sunday dinner. You've seen the tragic pictures. Oddly enough, really malnourished kids get distended stomachs, as if they've been eating far too many donuts. But you remember the skinny little arms and legs too, not a bit of flesh on them—and not enough muscle to walk.

We need food to live. People are not camels; we don't have humps for storage. But we can get along for quite some time on little more than a thimbleful of food. Not so with water. So much of our body is liquid that without it we literally dry up. It's not pretty.

A friend of mine who was in a concentration camp during World War II told me that the guards used to make the prisoners distribute the measly portions of water and bread and fat they were given each day at supper. Why? Because they knew the prisoners were so hungry that they'd hurt each other if there was any cheating.

People don't eat or drink themselves into existence. But eating and drinking nourishes us, makes us grow, builds strong bones and muscles, and keeps a shine on our skin. Eating and drinking, in other words, makes us healthy.

The Catechism thinks so too. You'll notice that it makes a distinction between the preaching of the gospel and the sacraments: The Holy Spirit *produces* faith by way of preaching and *confirms* it by way of sacraments.

Promise me you won't ever think you know exactly how the Holy Spirit works. Promise you won't try to say that God will only do this or that. God is God. We are not.

But just think for a moment about someone who has never, ever heard a thing about the gospel (that's a little difficult in North America, of course). Now put that person in a pew at a baptism. I doubt that he or she is going to come to faith on the basis of having seen some guy toss water over a baby or dunk somebody's head. If anything, it would all seem very strange.

Preaching is for everybody, but the sacraments are only for believers. They're what we eat and drink. They keep us alive in the Lord and make us strong.

Lord, thank you for nourishing us, thank you for keeping us strong. Thank you for giving us the Spirit to help us become all that you want us to be. In Jesus' name, Amen.

Swooshes, Signs, and Sacraments

Q&A 66

Sacraments are holy signs and seals for us to see.

God said to Noah, "[The rainbow] is the sign of the covenant I have established between me and all life on the earth."

—Genesis 9:17

You want to know the most successful advertising symbol in history? For my money, it's the Nike swoosh. You all know what it looks like because it's plastered on everything Nike makes: shoes, of course, and caps and belts and socks. Tiger Woods gets paid a mint for using Nike golf balls. These balls have no lettering whatsoever, only the famous swoosh. The swoosh says it all.

So how did the Nike swoosh get to be the most successful advertising gimmick ever? Because it's simple—nothing more than a curved line, the kind of line a kid might leave on a sheet of paper as he falls off a desk. Swoosh. Just a line says it all. I don't mean to demean Nike by making this comparison, but the only thing even close in terms of recognizability is the Nazi swastika. Anyone who knows about World War II can spot a swastika and immediately see the madman Hitler straight-arming a salute to thousands of loyalists.

If I were the CEO of Nike, I'd love it. Just think, all you have to do is put a swoosh on a golf ball and the whole world recognizes the make. Just one curved line says it all.

Think of the water of baptism as a kind of swoosh. Even though the water itself soon gets toweled off or dries up on its own, that doesn't mean the sign is meaningless. Baptism has never sold a running shoe or a golf ball, but for thousands of years it has identified Christians as members of a very royal family, the family of God.

The bread and wine or grape juice of communion are something like that swoosh too. They're signs that point us to Christ's own body and blood. Just as the swoosh identifies shoes and socks and golf balls made by Nike, these signs identify us as God's own children.

In a way, sacraments make us official. They signify what we are and whose we are. Baptism and the Lord's Supper feed us and nurture us spiritually—but they are also visible signs that remind us of who we are, now and forever.

Unlike the famous swoosh, which may well disappear someday, the sacraments forever remind us that we are children of God through Jesus Christ our Lord.

Thank you, Lord, for giving us signs of who we are. Thank you for making us official. Thank you for making us part of your blessed family. Amen.

Show-and-Tell

Q&A 67

And through the holy sacraments [the Holy Spirit] assures us that our entire salvation rests on Christ's one sacrifice for us on the cross.

For whenever you eat this bread and drink this cup, you proclaim the Lord's death until he comes.

—1 Corinthians 11:26

Here's how I teach writing. Take a look at this little paragraph: *Hamon Wiggledy is not a very handsome guy. Some people might call him ugly actually, but I don't know. He's just, well, different. OK, he's not very good looking.*

Now this: *Hamon Wiggledy's paunchy nose wouldn't be so massive if poor Hamon's whole head wasn't the size of an old grapefruit. And hair—yikes! I've seen growth more manageable on a prickly pear cactus. Once our hogs lost two months' growth because Hamon just stood there and looked at 'em. I'm not kidding.*

Which paragraph creates a better picture of poor old Hamon Wiggledy?

That's a no-brainer, right? The second paragraph *shows* us what Hamon looks like (by the way, there is no real Hamon Wiggledy—I hope), while the first one only *tells* us.

Here's another example. "Lyndsey is a great volleyball player." Compare that to "Lyndsey averages eight kills and three aces a match." The first tells, the second shows.

Writing isn't life, of course. Telling is important too, not just showing. But the writer who shows gets into the mind of readers in a wholly different way than the writer who only tells. Think of showing as pictures, word pictures.

Like a writer, a preacher can tell us about God's love in a million different ways, and the people in the church can certainly come to believe it. The Bible *tells* us the gospel, of course; but it's also packed full of stories and word pictures that *show* us God's love. I'm pretty sure Jesus used parables because he wanted to show and not just tell.

Sacraments do the same thing: They show us God's love.

Not long ago, our preacher held up the loaf of bread as if it were the very best thing he'd ever seen. He just held it up in the air for a long, long time, so that every last person sitting in church that morning could admire it. He *showed* us the bread. That moment was really wonderful.

We see God's love in the sacraments. We see the water and feel the cleansing of baptism; we see and taste the bread and wine and know Jesus' blood and body.

The sacraments show us the truth of the gospel.

Lord, thank you for showing us your love in the life and death of your Son, in the sheer beauty of rolling landscapes and mountain streams, in the love we have for others. And thank you for showing us by way of baptism and the Lord's Supper. Amen.

What's Sacred and What's Not

Q&A 68

How many sacraments did Christ institute in the New Testament? Two: baptism and the Lord's Supper.

"Take off your sandals, for the place where you are standing is holy ground."

—Exodus 3:5

Brisbane Street Church is far too small. They've got people sitting in every dark corner of the church on Sundays, and more on folding chairs—so many that they decide to hold two Sunday morning services. Soon enough, however, even those get full. Finally they decide it's time to build.

A committee comes up with a plan for a church that looks completely different from the old one: no spire, no bell tower, no cross on top. It's a cool place, complete with a gym, and the congregation votes to build it. The wrecking crew comes in to tear the old church down.

But before they can begin, the old cross has to come down. Now everybody in Brisbane Street Church knows that the cross on the tower isn't sacred—it's just treated wood, after all. At the same time, nobody thinks that some hard-hat with a wrecking ball should just bang it off the tower.

They decide to build a whole platform to take it down, a platform big enough to hold the preacher and the church elders. Very carefully those people climb the ladder to the platform and get hoisted up to the top of the spire. Very carefully they remove that cross, which had stood there for seventy-five years. Very carefully they bring it to the ground. Today that cross has a place in the new church—it stands just outside the room where the people worship.

The whole cross-removal operation cost thousands of dollars. But to the people of Brisbane Street Church, it was money well spent, because that cross stands for the death and resurrection of Jesus Christ as well as the history of Brisbane Street Church. Somehow that cross seemed almost sacred.

Sometimes it's tough to distinguish what is sacred and what isn't. So as we talk for awhile about the sacraments, it's important to understand that good people can have big disagreements about what is sacred, what is closest to their hearts and souls. Remember that good Christians can and do disagree.

According to the Catechism, the church celebrates only two sacraments, two sacred acts: baptism and the Lord's Supper.

Next time we'll find out why there are only two.

Lord Jesus, thank you for giving us the sacraments. Help us to know what we believe, and keep us from feeling somehow better than believers who disagree with us on the details. In your name, Amen.

126

Only Two

Q&A 68

How many sacraments did Christ institute in the New Testament? Two: baptism and the Lord's Supper.

"Therefore go and make disciples of all nations, baptizing them in the name of the Father and of the Son and of the Holy Spirit."

—Matthew 28:19

"Unless you eat the flesh of the Son of Man and drink his blood, you have no life in you."

—John 6:53

If you were raised in the Roman Catholic tradition, you would say that Reformed folks are dead wrong in accepting just two sacraments. You would say there are seven.

First, baptism.

Second, Holy Eucharist, known by Protestants as the Lord's Supper or communion. "Unless you eat the flesh of the Son of Man and drink his blood," Christ said, "you have no life in you" (John 6:53).

The third is penance, instituted by Christ, they say, on Easter Sunday night. Because Christ knew his people would fall into sin, he provided the means for bringing them back in this sacrament.

Holy Orders is fourth. Our mother church feels strongly that Jesus himself instituted the priesthood to ensure Christ's continued presence on earth.

Holy Matrimony is fifth. Since Christ said that the "two should be one," marriage is sacred.

Confirmation, or the sacrament of spiritual strengthening, is sixth. It's the event in each believer's life when he or she professes his or her faith.

Anointing of the Sick, also called the Sacrament of Anointing, is seventh, a sacrament usually given to the dying.

When the Heidelberg Catechism says there are only two sacraments, it is shouting defiance against the Roman Catholic Church, saying the Church is wrong in putting a priest between God and man. It is saying that a priest doesn't make us believers, only the Word does. It is saying that Jesus Christ himself "instituted" (established) only two sacraments, not seven.

One of the great rallying cries of the Reformation was *sola scriptura,* which means "only by the Word." We don't come to grace because the priest gives us penance or marries us or anoints Grandma at her death. We come to faith only by the Word. We are justified by faith.

Sola scriptura.

Lord, help us to understand that your Word is truth. Help us to walk ever closer with you in this life. Forgive us when we think we know it all. Forgive us our foolish pride and keep us safe in your arms. In his name, Amen.

Reminding

Q&A 69

How does baptism remind you and assure you that Christ's one sacrifice on the cross is for you personally?

The Holy Spirit . . . will remind you of everything I have said to you.

—John 14:26

OK, I'll admit it. I wasn't thrilled when some guy stood up with a video camera to record the baptism of his nephew. And it wasn't just that he made a spectacle of himself either, poking that camera here and there with so much commotion that he unfocused the congregation's eyes from what was really happening at the front of the church.

I didn't like the whole idea of videotaping the sacrament because it somehow suggested that baptism was something less than sacramental. What I pictured was a shelf full of videos in someone's house labeled "Timmy's Baptism," "First Soccer Game," "Eating Cake with Fingers." You get the idea. Cute moments in Timmy's life—want to see one?

Baptism, it seems to me, belongs in another category altogether than Timmy's first tooth or the day he swung on his kindergarten backpack and trudged off to school. Baptism isn't just another step toward growing up. It's bigger than that. That's what I was thinking when this guy was shooting the whole event on video.

But maybe I was wrong. After all, the Catechism asks this question first of all when approaching the whole idea of baptism: "How does baptism remind you and assure you that Christ's one sacrifice on the cross is for you personally?"

Remind. I don't know if you've ever thought about it, but it seems to me that there are loads of things we need to be reminded of time and time again. Not just older folks like me, either—all of us.

Maybe someday, in the middle of trying to figure out what he wants to do with his life, Timmy will look up at that video on the shelf and remind himself that, no matter what he does, he's a child of God. Maybe someday, after losing the district championship basketball game he and his teammates had set their hearts on, he'll glance at that shelf and remember that no matter what happens, one day long ago his parents brought him to church to be bathed by water that somehow represents Christ's own blood. Maybe someday, when his own parents die, he'll clean out their library and be reminded that no matter how much his grief hurts, he is part of the family of God.

Baptism, the Catechism says, *reminds* us of who we are.

Let's face it—there are tons of things about life worth forgetting. But that we belong, body and soul, to our faithful Savior Jesus Christ isn't one of them.

Lord, thank you for reminding us of whose we are. Help us remember. Every time we see someone baptized, remind us that we are yours, that even right now we live in the glory of your grace, your love. In Jesus' name, Amen.

Saul Sees the Light

Q&A 71

Whoever believes and is baptized will be saved. . . .

Immediately, something like scales fell from Saul's eyes, and he could see again. He got up and was baptized. . . .

—Acts 9:18

We don't know much about the apostle Stephen, except that he was "a man full of God's grace and power" (Acts 6:8), that he preached one powerful sermon, and that he became, on the basis of that sermon, the gospel's first martyr (Acts 7).

No one can ever know for sure, but it's possible that Stephen wouldn't even be in the Bible—and therefore we wouldn't even know of him—if it weren't for someone who was present when he was being stoned. The Bible says that Saul was standing right there, "giving approval to his death" (8:1).

Not Paul, but Saul. The Saul who became Paul. The Paul who, as Saul, had dedicated his life to deep-sixing all Stephen-type believers, people he thought were fanatic madmen seeking to destroy the whole religious establishment.

You probably know the story of Paul's incredible conversion to the cause of Jesus Christ. If you don't, check it out in Acts 9.

But there's one little part of the story we need to go over, one little footnote, because it will help us understand why the Christian church, over the centuries, has felt it so important that believers go through this water business, this immersion or sprinkling of baptism.

After the shocking light on the road to Damascus, the light that literally opened his eyes to darkness, Saul can't do much of anything. His eyes are worthless, so this guy who was once so dead-sure of how he saw the world is led into Damascus by the hand.

For three days, the Bible says, he couldn't see a thing. Neither did he eat or drink. Meanwhile, a disciple named Ananias got a vision telling him to head out to Straight Street and look for Saul of Tarsus, the sworn enemy of all Christians, who was staying at the home of a man named Judas.

Ananias can't believe what he's been told, but he goes and he finds Saul. Then he lays his hands on him and tells him why he's come.

Boom! Just like that the lights come on. Now Saul can see. Immediately, the Bible says—catch this—"he got up and was baptized."

There are several reasons the church, for centuries, has baptized believers, but maybe the most obvious is the example of Saul, who became the great apostle Paul. He was baptized. Baptism is what the Lord commanded.

Bottom line? Baptism is what we do.

Lord, thank you for baptism, a reminder that all our sins are forgiven because of the blood of Jesus. Thank you for washing us and making us clean. In Jesus' name, Amen.

Ritual

Q&A 72

Only Jesus Christ's blood and the Holy Spirit cleanse us from all sins.

But you were washed, you were sanctified . . . in the name of the Lord Jesus Christ and by the Spirit of our God.

—1 Corinthians 6:11

Maybe you've already read Shirley Jackson's short story "The Lottery," one of the most-read stories of all time. If you haven't, someday you probably will.

It's haunting and it's scary, and there isn't a single vampire in it. It's about a small town where every year people choose one of their friends and then kill him or her in a ritual that's done for no good reason, except that it's a ritual. They do it because they always have.

Why would such a strange story be one of the most popular short stories of all time? Probably because millions upon millions of readers have found themselves in it. In other words, people who've read that story think there's something "true" about what happens. Often enough in life, it seems, we do things because, well, because we've always done it that way.

In one of the most meticulously choreographed scenes from the movie *The Godfather,* Michael and Kay Corleone take their son, Michael Rizzi, to the altar to be baptized at the exact same time a gangland murder is carried out under Michael's direction. That scene is absolutely hideous because every viewer knows Michael doesn't believe in "God the Father, the Creator of heaven and earth," as he swears he does. His son's baptism is an empty ritual, a cover for the murder that takes place at the same moment.

Let's face it. Baptism—and the Lord's Supper—can be things we do because, well, because we've always done them. In our fingers, the bread and the wine can be nothing more than bread and wine, the water of baptism nothing more than two parts hydrogen to one part oxygen.

The Catechism makes very clear that there's nothing magic about baptism. Whether a kid is dunked or sprinkled, you can count on that kid getting dirty again. On its own, that water doesn't wash anyone from sin. Baptism itself isn't hocus-pocus. Wouldn't it be great if it were? Wouldn't it be wonderful if all we had to do was get sprinkled and that would be it for the rest of our lives?

Doesn't work that way. "Only Jesus Christ's blood and the Holy Spirit cleanse us from all sins," the Catechism says. By itself, baptism itself doesn't mean a thing.

"Then why do it?" you ask.

Stay tuned.

Lord, remind us each day that without your love we're doomed. Help us to know in the very center of our hearts and souls that all our sins are forgiven. Remind us that nothing is more wonderful, nothing at all. Thank you so much for loving us. In Jesus' name, Amen.

Why?

Q&A 73

God has good reason . . .

And now what are you waiting for? Get up, be baptized and wash your sins away, calling on his name.

—Acts 22:16

Yesterday we ended up with a question, remember? If baptism doesn't do anything by itself, then why do it?

"God has good reason," begins the Catechism's answer.

That reason has a lot to do with ritual—that is, something that's performed in a similar manner time after time. Think of it this way. One Friday night you decide to go to a football game. But something strange has happened: The coaches have decided to break the rules tonight, just for kicks. Instead of getting a first down after making ten yards, each team gets the ball indefinitely. What's more, there's no out-of-bounds. Players are free to run into the next county if they feel like it.

Chaos—that's what would follow, right? Who on earth would want to watch a football game if there were no rules?

Now don't get me wrong. Baptism isn't just a rule like "no face-mask tackles."

But there is a principle operating here. We organize our lives on rituals. We get up at a certain time, we eat at a certain time, we go to bed at a certain time. We go to church on Sundays, put out the garbage on Mondays (at our house), and go to ball games on Fridays.

Baptism? Jesus Christ was baptized, as were hundreds of his followers. Paul was baptized. The guard at the jail where Paul was set free was baptized, as was that guard's entire family.

God wants us to practice baptism because baptism gives order and meaning to our lives as God's children. "He wants to teach us that the blood and Spirit of Christ wash away our sins just as water washes away dirt from our bodies," says the Catechism.

Even more importantly, God wants to remind us, every time we see a baptism, that just as surely as water washes away dirt, his blood washes away our sin. Just as surely, and even more completely.

It's a drama that goes on in front of church over and over again. It's a great, great story. We were messy and dirty. We were all pigpens. But Jesus died on the cross, rose again, and made us all eternally clean. In a few drops of water.

What a story! Don't ever forget it.

Thank you for teaching us in baptism that all our sins are forgiven through the blood of Christ's death for us. There's no greater story anywhere, anytime. Thank you, Jesus. Amen.

Lydia's Story

Q&A 74

Should infants, too, be baptized? Yes. Infants as well as adults are in God's covenant and are his people.

The Lord opened [Lydia's] heart to respond to Paul's message. When she and the members of her household were baptized, she invited us to her home.

—Acts 16:14–15

For centuries good Christians have disagreed about who should be baptized. So before we say anything more, we need to say that baptizing babies—or *not* baptizing babies—shouldn't keep us from throwing our arms around fellow believers who don't believe exactly what we believe.

Reformed Christians believe that "infants as well as adults are in God's covenant and are his people," and therefore *should* be baptized.

Why? Take Lydia (Acts 16:13–15). A businesswoman, a dealer in purple cloth, the Bible says. On one of their missionary journeys, Timothy and Paul and Silas leave their ship at Philippi, one of the central cities of Macedonia. On Sunday morning they look outside the gates for a place to pray, and they meet a group of women. Lydia is one of them. She's a "worshiper of God," the Bible says, which likely means that she's come to believe in the God of the Jews even though she's a Gentile.

Things begin to happen outside those city gates. Soon enough, "the Lord opened her heart to respond to Paul's message," we read. Just like that, Lydia becomes one of them, a believer in Jesus Christ.

So far, so good, right? In the most conventional of ways, Lydia becomes a believer. Conversions like that happened often on the apostles' missionary trips, and they happen often today.

But then, the Bible says, she and the members of her household were baptized. Not just Lydia, but all of them—Lydia and her household—were baptized.

People like me who believe infants should be baptized argue that God's promise to be our God (Gen. 17:7) extends to every member of a believer's family or household. Babies, we believe, are not outside of those promises. If a mom and dad are believers, they're likely teaching their children right from the start about God Almighty.

Lydia's story is not unique. There are others in the Bible who also have their children baptized when they become believers.

So why did I baptize my children when they were babies? Because, as the old song says, "The Bible tells me so."

Thank you that way back in the Old Testament, you told Abraham that he and his children were all members of your family. Thank you that all your promises are for all your children, young and old alike. In Jesus' name, Amen.

The Command

Q&A 75

Christ has commanded me and all believers to eat this broken bread and to drink this cup.

"Do this . . . in remembrance of me."
—1 Corinthians 11:25

Now listen to me. Don't let your mind wander for a minute because this is really important. Don't think about school or soccer practice or going to some dance on the weekend. Keep your hands on this book and read slowly.

And clean up your room. When you're done reading these words, make your bed. Don't let your dirty socks lie around on the floor stinking up the place, and at least once in a while try to hang up your clothes.

Once you've read all of this and cleaned up your room, do your homework. Haul out that history book and read. Don't touch the computer and don't even think about switching on the television. Leave the radio alone too—and the Walkman. And that magazine you'd like to read—don't. Hit that history book or you're in real trouble.

Don't sleep either. Don't lie on the bed and read about the Peloponnesian Wars because sure as anything you'll conk out in a moment. Stay awake. Push that information into your head or you'll never pass. Don't touch that telephone. Be responsible.

Commands, all of it. Everything you've just read is a specific form of writing called the command form. Go back and sample a chunk—see what I mean? What's rather rudely missing from the command form is a subject. See for yourself. There are no subjects, really, because the command form doesn't try to be human.

What's important about the command form is the verb. Think of Nike's famous slogan "Just do it." That's addressed to you and me and every last citizen of the world. People don't matter all that much in the command form; they're not even there. They're only "understood," as English teachers say. What matters is action. Do it.

Jesus Christ himself uses the command form when he tells his disciples—and us—to take communion. He means what he says. "Just do it," he says, long before anyone's ever seen a swoosh.

When you use the command form, you're not pussy-footing around. The emphasis is on action. It's not a polite invitation, it's a command.

"Do this in remembrance of me." That's the way Christ phrased it. Communion for believers is not an option at all. It's a command.

Listen to Jesus.

Thank you for inviting us to your table, Lord. We know where you want us, and we know why. As you commanded, help us remember and believe. In Jesus' name, Amen.

Blood Brothers and Sisters

Q&A 76

We are united more and more to Christ's blessed body.

"For my flesh is real food and my blood is real drink. Whoever eats my flesh and drinks my blood remains in me, and I in him."

—John 6:55–56

It's kind of gross, but lots of kids, at some point during their childhood, become blood brothers or blood sisters with their friends. Maybe you've done it too. Here's what happens. Two kids prick their fingers so that a little blood starts running. Then they press their fingers together to mix their blood. That makes them blood brothers or sisters.

Mixing blood isn't a smart thing to do. Fact is, it's almost as dangerous as mixing chemicals. As you know, blood carries life. It's liquid life. What's more, what belongs to us belongs to us alone. And, of course, blood comes in different varieties or types. Only under very controlled conditions can doctors use other people's blood to pump life back into sick people.

There's another ritual involving blood that seems kind of gross too. It's called the Lord's Supper. When we participate in the Lord's Supper, what Jesus Christ wants us to remember through our eating and drinking is his body and blood. That bread? It's like his body. That wine? It's like his blood.

Face it. It's actually pretty gory stuff. When we eat Christ's body, we're cannibals, in a way. What's more, when we drink his blood, we're vampires. Ever think of it that way? Maybe you should.

I'm overstating here, of course. Although we're not really cannibals and vampires, what we do during the Lord's Supper is no less shocking. Even if the bread and wine are only symbols of Christ's body and blood, remember what it is you're symbolically doing next time you put that chunk of dough into your mouth: You're eating Christ's body.

But that's what Christ commanded.

So what does this eating and drinking do for us? In a way, it's like a transfusion. We get something new in our systems, something of Christ—because the bread and wine connect us to his body and blood sacrificed for us on the cross.

This very strange but very powerful "feast," as we sometimes call it, brings us closer and closer to Jesus Christ.

Why do we do it? Because Christ commands us. What does it do for us? It brings us closer to him. We become, in a way, blood brothers and sisters with the Lord of heaven and earth.

Dear Lord, this world has lots and lots of good things, things that sometimes keep us from remembering your precious love. Thank you for commanding us to eat and drink the bread and the wine. Thank you for bringing us closer to you. Amen.

Commemoration

Q&A 77

"The Lord Jesus, on the night he was betrayed, took bread, and when he had given thanks, he broke it and said, 'This is my body, which is for you; this do in remembrance of me.'"

"For whenever you eat this bread and drink this cup, you proclaim the Lord's death until he comes."

—1 Corinthians 11:26

In a way, I'm not looking forward to tomorrow. Maybe I should—after all, tomorrow is Thanksgiving. But tomorrow will be the first Thanksgiving in twenty-two years that neither of our kids will be here with us.

Not to worry—we won't be alone. My wife's parents will be here, and a whole family of friends who come every year for Thanksgiving dinner. We'll have a great time.

But something will be different for my wife and me, and I know both of us will think of it.

Holidays like Thanksgiving are important because they lug in a backpack full of unseen memories of similar get-togethers that have come before—the perfect crust on Mrs. De Smith's pies, the wonderful smell of turkey, the sharp linen tablecloth beneath the plates and silverware, the dark red cranberries. Over the years Thanksgiving celebrations resemble each other. That's part of the joy.

In the United States, we celebrate Thanksgiving because the pilgrims did. After their first year in a wilderness town they called Plymouth, after losing half of their number to starvation and disease in that first year, they got together with the native peoples and had a feast to thank God for his blessings.

Most of us probably don't tell each other that story on Thanksgiving. But maybe that's OK. After all, we create our own commemorations.

The Lord's Supper isn't a holiday exactly, even though, finally and surely, it brings us much more joy than a perfect turkey. The Lord's Supper commemorates one specific Passover night, a night Jesus gathered his faithful followers around him and commanded them to take up the bread and wine and to remember and believe. Every time we do it, we remember.

We'll have a great Thanksgiving tomorrow, even though our kids will be far, far away. The turkey will be great—my wife never misses. Mrs. De Smith's pies will be scrumptious. Grandma's gravy will be to die for.

But the real reason we'll give thanks isn't turkey or cranberries or pilgrim fathers. At our house, we'll give thanks most deeply because we know we belong to our faithful Savior, Jesus Christ—every one of us, even our faraway kids.

We celebrate our belonging in another feast, a different commemoration, a whole different kind of holiday. "Remember and believe," he said. And we do.

Thank the Lord, every day, as we will tomorrow—Thanksgiving.

Lord, every time we celebrate communion we remember what you have done for us. Thank you from the bottom of our hearts. Amen.

Horror Movies

Q&A 77

"We, who are many, are one body, for we all partake of the one loaf."

Now you are the body of Christ, and each one of you is a part of it.

—1 Corinthians 12:27

The skinny guy who gets lost in cartoons wasn't really the first famous Waldo. There have been a few others along the way, but none as famous as Ralph Waldo Emerson, a nineteenth-century American writer I happen to like a lot, a man whose friends called him "Waldo."

This Waldo never got lost. He was a high-profile kind of guy, a preacher, and if he were around today, he'd likely be the toast of talk shows. He and his friends created a religion of their own called "transcendentalism"; one of its central ideas was the oneness of all people. Listen to what he said in one of his earliest essays:

> The state of society is one in which the members have suffered amputation from the trunk, and strut about like so many walking monsters—a good finger, a neck, a stomach, an elbow, but never a man.

Sounds like a horror movie, doesn't it? See, Ralph Waldo Emerson felt that people in his time were becoming separated from whatever glue held them all together, some kind of brotherhood or faith. When he looked around himself, he said, human beings were all going their own ways, so that instead of simply being parts of humanity, they were all walking monsters. Here a hand, there a big toe, here a massive kidney, there a little epiglottis. Gross.

Just for a moment I want you to think about Emerson's horror movie, where people aren't people but walking body parts.

And now I want you to remember what the Bible says about the Lord's Supper: "We, who are many, are one body, for we all partake of the one loaf" (1 Cor. 10:17). The Bible seems to agree with Ralph Waldo here: Without something holding us together, we're all just body parts. The "glue" that holds us together, says Paul, is the loaf, the bread, the body of Christ. He's our body. He's the Superglue.

Listen: Two things happen when believers participate in the sacrament of the Lord's Supper, and they happen at the same time. First, we're remembering what Christ said and did and commanded us to do in that final supper before he died. Second, we're coming together as believers because Christ himself is the glue that holds us together.

In the sacrament of the Lord's Supper, Jesus Christ himself keeps us from becoming the walking monsters of a horror movie.

Dear Lord, thank you for reminding us that you hold us together with all those who confess your name in every nation, every time, every place. Amen.

Nourishment

Q&A 79

His crucified body and poured-out blood truly nourish our souls for eternal life.

I am the living bread that came down from heaven. If anyone eats of this bread, he will live forever.

—John 6:51

OK, I confess. Yesterday, I came home from Wal-Mart with not one but two cans of mixed nuts. I can't control myself.

My wife is powerless if an open bag of potato chips is on the table. We both deny ourselves a certain kind of cream-filled cookie *most of the time* because if we don't, we just go bonkers. I know a man who can eat an entire bag of chocolate chips while correcting his students' papers—an entire bag!

Bill Clinton, it was rumored, couldn't pass a McDonald's without stopping for French fries. If I lived in Canada, I know it would be painful for me to pass by a Tim Horton's because a fresh bear claw (ever see those things? Big as a baseball glove) turns me into a stuttering idiot. Pie? Make mine pecan, please.

I've got to hand it to my son, who's got far better eating habits than I do. He eats lettuce like a rabbit, prefers stir-fry to sausage, rice to raised donuts. He'll choose—actually choose—a spinach salad, even when there are hot dogs in the refrigerator! I don't know where he picked up his values.

Last night, along with a steak, I had hash browns complete with cheese and onions. Good? Sure. Good for me? Are you kidding?

What I want is taste, but what I need—what we all need—is nourishment.

The Catechism says that our souls are *nourished* by Christ's body and blood. In the same way that our bodies are nourished by good food—like spinach salad and stir-fry—so our souls are nourished by Christ's body and blood—by bread and wine or grape juice.

When we take communion, we're symbolically eating the body and drinking the blood of Christ. We "participate" in Christ, says Paul. "All of his suffering and obedience are as definitely ours as if we personally had suffered and paid for our sins," says the Catechism.

Eating the bread and drinking the blood is a string around your finger, a note on the refrigerator, something scribbled on your hand. Don't forget what Jesus did. Don't ever forget. Don't you dare!

Remembering Christ's body and blood, broken and shed for us, makes us stronger in every single way. It nourishes. The bread and wine are soul builders.

They are the most substantial food we can have. Ever.

Make us hungry, Lord. Give us an appetite for your righteousness that won't quit. Feed us with your body and your blood so that we can be strong. Nourish us with your love. Amen.

Post Toasties

Q&A 80

How does the Lord's Supper differ from the Roman Catholic Mass?

Now these three remain: faith, hope and love. But the greatest of these is love.

—1 Corinthians 13:13

When I was a boy, I went to a Christian school. So did my children. Fifty years ago kids who went to Christian schools were sometimes called "Post Toasties," the name of an old breakfast cereal that claimed it was "just a little bit better."

In a way, I used to think of myself as being "a little bit better." I thought going to a Christian school was somehow "better" than going to a public school.

But I was dead wrong—and I'd be dead wrong today—if I really thought that I or my children were any "better" than other kids. No way. They're all kids. They're all human. Every one of us is capable of being nasty at one moment and nice the next.

The Heidelberg Catechism has three questions and answers in a row about the Lord's Supper. All three argue that Roman Catholics don't do the Lord's Supper right. Like I said before, reading this Catechism is sometimes like walking into a museum. What you find in questions and answers like these are issues that were really, really important to believers back then.

In a way, I believe those answers are still important. But I'm not sure they're as important now as they were then. One thing I do know for sure: If we want to break up the body of Christ into a horror movie, there's no better way than to start by saying that I'm right and you're wrong. We need to know what we believe, but we shouldn't poke our beliefs into the eyes of our fellow believers.

Not that I don't believe what the Catechism says here about the Roman Catholic Mass. I'm just not convinced that what people fought about in the sixteenth century is worth more bloodshed. I believe the Catechism, but I don't think beating up on Roman Catholics is what Christ has in mind for us these days.

So here's an even bigger question: How do we live in a world where good Christians disagree?

Read 1 Corinthians 13. "Now these three remain," the Bible says, "faith, hope and love. And the greatest of these is love."

You think loving isn't hard at all? Then you're a Post Toastie.

Don't be.

Help us, Lord, to understand your promises and to find your will for our lives and our world. Keep us from hurting others, especially those who also pray to you. Forgive us for our pride. Keep us from being Post Toasties. In your name, Amen.

Some Mayn't

Q&A 81

Who are to come to the Lord's table? Those who are displeased with themselves because of their sins, but who nevertheless trust that their sins are pardoned. . . , who also desire more and more to strengthen their faith and to lead a better life.

Whoever eats the bread or drinks the cup of the Lord in an unworthy manner will be guilty of sinning against the body and blood of the Lord.

—1 Corinthians 11:27

We've been going over how important the Lord's Supper is to believers. When we eat of the bread and drink of the cup, we commemorate what Christ commanded us to do. But we also become one with other believers.

Then why don't we just say anyone who walks into the church can take communion?

Because the Bible says not to. Take a look at the verse at the top of this page and see what I mean.

Now prejudice is a horrible sin, and it's hard to imagine that the Bible would discriminate by saying that some folks can't come to the Lord's table. But that's what it says. That kind of thing doesn't go down easily in our society. Some can eat, some can't. Some can be there, some must stay away.

My sisters used to love to say two words to me, one of which is an old contraction people don't use much anymore. "Jim," they'd say, "you mayn't."

The Catechism says it too—some may come to the table but some mayn't.

Who mayn't? Here comes a double negative—those who don't wish they weren't sinners. Those who think they're right about everything.

And more: those who don't believe their sins can be forgiven. Those who don't believe, really, that they're God's children.

And more: those who don't want to live better lives. In other words, those who aren't interested in serving the Lord Jesus Christ.

That describes those who mayn't come.

Who may? Those who know their sin, know they're loved, know they want to do better. Know all of that, the Catechism says, and you're welcome.

Amazing. What we've got in Q&A 81 is a mini-catechism. This Heidelberg thing starts with sin, remember? What we need to know is that we can't make it on our own. Knowledge of sin leads us to know our need for a Savior. And once we have that, we're thankful as can be. Know your sin, know you're saved, and know you want to do better. That's our ticket to the Lord's Supper.

Sin, salvation, service. That's the way the whole Catechism goes, and that's what we have to know to eat of the bread and drink of the cup.

You help us in our weakness, Lord. You give us strength when we know we don't have it ourselves. Thank you for your gifts of grace. Thank you for the sacraments. In Jesus' name, Amen.

Supervision

Q&A 82

Therefore, according to the instruction of Christ and his apostles . . .

It is not the Lord's Supper you eat, for. . . each of you goes ahead without waiting for anybody else. One remains hungry, another gets drunk.

—1 Corinthians 11:20–21

If you'd never heard the word *supervision* before, it might sound like something out of a comic book. It might even sound flashy, you know—as in, "armed with his super vision, Superman located those six hog-tied hostages in the basement of the Acme Funeral Parlor."

But we've all heard the word before, probably lots of times. Somebody, after all, has to supervise. When you're a kid, it's usually an adult, like a traffic cop or a teacher or a parent. The person who supervises is called the *supervisor*, and there's nothing very exciting about that job. When I was a high school teacher, I used to have to chaperone dances. *Chaperone* is only a supervisor with a French accent. My job was to supervise, to make sure, for instance, that kids didn't start putting on a smoochy show with their partners on the dance floor.

I know some people who love to supervise. Some people would love to drive your life through the next five years. Some people want to be the honchos.

Not me. And not most of us, I'd guess. I never liked to be a chaperone at a dance because the job always meant keeping kids in line. I'd rather let them go.

But you can't, really. Face it: We need supervisors. Even senior citizens on a two-week trip to Finland need somebody to make sure everything is taken care of. Tour guides supervise too.

Paul's most explicit instruction concerning how to do the Lord's Supper comes in 1 Corinthians 11, and it comes after a note about how the Corinthians ought to conduct themselves in worship itself. They were a young church, full of brand-new Christians, and they did some pretty stupid things at the Lord's Supper. They needed supervision. Fact is, we all do.

The Catechism says that when a church serves the Lord's Supper, someone has to supervise. Someone has to make sure that the sacrament doesn't end up looking like just another church supper. Someone has to make sure that those who are professing their faith, partaking in the ancient sacrament, and following Christ's own command are getting it right.

Because what happens in the Lord's Supper is far too important to get wrong.

And lest we forget: God Almighty is the head supervisor.

Sometimes it's hard to thank you for our supervisors, Lord: teachers, counselors, pastors, parents. Sometimes it's not at all fun to be told what to do and not to do. But thank you, Lord, for supervising our lives. Thank you for watching over us in so many ways, even when those ways burn a little. Thank you for loving us. Amen.

King of Kings

Q&A 83

What are the keys of the kingdom?

He will reign on David's throne and over his kingdom . . . from that time on and forever.

—Isaiah 9:7

Not so many years ago, Great Britain went through a period of national mourning. Maybe you remember. Princess Di was killed in a horrifying auto accident, and the English couldn't contain their grief.

Princess Di had already walked away from her husband, Prince Charles, heir to the throne. What's more, she hadn't acted anything like a storybook princess: She'd taken up with some man who wasn't even British, and she'd been living a life some might call reckless. You wouldn't have thought her death would be so big, but she was royalty, after all.

Along with much of the world I watched the royal funeral, even though it happened in the middle of the night, North American time. It was a huge event.

It's hard for those of us who live in North America to understand royalty. Princess Di really never did much of anything by our standards. All she did is marry a prince. She never ran for office or fought off Nazi tanks. She didn't eradicate poverty from London's ghettos. Still, she was royalty.

In the United States we don't have royalty. As I write this, the 2000 presidential election is a mess. More than two weeks after the election we're still trying to count ballots. In fact, we haven't even figured out what kinds of ballots we should count.

Nobody I know thinks of George W. Bush or Al Gore as royalty. I don't think anyone would vote for either as king. When it comes to royalty, we just don't get it.

So the idea of a *kingdom*—except maybe for Disney's Magic Kingdom—seems kind of strange to us. That we are servants of a King is a real stretch. But it's true—we are servants of the Almighty King. You can't bejewel a crown regal enough for our King.

But what do we really mean by *kingdom?* Maybe you're thinking that kingdom refers to heaven, the afterlife. Lots of believers might define *kingdom* as eternity, when God will rule.

But that's not quite right because God *already* rules. We've seen the King—not with our own eyes, but through the gospel writers. Jesus Christ was here; and now, after the ascension, he rules the world. He rules today.

Thank goodness he's not the President or Prime Minister or Princess Di. Our king is the King of kings.

You are our Lord. You are our Redeemer. You gave us life. You conquered death. You ascended into heaven, and now you are our King. Thank you, Lord, for ruling our lives and ruling this world. Help us be your servants. Amen.

In Our Lives

Q&A 83

What are the keys of the kingdom?

But seek first his kingdom. . . .

—Matthew 6:33

You may never have thought of it quite like this, but it's true: We live in a kingdom. I don't mean the kingdom of the United States or the kingdom of Canada. We are citizens of another country altogether, a kingdom that has no border patrol, no freeways, no zoning regulations, no flag, no state bird. You don't have to have a passport to get in, although once you're in it takes some effort to get out.

This kingdom has an army, and everyone is in it. It has taxes, so to speak, and laws. What's more, it has an educational system. It has plumbers and farmers, homemakers and homeopaths, tort lawyers and bassoonists, meat cutters and film gaffers. It's got just about every kind of citizen you can imagine.

On Ascension Day, a day we ought to celebrate a lot more than we do, Christ took a throne on high to rule as our king. His kingdom isn't something we get into when our lights go out. We're in it right now.

Research has shown that people who believe in God live much happier lives. They marry better and longer, they have fewer health problems, they live longer, and they're less burdened with emotional distress. That's not to say believers don't get divorced or suffer mental breakdowns. Don't ever think that. But research shows that human beings who are citizens in the kingdom of God are different.

That kingdom really exists. Maybe you think I'm saying this too often, but I don't think I can. There is already a kingdom, and you're a part of it if you believe in Jesus Christ. You're in.

Maybe the biggest question is this: Now that we're in, how do we live? How do Christians, who are citizens of God's kingdom, live in a world in which not everyone is? How do we do what humans do when we're really citizens of another kingdom? Let's get personal. How does someone like me—someone who likes to write—do that, first of all, as a citizen of God's kingdom? Those are the tough questions.

How do you play soccer as a citizen of God's kingdom? How are you going to be a student as a citizen of God's kingdom? How are you going to go to movies as a citizen of God's kingdom?

Sure, we're citizens of Canada or the United States or whatever country we come from, but far more importantly, we're citizens of another kingdom altogether. The Lord Jesus Christ is our King.

Lord, help us to be citizens of your kingdom in every task we do. Help us carry your name into our work today and for the rest of our lives. Thank you for making us part of your family, for hiring us on as your servants. Amen.

Carry the Keys

Q&A 83

What are the keys of the kingdom? The preaching of the holy gospel and Christian discipline toward repentance.

I will give you the keys of the kingdom of heaven; whatever you bind on earth will be bound in heaven, and whatever you loose on earth will be loosed in heaven.

—Matthew 16:19

By themselves, keys are nothing more than little chunks of metal cut like puzzle parts. Bring a dozen in to a salvage yard, and you'd likely not make more than a penny. Pick one up on a street somewhere and there's not much to do but throw it out. Useless.

But like dollar bills and wedding rings, keys are also symbols. They are what they are, but they mean a whole lot more.

The kingdom of God we've been talking about has keys too—not silver-plated keys like the ones on a janitor's belt, but keys nonetheless—things we use to get inside that kingdom. The keys of the kingdom open the doors of that kingdom—and close them shut.

What are these keys? "The preaching of the holy gospel and Christian discipline toward repentance."

These keys don't make good rattles. But the King himself has given them to his church.

Now I happen to believe that the best thing about Sunday worship is preaching. Wonderful music is great, a little drama is OK, and now and then a couple of jokes keep the ears open. But pancakes and syrup without the pancakes is just so much sweetness. For me, the preaching in worship is more important than anything else. What's more, says the Catechism, preaching has the power to open and close the doors of the kingdom.

But statistics show that most people who become Christians don't wander into church, hear a terrific sermon, and then sign on the dotted line. Most people come to faith because they see it at work. They see the kingdom lived out in the lives of people they know well.

Now I know that preaching is one of the official keys Christ has given the church. But listen: We bring God's Word too. As I've said before, we're all preachers of sorts. You could even say we carry the keys of the kingdom around with us. Every time we tell or show others the joy of life in the kingdom, we are preaching. And we are helping to open the door of the kingdom to those around us.

Babies love keys, but they don't carry them. The church does . . . and when we bring God's Word to the world, so do we.

So carry the keys. And use 'em.

Lord, help us to be better preachers. Help us by what we say and do to show others the way into your wonderful kingdom. Amen.

When People Are Wrong

Q&A 84

The kingdom of heaven is closed. . . .

In your hearts set apart Christ as Lord. Always be prepared to give an answer . . . for the hope that you have. But do this with gentleness and respect. . . .

—1 Peter 3:15

Not so long ago, I was telling you about Ralph Waldo Emerson, a man who wrote that little passage about how separate parts of the body were walking here and there and everywhere. Here a leg, there an eye, and look—over there—a pair of kidneys.

I like this Waldo, always have and always will, I guess. He was a very religious man. He felt that Christ was the finest human being ever because Christ recognized something very clearly that the rest of us just can't get straight: Jesus Christ understood that he was divine. Nobody else really understands that, Emerson used to say.

This most famous Waldo was absolutely convinced that we are all Jesus Christs. That's right. Every last one of us, he said, is just as divine as Jesus. If only we could all get that lesson through our thick heads, he would say (in much more graceful prose), we could all achieve divinity. That's what he preached. Each of us is divine, but each of us thinks we're only made of dust. Not so. We're all gods.

Reading this Waldo is so inspiring! Trust yourself, he says. Don't give a toot what others think of you because you have to listen to the divine in you. If you want to get a silver stud in your tongue, go for it. Listen to the god in you. God is in you.

After a fashion, of course, Waldo was right—our bodies are God's temple, after all. But to say that we are God is dead wrong. God is something other than we are. God may live in the heart of Aunt Sadie, but Aunt Sadie isn't God. God is altogether something else. As much as I like Waldo, somewhere along the line, had I known him, I would have had to tell him what I thought. I would have had to tell him he was dead wrong.

Now I know that if Waldo were part of the church in those days, the church itself would have the job of telling him he was wrong. But as a member of that church and, let's say, as someone who knew Waldo pretty well, I would also have to speak up.

So how do you tell someone he or she is wrong? "In your hearts, set apart Christ as Lord," Peter says. "Always be prepared to give an answer to everyone who asks you to give the reason for the hope that you have. But do this with gentleness and respect."

Give us wisdom, Lord, to know what's right; give us strength to know when to say it; and give us love to know how. Help us be more like you in everything we do. Amen.

Keys and Swords

Q&A 85

Such persons the officers exclude from the Christian fellowship. . . .

If he refuses to listen even to the church, treat him as you would a pagan or a tax collector.

—Matthew 18:17

Guess what—those keys of the kingdom we've been talking about, the keys given to the church? They're keys all right, but they're also swords. They can cut and wound—even kill.

If you think of Jesus Christ as the great peacemaker, you're not wrong. But listen to what he says in Matthew 10:34: "Do not suppose that I have come to bring peace to the earth. I did not come to bring peace, but a sword." Ouch.

So think of those keys as swords. Why? Because sometimes, very rarely, the church has to lock its doors against someone . . . until that person repents. And that hurts.

The Catechism says the officers of the church hold the most important keys. Not all of us are officers. Twice I served as a church officer, and both times I was scared because I knew being an officer meant I'd have to rule—guilty or not guilty—in some tough cases.

Maybe it will help to think of what we're talking about as a trial, say a divorce trial. A mom and a dad can't get along. They fight like cats and dogs. Each blames the other; both want custody of the kids. So they take the case to court and throw the whole question into the lap of the judge, who has to decide. He's the one with the keys, but at the same time he's the one with the sword, because in all likelihood someone is going to lose.

Being a judge must be a terribly difficult job. Take it from me, being an elder or a church officer is too. Sometimes you have to wield that sword. You have to tell someone that he or she is wrong—wrong about stealing, wrong about adultery, wrong about pride or envy or wrath. You have to tell that person that unless he or she changes, the gates of the kingdom will swing closed. Sometimes—very rarely—you have to lock the door.

Judges have been wrong about things, and so have church officers. For that reason it's good for us all to remember that the keys of the kingdom are like swords.

Here's the big thing to remember: When the door closes in someone's face, we hope and pray that one day that same door will swing wide open. We hope and pray that someone who once lost the way will find it back, by the grace of God.

The whole point of locking the door is to be able to open it again.

Lord, help us to know when to wrap our arms around people and when to tell them we can't. Help us to love as you loved. In the name of the one who loved us more than anything, Amen.

Forever Thankful

Q&A 86

Then why must we still do good?

Therefore, as we have opportunity, let us do good to all people. . . .

—Galatians 6:10

I'm a brand-new grandpa! And now I understand why everyone who's a grandparent crows about it. We can't help it.

Chances are, I'd be a grandpa even without Delores, but let me tell you about her anyway. No, Delores isn't my wife, she isn't my daughter, and she isn't Jocelyn, my brand-new granddaughter. Delores is a nurse.

She wasn't the nurse on duty when Jocelyn was born. If the truth be told, Delores didn't even have to attend the birth of my granddaughter. But she did, and my wife and I will never, ever forget.

Today Jocelyn is only six weeks old, and she's just fine. Did I mention how beautiful she was? Trust me. She'll knock your socks off.

So my son-in-law called my wife, who was visiting at their house waiting for Jocelyn's birth. "Can you come to the hospital right away?" he asked. "Delores is just finishing her shift—she'll pick you up and bring you back." Delores did, even though she didn't have to.

Jocelyn's umbilical cord was wound around her forehead, so every time my daughter pushed, the graph on the machine monitoring her daughter's heart would flatten. I'm glad I wasn't there.

But my wife was. She saw the nurses' concern and the doctor's fear. Jocelyn's birth wasn't normal; there were even more complications.

Now listen to this. Delores stayed the whole night, even though her shift had ended hours and hours earlier. She stayed because her children are friends of our children, and she knew that everybody at the hospital—mom, dad, and grandma—needed her. She didn't get a dime, and, that night, not a moment's sleep. That night God gave my wife Delores for comfort.

Why do we do good works? Delores didn't get rich or famous or win a trip to Cancun. She gave a whole night of her life simply because my family needed her. Thanks be to God.

Maybe twenty souls in all of North America know Delores is a hero. I do and so does my wife, of course. So does my daughter and my son-in-law, and someday so will beautiful Jocelyn.

But someone else knows too. The Lord God Almighty. God knows.

Lord, please bless everything we do in our lives, every moment. Make us witnesses of your love. Help us bring your love into a world that needs it. And thank you, Lord, for the Deloreses in our lives. In Jesus' name, Amen.

From the Inside Out

Q&A 86

We do good because Christ by his Spirit is also renewing us to be like himself. . . .

Therefore, if anyone is in Christ, he is a new creation; the old has gone, the new has come!

—2 Corinthians 5:17

Just for a minute, let's rewrite the Bible. Let's pretend that instead of saying, "Today, you will see me in paradise" to the believing thief on the cross, Christ had said, "OK, your sins are forgiven—now step down and go home."

I know, he didn't say that, but let's just pretend that the thief went home.

Home, where he's known as a felon, an armed robber. Home, abandoned ages ago by the wife and kids because of endless scrapes with the law. Home, with no job, no income, no way of life except picking locks.

It's no picnic in his apartment. Christ cleaned him up on the cross, but the place he lives is still a pigsty.

He sits down on an oily couch, and the phone rings. It's Lefty. "Heard you came down off that cross, Biff," he says. "Hey! That's way cool!" Just like that, Lefty tries to pull him back in. "Listen, we got this thing goin' down tonight—you in?"

Now remember, Biff has been changed from the inside out. Not many hours before, he'd come to believe in Jesus, and that faith was confirmed when Christ helped him step down off the cross. In place of the old darkness that characterized his life, there's now incredible light.

So what does he tell Lefty? "No, you worthless, ignorant con—now I'm a Christian!"

I doubt it.

But he's not the man he was either, no way. So he's going to have to deal with people who were his friends, those friends in all the wrong places. He's going to have tell them, one way or another, that Jesus Christ has changed him from the inside out.

The Catechism says that once we have been delivered from the darkness, we become wholly (and holy) different. Not because we earn our own salvation by being nice, but because the Holy Spirit rebuilds our insides so we're not what we were, but—listen to this—we're like Christ himself! That renewal of ourselves, says the Catechism, is one reason we "do good."

Had Christ sent the thief on the cross home, he would have given him a new "inside" friend. He would have given him the Holy Spirit.

Thank you for never leaving us alone, Lord. Thank you for promising and delivering, for giving us your Spirit, to guide, to bless, to make us better, to make us more like you. Amen.

Doing Good, Feeling Good

Q&A 86

And we do good so that we may be assured of our faith by its fruits. . . .

Every good tree bears good fruit, but a bad tree bears bad fruit.

—Matthew 7:17

In a way, this one is a no-brainer. Take Corrie. She and about fourteen others went down to a little out-of-the-way town in Central America where people were building a health clinic. Corrie is sixteen and has no plans to be a medical doctor; in fact, she's thinking about majoring in music when she goes to college. Anyway, she went down with a bunch of friends and spent almost two weeks doing masonry work.

Would Corrie have done masonry work back home? Doubtful. Did she like it? The sweat and aching fingers? No. Is she thinking about a career laying block? No way, especially after ten days of hoisting too many of them. Talk about sore arms and legs—she was sore in places she didn't even know she had.

But Corrie said she had a great time in rural Mexico.

"Are you kidding?" she said. "I'd do it again in a heartbeat. We worked like dogs, and I could hardly sleep at night because my whole body ached. But we had the greatest team—all kinds of support from each other and from the people of the town.

"Every night we had devotions together. Everyone was open and honest. I've never experienced anything like it.

"Would I recommend it to other kids? In a flash. It was wonderful. I got to see a whole different way of life, felt a great spiritual high, and came back sure that what I'd done was going to be a big help to those people. They're not rich, you know, and they don't have very good health care. This new clinic is going to be a miracle."

The Catechism tells us something that life itself makes very clear: Do good things, and you'll get your reward; act like a jerk, and you'll turn into one.

Why do believers do good? The Catechism says doing good assures us of our faith by its fruits. We see the fruits or results of our faith in the good we do. "Every good tree bears good fruit," says Jesus. And when we see those fruits in our lives, we're reminded that we are, by grace, among God's children. We are assured of our faith.

Like I said, this one is really a no-brainer.

Thank you, Lord, for teaching us what we know—that being good and doing good assures us of our place in your family. Help us remember the opposite too—that dancing with the darkness isn't good for us, inside or out. Open our eyes, Lord, help us see clearly. Assure us again that we belong to you. In Jesus' name, Amen.

By Our Love

Q&A 86

By our godly living our neighbors may be won over to Christ.

Let your light shine before men, that they may see your good deeds and praise your Father in heaven.

—Matthew 5:16

Old Mrs. Thornapple's greatest joy in life was her garden. Our greatest joy was the baseball field that lay right beside it. When I was twelve years old, my greatest joy was slamming a home run over the left field fence and into Mrs. Thornapple's garden.

But my triumph was Mrs. Thornapple's misery. My home run meant a swarm of kids would trek through her cauliflower to try to find the dumb ball. We weren't always charitable to her carrots. And I don't doubt we banged a couple of green beans off the stalks while we were at it. We had to have the ball. Can't play a game without the ball.

We were sure that Mrs. Thornapple hated us. Of course, she really didn't know us as kids; she knew us only as those worthless brats who created havoc in her precious garden. So she'd yell and she'd scream and she'd call the principal of the school. She'd come out with a broom and threaten us like the Wicked Witch of the West. To us, she was truly evil.

Sure, I knew she wasn't always to blame. Maybe we should have asked *her* to retrieve home-run balls. But then we'd have had to wait forever, right? What do kids know about time?

What I know is this: We really, really disliked Mrs. Thornapple. I guess you could say we even hated her, at least for long periods of several springs and summers.

She's dead now—has been for years and years. I wouldn't doubt for a minute that Mrs. Thornapple is somewhere tending a heavenly garden right now, a heavenly smile on her face. I don't doubt she was a believer. But there's no way I would have called her a Christian when I was twelve. And I suppose she never thought of us as angels either.

Godly living, doing good, says the Catechism, brings neighbors to Christ. Let's face it: We weren't exactly godly neighbors, not the home-run hitters or the gardener on the other side of the barbed-wire fence. Neither brought the other any closer to Christ.

Love is the name of the game, Jesus says time and time again. Love will heal. Love will make more love. Love will bring others to the love of the Lord.

But we've got to work at it.

It's not hard to love the people we love, Lord. But you tell us to love others, regardless of whether or not they're lovable. That's what you do. Help us show others the way to faith by our good deeds, by our love. In Jesus' name, Amen.

Conversion Software

Q&A 87

Can those be saved who do not turn to God from their ungrateful and impenitent ways?

Repent, then, and turn to God, so that your sins may be wiped out. . . .

—Acts 3:19

It may surprise you to know that my parents are my most loyal readers. Maybe that's the way it should be, right? Trust me on this: Your parents share in your hurts and your joys in ways that you won't begin to understand until you have your own kids.

Anyway, because my parents really like to read what I write, I often send them things—stories and essays—long before they ever appear in print.

Here's the problem. I send these meditations to them, but their computer can't read my WordPerfect software. They try to open the attachments in their e-mail, and it's all gibberish because their computer reads only Microsoft Word. That's Bill Gates's fault. Unless we have compatible software, it's impossible for them to read these words.

So I've got to convert these files to their software, or they've got to convert them. We've got to change it somehow or it's all gibberish.

Spiritual conversion is kind of like that. The Catechism's list of tough sins reads like a rap sheet. "Scripture tells us," it says, "that no unchaste person, no idolater, adulterer, thief, no covetous person, no drunkard, slanderer, robber, or the like is going to inherit the kingdom of God." Want to know the key words here? *"Or the like."* Reading that list of sins, you might get the idea that the only real sinners are the ones on WANTED posters. Not so, of course.

The truth is, *no* sinners are going to inherit the kingdom of God. Not a single one. We all need to be converted, like these meditations need to be converted for my parents to be able to read them.

We're gibberish without grace. We're unreadable. We don't make a dime's worth of sense. We're a mess.

"Jesus loves me, this I know" may well be the most precious and important six words in the whole Christian vocabulary. But knowing that—really knowing it deeply and eternally in your heart of hearts—means that you and I are going to be converted, just like these meditations, into something clear, understandable, and even pure.

Think of it this way: *L20lesxxx.asdf.ffff*, slowly but surely, in conversion, becomes *love.*

Dear Lord, Sometimes the typos in our lives start to feel like roadblocks, not just speed bumps. Help us to repent. Then convert us to your will, Lord, and help us live every day for you. Amen.

Getting Cranked

Q&A 88

What is involved in genuine repentance or conversion?

Even youths grow tired and weary . . . but those who hope in the Lord will renew their strength. . . . they will run and not grow weary. . . .

—Isaiah 40:30–31

Remember Corrie? A couple of readings ago, I told you about her experience working in a small town in Mexico. She came back completely cranked about love, about Jesus, about helping others, about herself. She never felt better in her life.

But guess what? All of a sudden she's back in town, and nothing has changed. Coming back home was a bigger culture shock for Corrie than going to Mexico. She would have liked to be met at church by a rock band banging out praises to God. Instead she got the same old people in the same old pews with the same old preacher trying to energize the crowd like some flunky cheerleader.

When we get cranked, when we get ourselves spinning like some kids' top, when we feel as if we're wired for God and then come back to the same-old, same-old, we sometimes crash and burn. Some of you know what I'm talking about.

Now hold on for a minute. Let's say that when Corrie returned, the whole sanctuary was dressed up in streamers and banners. A rock band was playing up front, everybody was standing up, waving their arms to "Shine, Jesus, Shine." Let's say they had cake—"Death by Chocolate"—in the back after the service that everybody gorged on. Let's say Corrie's youth group couldn't have felt more welcome on the day they came back to their church.

Great! But the next day she'd wake up with bad hair. The next day she'd have to brush her teeth. The next day it might be raining.

Sometimes believers get torqued like those little furry gizmos you wind up tight. And sometimes, like those same toys, they run into walls, back up, run into walls, back up, run into walls again until they finally run out of steam.

Corrie came back on a high, then she ran into the same-old, same-old. She felt different, somehow, but then Mrs. O'Hare was still playing the piano at church as if worship were a funeral.

The same thing happened to the apostle Paul. On the road to Damascus his lights were knocked out. But later, like other Christians, Paul became discouraged when he had to slug it out in the trenches with the same-old, same-old.

Just remember, conversion isn't a party drug. It's not a high. It's a lifelong thing. Buck up—we're in this for the long haul.

Thank you for moments of real joy, Lord, moments when everything sings your praise. Help us carry those moments into the real world, the world that's broken and torn. Help us to be your servants for the long haul. Amen.

Death of the Old Self

Q&A 89

What is the dying-away of the old self?

Put to death, therefore, whatever belongs to your earthly nature. . . .

—Colossians 3:5

Someday maybe you will read (or maybe you have already read) a story titled "The Swimmer" by John Cheever. I read it first about twenty years ago or so; it's one of those stories that just sticks with you, like good oatmeal.

On first reading, you might think it strange. I know I did. It's about a man named Neddy Merrill who lives in an exclusive suburb of New York City. One summer morning, Neddy decides to swim back home from the friends' place he was visiting by way of the eight miles of fashionable swimming pools that lie in backyards between their homes.

Strange, I know, but Neddy thinks it's a grand idea, a kind of triathalon test of his manhood. Anyway, the whole idea ends up really testing his soul, because as he gets in and out of pools, a kind of *X-Files* thing happens. The seasons change, for one thing: Night and fall come as if out of nowhere, and he ends up in a thunderstorm at the door to what seems like a haunted house.

When my college students read the story, they generally think it's weird until we talk about it a little. You see, Neddy Merrill disintegrates as a character. He self-destructs, which is something you would never have guessed, given his bucks and his status. Neddy loses heart, grows weary, gets old. By the time it's over, Neddy has lost everything that ever meant anything to him. He's a sorry case.

"The Swimmer" is a story drawn right from the Catechism. Conversion is what we're talking about, and the Catechism says it happens in two steps. One of these steps—the death of the old self—is often very, very painful.

My students don't really like the story much because it ends so drearily, with Neddy just about dead and freezing cold. But the story suggests "the death of the old self." Everything Neddy Merrill held important, everything he worshiped, was washed away in a succession of backyard pools.

The Bible says conversion begins to happen when our old values crash and burn, when what we held dear becomes trash. A part of us dies then, and that can be ugly, as it was for Neddy Merrill. But only when the old person dies can the new person be born.

That's the story of Neddy Merrill. It's my story too, and yours.

Lord, scrub us and we will be whiter than snow. Help us understand that when we become truly yours, something has to go, something has to die. Bring us through that pain to glory. Amen.

Hear the Joy

Q&A 90

What is the coming-to-life of the new self? It is a wholehearted joy. . . .

Let me hear joy and gladness; let the bones you have crushed rejoice.

—Psalm 51:8

Everyone in the community in which I live, as well as the whole Midwestern part of the continent, will remember December 2000 as one of the coldest, wind-driven, snowy Decembers on record. Our average daily temperature was just five degrees, with eleven days of below zero temperatures, and the month wasn't even over. People die in this bone-chilling cold, believe me. Winter here is a killer.

But sometime in March, spring's warm winds shove out the cold and begin their warm and wonderful transformation of the prairies. When it does we forget winter's bitter midnight. Snow melts into rivulets that sing with warmth of the new season. As always, spring dances in like joy itself.

That transformation makes spring what it is—not just a time of year but a symbol. If you have spring in your heart, every last form of winter is bearable.

In John Cheever's story "The Swimmer," Neddy Merrill feels his faith in this life freeze into nothingness. He's left with nothing but his own human weakness. That's all. But Cheever had it only half right.

The Catechism gets it all right when it explains the gospel. It doesn't leave us in pain when the old person of sin is buried forever. In place of that old person of sin, a brand-new person arises in each of us. That new person is born in Christ and arises on the strength of Christ's own incredible resurrection.

Conversion requires a death that brings life. What a remarkable juxtaposition! The pain of losing is deleted from our screens by the wholehearted joy of new life.

New life in Christ makes frogs into concert sopranos, three-toed sloths into eye-popping beauties, every last ugly duckling into a graceful swan.

Want to know the truth? New life in Christ turns a wind-driven blizzard, bitterly cold, into an unforgettable wonderland. New life in Christ turns winters into springs. We are born again in a new life in Christ. That's not half-hearted—that's *wholehearted* joy.

"Let me hear joy and gladness," David says to God after he has confessed his sin. Hear the joy?

Lord Jesus, by your life and death and resurrection, we know what joy means. We who have seen the darkness have also seen the new light. If we'd thank you every day, it wouldn't be enough. Help us sing all our lives. Amen.

A Wildfire of Joy

Q&A 90

It is a wholehearted joy in God through Christ. . . .

Rejoice in the Lord always. I will say it again: Rejoice!
—Philippians 4:4

Last night, on Christmas, a local TV station interviewed people coming out of Christmas worship. "What does Christmas mean to you?" they asked. "The birth of Jesus Christ," the people all said, "and getting together with family and friends."

Most Christians would say the same thing: Jesus' birth *and* coming home, Jesus' birth *and* presents, Jesus' birth *and* a wonderful dinner with the whole family.

At Christmas, the whole world—Mr. Scrooge and the Grinch excepted—becomes an angel-shaped, frosted cookie. It's a wonderful time for wonderful joy, usually for two wonderful reasons: Jesus' birth and the grand hoopla that goes with Christmas in North America.

One of the most interesting writers in American literature is a grand old Puritan named Jonathan Edwards, a brilliant, brilliant preacher. Even though Edwards's most famous piece of writing is a wild-eyed, fiery sermon titled "Sinners in the Hands of an Angry God," he likely never slammed the pulpit himself; he really wasn't a fiery preacher.

Of all the things he wrote, his own story is perhaps the most interesting. It's called, simply, "Personal Narrative," and it's about his love for God. All through it, you'll find sentences like this: "Holiness . . . appeared to me to be of a sweet, pleasant, charming, serene, calm nature, which brought an inexpressible purity, brightness, peacefulness and ravishment to the soul."

The Catechism says conversion in our hearts brings about a wholehearted joy—not just any joy but a wholehearted joy *in God through Christ.* The kind of thing Edwards felt but couldn't quite describe. Not joy in Christmas presents, but joy in Christ himself. Not joy that comes from being with family, but joy in the Lord—right?

Maybe, maybe not. Try to imagine someone who could find joy in God but not in God's world. Try to imagine someone who could find joy in God, but not in those who bear God's image (like all of us).

"A wholehearted joy in the Lord" begins in God, but spreads like . . . well, like the joy of Christmas. Go ahead. "Rejoice in the Lord, always. I will say it again: Rejoice!"

Lord, families aren't always sweet, friends aren't always friends, life's paths have switchbacks and landmines. But when we know we're yours, we can get through the tough times. Thank you for converting us, for giving us a real job, for making us yours now and into eternity. Amen.

Love and Hate

Q&A 91

What do we do that is good? Only that which arises out of truth faith. . . .

If anyone says, "I love God," yet hates his brother, he is a liar. . . . Whoever loves God must also love his brother.

—1 John 4:20–21

One of the finest men I know taught me how to hate. I can't say enough about him. He taught me a love for the outdoors that I carry with me even today. He knew every last tree, every last flower, every last piece of undergrowth vegetation in the woods near the lake where I grew up. He knew the paths in those woods like the back of his hand. Every year he hunted deer, but he never shot one. I'm sure he couldn't.

But this wonderful man was scared to death of communism, perhaps with good reason. One night when I was a kid, he took me and his son to a meeting of anticommunists, and we watched a slide show that featured Dr. Martin Luther King. Dr. King, said the show, was an undercover communist, an enemy of America worthy only of hate.

The only people in that room were white. I think I was fourteen years old or so. At that age, I wanted to believe everything good people told me.

What may be hard for you to understand is this: Frank, the man I thought was the greatest, was capable of hating with a righteous heart. He honestly and truly believed that his hate for Dr. Martin Luther King grew out of God-glorifying reasons. He honestly believed that God wanted him to hate Dr. King.

The Catechism asks a very simple question, "What do we do that is good?" and then gives a very simple answer: "Only that which arises out of true faith."

Seems simple enough, doesn't it? But good Christians in Salem, Massachusetts, hung eighteen people they presumed to be witches. Good Christians persecuted Anabaptists, Mormons, Quakers and, in general, most of those who didn't see the world just like they did. In my life, good Christians taught me how to hate.

The real lesson of this question and answer is the one you find between the lines: "Don't ever start to think you know it all."

Humility is not only a virtue but a requirement for those who try to live by God's rule of love. Too often in history, good Christian people, for good reasons, have taught their children how to hate.

And when they did, they always thought they were doing God's own will.

The difference between *righteousness* and *self-righteousness* is just four little letters that mean *me*.

Lord, help us to do good. Let us be your hands in this world. But keep our hearts pure. Help us to love, not hate. Give us wisdom to guide us how to act in your name. In Jesus' name, Amen.

"Only What's Done for Christ Will Last"

Q&A 91

Only that which arises out of true faith, conforms to God's law, and is done for his glory . . .

So whether you eat or drink or whatever you do, do it all for the glory of God.

—1 Corinthians 10:31

Non-Christians have created some of the world's greatest masterpieces. They've written some of the best novels, painted some of the best paintings, created some of the finest bridges and buildings, acted in some of the world's finest plays.

Non-Christians have helped to relieve some of the world's pain and sadness by developing medical cures that ended life-threatening illness. Non-Christians have been among the finest judges, the best lawyers, the wisest politicians.

Non-Christians risk their lives each day as firefighters and police officers. Non-Christians make great teachers. Non-Christians make movies that entertain and educate us, create TV shows that make us laugh and cry. Non-Christians are often on the cutting edge of change and innovation in the way we see ourselves, our families, and our culture. Non-Christians are smart and engaging, and often they are very interested in making this world a better place.

I'm not lying.

Upstairs in my childhood home, my parents kept a plaque on the wall that says "Only one life will soon be passed; only what's done for Christ will last."

I've fought with that plaque's moral lesson for most of my life, perhaps because I love literature, and most of it isn't written by Christians. Was Shakespeare a Christian? Who knows? But he's written plays that will still be read and produced years after you and I are popping daisies in some cemetery. Certainly Shakespeare produced *lasting* literature, whether or not it was done "for Christ." Is it eternal? That may be another question.

The Catechism sounds like that old plaque: "Only that which arises out of true faith, conforms to God's law, and is done for his glory"—only those things are real good works. *A Midsummer Night's Dream?* Bah, humbug!

Can unbelievers do good works? For centuries the church has fought about this idea. To say no is to toss out Albert Einstein.

I say, cool it. The moment you feel like judging other people, step back and take a deep breath of fresh air. There's only one Judge of the living and the dead. Let God make the calls. God will determine who and what are truly lasting.

Meanwhile, remember what John said: "Whatever you do, do it all for the glory of God."

God Almighty, you've used millions of human beings in millions of wonderful ways, often regardless of their faith. Teach us how to love as you do. Amen.

Here's the Story

Q&A 92

God spoke all these words. . . .

Then the LORD said to Moses, "Tell the Israelites this: 'You have seen for yourselves that I have spoken to you from heaven. . . .'"

—Exodus 20:22

Define yourself.

Maybe you'd say, "I'm 5'8" and I'm a student at Last Ditch High School." Maybe you'd say, "I live in Toronto and I've got freckles and brown eyes." Maybe you'd say, "I like chocolate ice cream and the Blue Jays." Maybe you'd say, "I'm a Christian."

What you probably wouldn't say is something like, "Here's my story." When you're in your teens, your story is still in its preface.

But if I'd ask you to define your grandma, most of you would probably tell a story. Grandma was raised in Winnipeg (or wherever), married John Q. Last Name, had four kids (more or less), and worked most of her life as a teacher (or whatever).

You've heard of "scratch and sniff." I believe in "scratch and story." Strip away everything else, and what you've got left is a story.

The Israelites believed that too. When they'd get depressed, they'd ask some poet (maybe King David) to tell them the story of God's guiding them out of Egypt. "Tell us," they'd say, and the storyteller would remind them once again of the frogs, the water like blood, and the long night of the Passover.

Now define Jesus. Well, he was born in a barn, his mother was a virgin, he got himself into trouble he didn't deserve, he died a horrible death on the cross, but then—wonder of wonders—he came back to life, resurrected. Scratch and story.

For the next few readings, we're going to look at the Ten Commandments, which are themselves a chapter of a bigger story. The Lord God Almighty *first* delivered the Israelites from Pharaoh and his army, *then* gave his people the commandments. First, God saved them, and then told them how to live.

Check out this book—we're far more than halfway through. Why do the Ten Commandments come so late in the game?

The Ten Words are for the delivered, the saved, that's why. The Ten Commandments are for the family of God. Remember where we've been in this book: we've looked at our sin, then our salvation (thank God!), and now our service—out of gratitude to him. Sin, salvation, service.

The Ten Commandments are rules for beloved believers. That's me and that's you—and all those who believe the gospel.

"This," God says, "is how I want my people to live."

Lord, we are who we are because you saved us. Thank you for giving us a story—yours and ours. Help us learn to live as your family. Amen.

The Ten Commandments—for Israel or Us?

Q&A 92

. . . who brought you out of the land of Egypt, out of the land of slavery.

And God spoke all these words: "I am the LORD your God, who brought you out of Egypt, out of the land of slavery."

—Exodus 20:1–2

God defines himself by referring to a story. Even before the commandments begin, in the foreword of "the Ten Words," the Lord God Almighty steps up to the plate and says, "You want to know who I am, just remember the story. I'm the one who brought you out of the land of Egypt, out of the land of slavery." The Israelites knew very well who God was.

I'm not an Israelite. My ancestors were not told to make bricks with straw they had to scrounge up themselves. My great-grandparents were not persecuted by some hardhearted Pharaoh. Nobody in my family history ever walked through the dried-up bed of the Red Sea or wandered through the Middle Eastern wilderness for forty years. That's not my history.

The truth is, I got into this family only because of Jesus Christ. I'm adopted into God's chosen people. I can't trace my lineage back to some Levite priest. Not a single believer in my whole family tree ever did that strange, rocking prayer thing at the Wailing Wall.

I came into faith because of Jesus Christ, who never burned a word into tablets of stone but told his followers that the only way to live is by loving other people. I'm not Jewish; I'm Christian. Those "Thou Shalt Nots" sometimes seem a country mile from the Sermon on the Mount and all that love stuff. The Ten Commandments were fine for desert wanderers who ate doughy dew and dead pigeons, but we're in a whole new age, right?

Yes and no. On one hand, we do see things differently, now that we're on the other side of Christ's birth, his life, his death, his resurrection, his ascension. We've known a Savior, a Messiah the old Israelites didn't know. We live in a new relationship to God, something the Israelites of the Exodus never knew. "Jesus has become the guarantee of a better covenant," says the Book of Hebrews.

On other hand, there's only one theme to the whole Bible, all of it, Old Testament and New. That theme is God's love for us. The Bible is about deliverance—for the Jews and the Gentiles. The Bible is about forgiveness—for the Jews and the Gentiles. The Bible is about being made new, all of us. The Ten Commandments are the same, today and yesterday. For the Jews and the Gentiles.

The Ten Words still have oomph. You'd better believe it.

Lord, help us to bring your commandments into our hearts. In our kitchens and gymnasiums, in our classrooms and pizza places, help us live by your Word and words. In Jesus' name, Amen.

The Cross and the Ten Words

Q&A 93

How are these commandments divided?
Into two tables.

Jesus replied, "Love the Lord your God with all your heart. . . . Love your neighbor as yourself."

—Matthew 22:37, 39

Find it on churches all over the world. Find it hanging around people's necks. Find it on bumper stickers, outside downtown missions, in little huts in the bush, on billboards, and just about everywhere in the Vatican. The cross is so ubiquitous it's almost not there.

It's been around for centuries, twenty of them at least. Think of it: two narrow strips of wood, nailed together in one spot. That's a cross. You can fashion it of almost anything. Just cross two lines and you've got one.

Put one up on your lawn and you're making a statement. Burn it on someone else's and you're committing a crime—an obscenity. Wear it around your neck and it's not just jewelry.

To me, a cross will always be a memorial of Christ's suffering; it's the tree from which he hung. You've seen a crucifix, I'm sure, one of those crosses that depicts Christ hanging. That kind of cross says something different from empty crosses, but they both suggest the story.

A cross makes a perfect Christian symbol for another reason: It joins two lines, one of which goes up and down, the other of which stretches out horizontally. Jesus Christ, the man who was God and the God who was man, joined heaven to earth like no one else in the history of humanity. He joined the forever with the now, linked spirit and flesh, married this world and the next.

The Catechism says the law is divided into two parts: principles about God and principles about people. Two tablets, two directions (horizontal and vertical). Because in Christianity, this world and the next are wed.

Some people call Christianity a "worldview" because, to those who accept the gift of grace, every last element of life is affected. What we eat, how we eat, whether or not we eat. What we watch, how we watch, whether or not we watch. What we do, how we do what we do, whether or not we do it at all. In all these things, we remember that all of life belongs to God.

It's all there in the symbol of the cross. And it's all there in the Ten Words Moses carted down from Sinai. Christianity is a way to see the world. For some of us, it is "the Way."

Our faith affects all of this life and the next. That truth is visible in the very shape of the cross; and it's here in the Ten Commandments too.

Your light lets us see, Lord. Thank you for giving us the gift of grace, the light that makes our way clear in the darkness. Thank you for helping us know how to live in that light. Amen.

Foundations

"You shall have no other gods before me."

—Exodus 20:3

Q&A 94

What does the Lord require in the first commandment? That I sincerely acknowledge the only true God, trust him alone, . . . love him, fear him, and honor him with all my heart.

If you ever come to our house, you'll likely drive up in the backyard. Most people do. We've got a nice front door and everything, but the driveway is in the back and that's where most people show up.

If you do, you can't help but notice our barn. That's right, even though we live in the very heart of town, we've got a barn. It's even got a manger, where, almost a hundred years ago, horses once munched hay. It's got a two-holer too, although we don't use it anymore, of course. (If you don't know what a two-holer is, ask your grandparents.)

There's an upstairs in that barn, a nice one with lots of space. My son and his friends used to hang out up there a lot. It's a great spot.

Our barn would also be a great place for a studio. I could sit there and write my books. Seriously, it's slightly away from the house, it's rustic, and it's unusual—not everybody has a town barn and a loft. I could put some skylights in and maybe a window or two, fill the place with light. It would be great.

Unfortunately, the computer wouldn't run because right now there's no electricity. No heat either. Right now, I'd freeze up there.

But an electrician could run power out to the barn, and it wouldn't take an Act of Congress to get heat out there either. It wouldn't be too hard. I could redo that whole upstairs and make it into a studio. When important people would come, I could say, "That's where I write," and point proudly to the loft in the barn.

The problem is, our town barn is almost a hundred years old. The walls are bending a little. There's no insulation, and the whole foundation is a mess. If I were to have a studio in our barn, I'd have to rebuild the whole blessed thing, from the bottom up. And that would cost a mint. You know how it is—you can't build something great on a cracked foundation.

So it is with the commandments. The first one says, "God is number one." Period. That's the foundation. That's where life starts. You can't build a sweet second-story studio if the foundation is a mess.

There's a bottom line with God, and it's not hard to remember: God is first. That's it. No questions. End of discussion.

In believers' lives, God's at the foundation of everything, or we are nothing at all.

Lord, nothing sits at the foundation of our lives like you do. Nothing is as important to our lives as your love for us. May you, O God, always be first in our lives. Amen.

Other Gods

Q&A 95

What is idolatry? Having or inventing something in which one trusts in place of or alongside of the only true God. . . .

So, if you think you are standing firm, be careful that you don't fall!

—1 Corinthians 10:12

Consider Marcus. Great guy. Good looking, neat personality, better than average in the classroom, fun at a party. He's everybody's buddy, really.

In high school he was in everything: student council, chorus, even a play or two. But mostly he was a jock. Basketball (off-guard), football (all-conference defensive back), track (third in the state in hurdles his senior year), and golf (handicap of five or six).

At college he didn't make the basketball team. He ran track only one year and played golf only now and then. But all that high school athletic stuff made him into a junky. He went to the gym every day simply because if he didn't go he felt weird. Working out was a ritual, and after all, those sports in high school were his best experiences.

Something about the inside of a gym turned his crank. He had to go, you know? He had to be there. He didn't feel alive unless he could work up a sweat, play a little three-on-three or something. Anything. He just had to be there every day for at least a couple of hours.

Marcus says he's always been a Christian, and I don't doubt him. But if anybody'd try to tell him that athletics is like another god to him, he'd laugh in that person's face.

Maybe he'd have a right to laugh. But then again, maybe not.

Marcus's bedroom is almost a shrine: Every medal he's ever earned has a place. It's fair to say he practically lives at the gym. His scrapbooks are full of memories from his high school sports career.

The Catechism talks about "other gods" in terms of idolatry, prayers to saints, witchcraft, and superstitious rites. All bad. But if you believe that you're off the hook because you don't pray to Satan or drink cat's blood or bow down to tree toads, check out Paul's warning on this page.

Remember—you're human. Humans need something to worship, even if it's a gym or a roomful of trophies.

But God won't have it. The foundation, says the first commandment, has to be God. God Almighty is the only rock to build on. Anything else isn't real.

Who empowers us? Where do we look for joy? Whom do we most honor? God, God, and God. Amen.

Forgive us for judging others, Lord. Forgive us for pointing fingers when each of us has things, does things, worships things other than you. Remind us that you are the foundation we can live on. In your Son's name, Amen.

God and Money

Q&A 95

. . . alongside of the only true God . . .

[Jesus said], "No one can serve two masters. . . . You cannot serve both God and Money."

—Matthew 6:24

Years ago, in a church in which I was a leader, I talked to kids who wanted to make public profession of faith. Public profession is something individuals do when they want to declare to everyone in the congregation that they accept the promises of faith, the gift of grace in their lives.

Prior to that public profession, those kids (they were usually in high school) would meet with the church leaders and discuss their faith. We'd ask questions; they'd answer.

I heard lots of good answers and some pretty lousy ones. But one sticks in my mind so tightly that today whenever I see this person—he's now what some of you would consider an old guy—I remember his answer.

"What do you want out of life?" someone asked.

The kid sat in the chair, eyes lifting to the ceiling as if maybe he could find an answer there. Then he straightened up, looked back at us, and said, "I'd like to be close to God—and well off."

It doesn't take a rocket scientist to know what he meant. "Well off" means rich. The fact is, he wanted to be "well off" with bucks and with God.

Let's face it: Everybody does, right? I mean, very few of us really aspire to be Mother Teresa. Most believers would like to be close to the Lord and relatively comfy. How many people do you know who aspire to a life of suffering?

Should I have said he wasn't ready to profess his faith because he wanted God *and* money? Jesus himself said we can't serve God and money because that would be like having two masters. He also said it was easier for a camel to go through the eye of a needle than for a rich man to enter the kingdom of God (Mark 10:25). But then Abraham, the father of believers, was one of the richest gents in the whole kingdom. Miracles happen.

I didn't say anything, but his answer sticks with me, especially when I read through the Catechism's answer to what the first commandment requires.

It's not that you can't have both, of course; maybe you just can't *serve* both. Obedience is the whole deal here, isn't it? You can't serve both because the first commandment says we are to serve God alone.

Call God arrogant, jealous, demanding—the Creator of heaven and earth wants every last inch of us, inside and out. God wants us to seek him only. Maybe that's what I should have said.

Lord God, forgive us when we want more than we should and less than you demand, something other than you in our hearts, souls, and minds. Thank you for loving us. Amen.

Fashioning God

Q&A 96

What is God's will for us in the second commandment?
That we in no way make any image of God. . . .

"You shall not make for yourself an idol in the form of anything in heaven above or on the earth beneath . . ."

—Exodus 20:4

You know the kind of Saturday afternoon walk-around place I'm talking about: part art show, part flea market, part street bazaar. Lots of food, lots of music, lots of stuff to buy. This one was in Brazil. I was there to do a few stories for a book I was writing when my hosts brought me to this colorful folk fest in a city park. Everywhere you looked people were trying to sell you things, mostly their own creations. Many were really beautiful, others really bizarre.

I loved the wood sculptures one man had laid out on a blanket in front of him. They were slender and willowy, tall, graced with flowing images carved into the soft wood. Think of a baseball bat fashioned into an image of the virgin Mary and baby Jesus. I thought they were beautiful.

I stooped down beside the artist and turned one of his creations in my hand.

"You don't need that," my friend said, only half jokingly. "You serve a living Savior." And then she repeated it in Portuguese so the artist could hear it too.

She was right, of course. I didn't need one. But I bought one anyway, and today it's in my office, right beside a fat little sumo wrestler from Japan and a miniature South African flag, all mementoes of trips. I love the sculpture, I really do. It's as thin as your finger, painted delicately in soft earth tones. If you look closely, the virgin Mary is there, and so is baby Jesus.

I'm not sure the second commandment prohibits my having that nativity in my office. After all, I don't worship it any more than I do the sumo wrestler. Still, my friend, a missionary, wasn't wrong in telling me I didn't need it.

Somehow it's comforting for humans to have idols around, images of clay and wood and stone that either represent or are some kinds of deity. Remember when the people of Israel made a golden calf? Nearly all religions have idols.

Our God says no. Don't worship idols. God Almighty doesn't want us to believe that something human beings make—no matter how beautiful, no matter how graceful—can compare to God in beauty and grace.

God is bigger than anything we can imagine or make or design. He won't let us believe that we can fashion him. God, after all, fashioned us.

Thank you for creating in us a will to worship. Thank you for your commandments, which teach us to know how to worship you, and you alone. Amen.

The Cathedral at Canterbury

Q&A 97

God forbids making or having such images if one's intention is to worship them or to serve God through them.

Therefore since we are God's offspring, we should not think that the divine being is like gold or silver or stone—an image made by man's design and skill.

—Acts 17:29

Visitors enter the Canterbury Cathedral grounds by passing beneath a huge statue of Jesus Christ. That statue is new; the cathedral itself isn't. For almost fifteen hundred years people have come to the cathedral at Canterbury because it's one of the most beautiful examples of Gothic architecture in England.

Geoffrey Chaucer's *Canterbury Tales* is a series of yarns (some of them R-rated) told by pilgrims on their way to Canterbury to visit the spot where Saint Thomas à Becket was murdered on December 29, 1170, on the orders of King Henry II. Once there was a shrine there, but Henry VIII ordered it removed. Today you'll find a plaque marking the spot.

The cathedral is spectacular. The ceiling is a series of flying buttresses, incredibly huge gateway-looking structures that rise from the walls and reach upward, joining in a series of peaks at the very top of a huge dome.

The marble baptismal font is immense. Figures of the gospel writers ring the base, and the twelve apostles are on a cover so heavy it requires pulleys to raise it for baptism.

People are buried here, important people like Edward, the Black Prince; King Henry IV and his queen, Joan of Navarre. They rest under the glow of stained-glass windows, some of which were created in the late twelfth century.

But like I said, that huge image of Christ outside is new. An old statue of Christ once stood there, but centuries ago the Puritans ripped it down and burned it, just as they destroyed some of the stained-glass windows.

Visit an historic Puritan church and you'll be in and out faster than you can recite the books of the Bible. Puritan meeting houses were incredibly boring. Canterbury takes your breath away.

Puritans had this thing about the second commandment, the one about the making of images. When they took a wrecking ball to cathedrals, they did us all a disservice, I think. But visit a place like Canterbury and you begin to understand how the Puritans felt. To them, the place had become a shrine, a place for idol worship—and maybe they weren't all wrong about that.

God wants nothing we build to take God's place or to stand between us and God. It's that simple. That's what those Puritans who wreaked havoc on Canterbury believed. And so did those who wrote the Heidelberg Catechism.

Lord, you are an awesome God, yet what you've given us never seems to be enough. Help us keep the channels between us uncluttered so we worship only you. Amen.

Snake Worshipers

Q&A 98

. . . not by idols that cannot even talk.

[Hezekiah] broke into pieces the bronze snake Moses had made, for up to that time the Israelites had been burning incense to it. (It was called Nehushtan). Hezekiah trusted in the L*ORD*. . . .

—2 Kings 18:4–5

Everybody says the North America we live in today is the most "spiritual" that it's been in generations. I agree. At the school where I've taught for almost twenty-five years, students have never been as openly religious as they are today. They wear Jesus T-shirts and WWJD bracelets. They attend huge praise-and-worship gatherings, form Bible studies, and likely do more and better personal devotions than any students who've ever been here, including their own parents.

Why? Partly, I think, because we're all more spiritual—*we* meaning the whole culture. New Age religion has made spirituality really cool. Believing in some kind of spirit or power larger than we are is hip. Just a decade ago, it wasn't.

We really don't need the wise men to explain what God is telling us in the second commandment. For as long as I've lived, the seventh commandment was the one that got all the ink; the second barely rated an asterisk. But today, in this world where spirituality is hip, I wonder whether the second commandment might need to be hauled out of mothballs.

Here's a true story about that commandment. Look it up if you wish.

God Almighty got sick and tired of the Israelites' whining, so God sent snakes among them (Numbers 21:6). They bit people, and many died. Those who lived understood why God was angry, so they went to Moses and confessed. "We sinned when we spoke against God and against you," they said (v. 7).

As always, God forgave them. "Make a snake and put it on a pole," he told Moses (v. 8); "anyone who is bitten can look at it and live."

Bingo. It worked. Read it yourself.

Generations later, Hezekiah, a real Israeli puritan, smashed that same snake (2 Kings 18:4). You know why? Because the people of Israel were burning incense to it. In fact, they even had a name for it—Nehushtan.

Amazing, isn't it? Their worship of God had burned out like a third-rate candle, but the idol continued to get the full flame of their devotion.

Something in us loves an idol, a "graven image," as the King James Bible used to say. Something in us wants to worship something we can see, something we can make with our hands, something we can put on a shelf.

The second commandment makes very clear that God Almighty will have nothing of that. No idols. Period.

Lord, help us to love and serve you only. Keep our attention and worship focused on you, our Creator and King. In Jesus' name, Amen.

Drivel

Q&A 99

What is God's will for us in the third commandment?
That we neither blaspheme nor misuse the name of God. . . .

To the angel of the church in Laodicea, write: . . . because you are lukewarm—neither hot nor cold—I am about to spit you out of my mouth.

—Revelation 3:14, 16

Of all the sports I played, baseball was my favorite, even though the practices were incredibly boring. In football and basketball, you could scrimmage all afternoon, beat each other up, and keep score. Track practice was all inside—not inside the gym, but inside the heart. Track and field is an individual sport; either you hit the hurdles right, or you don't. No teammate is going to do a thing to help you.

But baseball is a team sport that requires just two things: hitting and fielding, along with a few specialized plays. When I was a kid, baseball practice meant endless batting practice—everybody gets twenty-five swings or so—and then it's endless fungoes. I loved baseball but the practices seemed to stretch into eternity. Maybe it's different today.

Like baseball practice, worship can get boring. When it's done exactly the same this Sunday and next, when we can predict exactly what the preacher's going to say, when we could walk through Sunday morning blindfolded, then worship loses its punch.

Minds wander during long prayers. Minds wander when the sermon almost puts us to sleep. Minds wander too easily maybe. But a worship service that's dull as last week's bread violates the third commandment.

The third commandment demands that we reverence God's name. When we hear God's name, our ears and souls should perk up. What God can't stand is the opposite—somebody going on and on about God while the rest of us doze off.

God gets annoyed at boredom as much as we do. Even more so. In fact, God tells the church at Laodicea that they are lukewarm, indifferent, boring. And God hates that, then and now.

There's more to the third commandment, but it's smart for us to remember that when we go to sleep when God's name is spoken, we're misusing that name and we're making God angry.

Listen to me, says God. I am not drivel.

Keep us from going through the motions, Lord. In our prayer life, in our devotions, in our worship, keep us from taking you for granted, from taking your name for granted. As you always do, forgive us when we fail. Thank you for your love. Amen.

Abusing the Name

Q&A 99

. . . by cursing, perjury, or unnecessary oaths . . .

"You shall not misuse the name of the Lord *your God, for the* Lord *will not hold anyone guiltless who misuses his name."*

—Exodus 20:7

What Kurt said when he discovered what Doreen—his girl—was doing wasn't pretty. Merek and Khalil were there. Kurt got a call on his cell phone telling about Doreen's relationship to Danny. What killed him was that everyone seemed to know about Danny except him.

Anyway, when Kurt found out, he lost it. The air turned blue. Merek had no clue that Kurt had it in him to use that kind of language, but the poison that gushed out of his mouth was radioactive, you know?

* * *

"No way," Doreen said when she and Kurt got together. "No way."

"It's what I heard," Kurt said. He'd settled down some, but he still wanted his buddies there with him, in case he lost it, he said.

"You believe everything you hear?" she asked him.

And then he said something he shouldn't have, called her something he shouldn't have, accused her of something he shouldn't have, in language he shouldn't have used.

Strangely enough, Doreen didn't lose it. Her lip was quivering, but she didn't cry, didn't back off either. "I'll swear on a stack of Bibles," she said. "Kurt, I'm not what you say."

* * *

"I swear—God as my witness—I'm going to kill him," Kurt said, speaking of Danny, when they left. The meeting between him and Doreen became, well, really ugly. As far as Merek and Khalil were concerned, that relationship was dead in the water. Now Kurt wanted Danny's scalp, as if Danny were the real sinner.

"Let it go," Khalil said. "The whole thing is history now."

Kurt couldn't even see straight. Merek got behind the wheel of Kurt's car because he didn't think Kurt could even drive.

"As God is my witness," Kurt said again.

* * *

The third commandment makes clear that we abuse God's name in a number of ways—simply by profanity (like Kurt); by bringing God's name into our lies (like Doreen); by cheapening that name with silly oaths (like Kurt).

In every case, we're treating God's name—and God himself—like drivel. And God won't stand for it. That's what the third commandment says.

Help us to hold your name in reverence and awe, Lord. Keep us from abusing it. In the name of Jesus we pray, Amen.

Blasphemy!

Q&A 100

No sin is greater. . . .

Anyone who blasphemes the name of the Lord must be put to death.

—Leviticus 24:16

"She told us yesterday," Matty told her friends. "We're moving to Georgia in the summer. Dad's got a new job. The decision's been made." She shook her head sadly.

"Can't he find a job around here?" Chip said. "Gee whiz, Matty."

End of story. Some people won't read it any further, because Chip said, "Gee whiz!"

I was brought up to believe that all kinds of words like "gee whiz!" and "gosh" and "gee whillikers" were really substitutes for Jesus Christ and therefore swear words. That meant Chip was swearing just now, cursing God—and the author (me) was using God's name in vain, breaking the third commandment.

I remember thinking that the Mickey Mouse Show bordered on the sinful because one of the main characters, the one who sang the song "E-N-C-Y-C-L-O-P-E-D-I-A," Jiminy Cricket, was really named after a curse. You see, there's some kind of link between the name Jiminy Cricket and Jesus Christ. People say, "Jiminy Cricket!" when they hit their thumbs with a hammer; but what they really mean, you see, is, well, the other name.

The answer to today's question makes blasphemy sound like the very worst sin a human being could ever commit—God commanded the death penalty for it. To avoid that kind of extreme punishment, people thought, it's a good idea to avoid any hint of a word that even suggests blasphemy. The fact is, the Old Testament demanded the same punishment (death) for breaking five other commandments as well (1, 4, 5, 6, and 7).

Can Christians go too far? Darn right they can.

Oops! Can't say "darn" either. That's for sure.

In a way, I'm happy with the way I was reared. The "gosh" lessons taught me a respect for language, especially the language we use for God Almighty. Do I think those who use "geez" in a sentence should be slain for blasphemy? No.

But I do believe the third commandment isn't blowing hot air. If you're going to talk about God Almighty, Creator of heaven and earth, Lord of life itself, the commandment says, don't mess around.

You know a ton of worse words about God than those I've listed. Those are out too. But that you know already.

Help us not to make our very worst moments even worse than they are. Bless our language. Keep us vigilant. Forgive us when we err; love us in our weakness. Make us stronger inside and out. In Jesus' name, Amen.

Anachronism

Q&A 101

May we swear an oath in God's name if we do it reverently? Yes, when the government demands it. . . .

Men swear by someone greater than themselves, and the oath confirms what is said and puts an end to all argument.

—Hebrews 6:16

No one doubts the joys of multiculturalism. Our lives are enriched by knowing people who do not come from our own background. The world is a rich place full of fascinating people and places. The more you know about the world, the more you know about God's almighty wingspan.

Some wonderful Christians at the college where I teach think it's hilarious that some of their best friends—also wonderful Christians—wouldn't think of eating out in a restaurant on Sunday. Others wonder how on earth any Christian kid could ever light up a cigarette or drink a beer. Some really strict Christians are more like really strict Muslims than other loosey-goosey Christians, at least with respect to how they choose to live. Believers, like people, come in a host of different looks.

The founding fathers (and mothers) of the United States were all basically Christian. (We can fight long and hard about that, but the statement is basically true.) Today, however, North America is really multicultural; our towns and cities are peopled by members of literally hundreds of religious creeds—Muslims, Hindus, Sikhs, Confucianists, Wiccans, to name just a few.

Yet in court, when a witness is asked to tell the truth, he or she is asked to swear on a Bible using the Lord's name as witness: "so help me God." Let's face it: The Bible doesn't mean a whole lot to lots of people. So the practice itself is something of an anachronism—an act that really belongs to another era.

In a way, today's question is something of an anachronism too. Heidelbergian Christians lived in a community in which some believers felt that God had strictly forbidden the use of his name—as in an oath ("so help me God")—in public. Such God language, they argued, should not be used at all.

Some believers still feel that way, but it's hardly an issue in the twenty-first century. Like I said, the question is something of an anachronism.

Can we swear by God's name in a court of law or when taking public office? The answer here is simply yes—because such deeply meant swearing actually promotes "truth and trustworthiness for God's glory and our neighbor's good."

Such swearing, the Catechism says, can be a witness. Such swearing can teach others about God's truth.

And that's no anachronism.

Lord, when we're called to take an oath in your name, may we do so reverently and with all of our hearts. May what we say in public show others that we love and honor you, O Lord. Amen.

Saint Christopher

Q&A 102

May we swear by saints or other creatures? No. . . . No creature is worthy of such an honor.

Give thanks to the Lord, call on his name. . . . Sing to the Lord, for he has done glorious things.

—Isaiah 12:4–5

Years ago I was driving to the university where I was studying and teaching, when, out of nowhere, I hit glare ice. Suddenly the rear end of the car slid around completely; I did a full 180-turn in the middle of the road in the middle of rush hour traffic. I could have nailed a half-dozen cars in this freefall slide. I ended up face-to-face with traffic in the right lane of the freeway. But I didn't nick a bumper.

All I got was a mega case of the shakes. I could hardly hold the wheel. But I did. I turned the car around and kept going.

When I got to school, it was still early. The janitor was there, a tough guy with a string of bluish tattoos up his one arm. The other arm was a long plastic prosthetic with a hook. On Tuesday mornings he'd come into my office and dump the trash. He took one look at me and said, "You see a ghost?"

So I told him the whole story—how I did a kittybutt in the middle of the freeway, how nobody hit me, how I just turned the car around and kept going.

"You better get down on your knees, boy," he said. "You better thank Saint Christopher."

The truth was, I hadn't been down on my knees at all. I hadn't thanked Saint Christopher or God Almighty. In a way, God sent a one-armed prophet into my office to remind me who was in charge.

My prophet was a Roman Catholic who believed Saint Christopher to be the patron saint of travelers. By his estimation it was Saint Christopher who needed to be thanked for my painless doughnut in the freeway.

It may be difficult for most Protestant Christians to understand why this question should be included in the Catechism; after all, who swears by animals or other human beings? Actually, some might, and did.

During the Reformation, Protestants rejected homage to saints—like the janitor's homage to Saint Christopher. The Protestants who wrote the Heidelberg Catechism wouldn't pray to Christopher or any other saint, neither would they swear by him.

Neither do I. But that doesn't mean the janitor-turned-prophet didn't teach me a lesson. When he left, I thanked God—finally.

You are the God we serve with our thanks. You are the God who saved us, who forgave us all our sins, who sacrificed your Son for our salvation. To you we bring all our thanks. In your Son's name, Amen.

A Matter of Freedom

Q&A 103

What is God's will for you in the fourth commandment?

"Remember the Sabbath day by keeping it holy."
—Exodus 20:8

I just wrote an ex-student who e-mailed me to ask whether marriage is really all it's cooked up to be. He says he finds himself drawn toward this girl like no other he's ever taken a shine too. But the problem is he loves to travel; he loves his freedom.

"Is marriage worth the price?" he asks. "Do I want to give up my freedom for getting hitched?"

I told him no. If you're asking the question, then the answer is no because when you get to that girl you really love, you'll know you don't want to go through another day without her. Don't marry her if you're not sure, I told him. You'll know when you're sure because then you'll be willing to give it all up.

I'm no Ann Landers, and I told him that too.

This ex-student's question has something to do with the commandment we're now looking at—the fourth, the one about the Sabbath.

Really good Christians differ on what should and what should not be done on Sunday. When I was a kid, I wasn't allowed to play ball on Sunday. Today, my wife and I don't go shopping on Sunday. My mother-in-law says she couldn't use a scissors on Sunday—too much like work. My grandmothers would cook Sunday dinner on Saturday night just to avoid working on the Sabbath.

Were they right? I don't think so, but were they alive today, I probably wouldn't tell them so. Because it seems to me that what we do or don't do on Sunday is really a matter of freedom. Like I said, really good Christians disagree. Your rules may not apply to me; mine may not apply to you.

Now back to my ex-student. He says he doesn't know if he wants to give up his freedom. I'm saying that what he means by *freedom* will be completely different once some girl knocks him off his pins. Once we know God's love, our freedom will be disciplined (*discipled,* really) by our love for God, in the same way my ex-student's love for the girl he marries will make him think differently about his freedom.

If you think I'm not answering the question of what we may or may not do on Sunday, you're right. When you know the Lord, when God sweeps you off your feet, you'll know. That's the only real answer, and ultimately it's the answer of the Heidelberg Catechism.

But there's more, so read on.

Lord, help us to be your people in every possible way, from the way we vote to the way we dress to the way we work and play. Draw us ever closer to you so that we become more faithful servants of your love—on Sunday and Monday and every day of the week. Amen.

Church—Who Needs It, Really?

Q&A 103

I regularly attend the assembly of God's people. . . .

Let us not give up meeting together, as some are in the habit of doing, but let us encourage one another. . . .

—Hebrews 10:25

Some keep the Sabbath going to church;
I keep it staying at home,
With a bobolink for a chorister,
And an orchard for a dome.

So says Emily Dickinson, a long-dead writer whose poetry I love. Some people keep the Sabbath, she says, by being in church. She stays at home. For a soloist she has the birds, and her orchard suggests the dome of a great cathedral. She doesn't need "church."

Most Christians feel the same way at times. Maybe you do too. Church can be a hassle—getting up on Sunday mornings when you'd rather sleep in, worship services that sometimes put you to sleep, pews full of smiling people wanting you to be sweet. Church can also add to your already impossible schedule—what with church school and/or Catechism, youth group, softball team, praise team, drama team, potluck dinners, service trips, family nights. . . .

I prefer a bobolink myself sometimes. I really do.

The Catechism says that God's will in the fourth commandment is that "we regularly attend the assembly of God's people." How often? Doesn't say. What time of day? No mention. Which service? No answer. What should that assembly look like? Doesn't say that either.

Look, we need each other. Every book of the Bible mentions the assembly of believers—every single book. "Where two or three come together in my name," Jesus says, "there am I with them" (Matt. 18:20).

Worship is why we come together; not "church." Worship is what believers do. We need to celebrate the sacraments. We need to learn and grow in faith. We need to bring God's love to others. We need each other.

From the very beginnings of the holy catholic church, when the apostles met secretly, to this very week, Christ's followers have come together to worship, to praise, to glorify, to exalt, to bring their joy like an offering.

If you were stranded on a desert island, could you be a believer? Of course. But sooner or later, I bet you'd really, really miss not being with those who, like you, confess the name of Jesus Christ, the name above all names.

God's will for his people is worship, public worship. The Bible says so over and over. We need each other. It's what God wants.

Thank you for your promise, Lord, that when and where we come together, you'll be there. Thank you that we're part of your family. Thank you for bringing us together as your children. Amen.

The 24/7 Sabbath

Q&A 103

Every day of my life I rest from my evil ways. . . .

Then [Jesus] said to them, "The Sabbath was made for man, not man for the Sabbath. So the Son of Man is Lord even of the Sabbath."

—Mark 2:27–28

The Catechism gives two answers to the question of what God's will is for his people in the fourth commandment. The first, as we've said, is worship; God wants us, together with other believers, to worship him.

The second seems more confusing, especially if you have been brought up, as I have, to believe that the Sabbath is set aside for rest. But listen to the Catechism: "That *every day* of my life I rest from my evil ways, let the Lord work in me through his Spirit, and so begin already in this life the *eternal Sabbath.*"

What does "every day" have to do with the price of eggs? We're talking about the Sabbath here. And what on earth is this "eternal Sabbath" business? Isn't Sunday, the first day of the week, the Sabbath? Doesn't the fourth commandment require us to stop working and rest every seventh day?

Most Christians believe that the fourth may be the most difficult of all the commandments to understand today. Do God's ceremonial laws for the seventh day of the week still apply today? We don't set our lives by other ceremonial laws. For instance, we don't build churches by the standards God gave the Israelites for the temple. We don't buy baby lambs to sacrifice either.

What God refers to as "the Sabbath," most believers say, is a matter of the mind more than the calendar. "The eternal Sabbath" refers to a relationship we have with God, not a day of the week. When Christ answered his critics by telling them that the Sabbath was made for man, not man for the Sabbath, he was telling them to lighten up. He was telling them to remember that no matter how they interpreted Old Testament law, they should never, ever forget the real goods: The law is all about love, loving God above all and your neighbor as yourself.

So what God requires of us in the fourth commandment is not necessarily that we refrain from schoolwork or ice hockey or going to the mall on Sunday. What God requires of us is a whole lot bigger than that. God wants from us is every day of our lives, not just the seventh (or the first). God wants to build an eternal Sabbath with us, an eternal relationship of love and joy.

What is God's will in the fourth commandment? An eternal Sabbath, an every-day-of-the-week relationship of love and joy.

A 24/7 Sabbath.

Take my moments and my days, Lord, let them flow in endless praise to you—the engineer of the Sabbath. Make our Sabbaths eternal. Amen.

Deadbeat Dads

Q&A 104

What is God's will for you in the fifth commandment?

"Honor your father and your mother. . . ."
—Exodus 20:12

Just yesterday, I saw a new TV commercial, a public service announcement that didn't sell shampoo or gym shoes or some life-changing dot.com. The only visual image for a whole minute was a baby.

The voice-over laid out the pitch. I can't quote it exactly, but it went something like this. "Today this little boy's father left the family. When he did, he increased this baby's chances of never finishing high school, of having a drug problem, of living a life of crime. In fact, this baby's chances for medical problems jumped much higher just this morning, even though he has no idea his father is gone."

Then the commercial took aim at fathers. If you leave home, it said, don't neglect your children. Support your kids and encourage them, because children need your love far more than anything from Toys-R-Us.

We've seen that the first four commandments have to do with our relationship to God Almighty. Next we'll look at commandments five through ten, all of which have to do with our relationship to the folks around us. Today we start with the family in the fifth commandment. It's the foundation for the rest.

People who claim that the family is the foundation of any culture aren't wrong. After all, at the bottom of a functioning, healthy society is a functioning, healthy family. The commercial I described focuses on deadbeat dads, fathers who go their own way rather than attend to the needs of those who really need them.

The fifth commandment isn't about deadbeat dads, however. It's about healthy children, kids of all ages. The fifth commandment makes it clear that peace in the kingdom means an open, loving family, a family where children of all ages respect their parents—of all ages.

Some people believe that the family is under a greater assault today than it ever has been. I'm not one of those. I've lived through a time—the late sixties—when relationships between parents and children were, I believe, a great deal worse than they are today.

But it's clear that sin, being the scoundrel it is, seeks destruction in every which way it can; it's clear that the family is always under attack by Satan's forces. Break down the family and things go to pot. It's that simple. What Satan wants is a mess.

The commandment isn't given to deadbeat dads. It's given to children. Respect, honor, obey, submit—that's the command. To you, to me, to all of us.

It's not hard to find families in trouble, Lord. Where moms and dads are split, bring healing, peace, and trust. Where kids are at war, melt their weapons into party favors. Bring us joy in our families, Lord. Help us learn to give, not just get. Amen.

Honoring

Q&A 104

Honor, love . . . obey and submit. . . .

Children, obey your parents in the Lord, for this is right. "Honor your father and mother."

—Ephesians 6:1–2

The United States presidential election of the year 2000 will go down as one of the most bizarre in American history. For more than a month after election night, the outcome was still in doubt. Some Floridians nearly went blind trying to determine which candidate should get a vote when all they could see on a ballot was a little dent, a dimpled chad. It was nuts, really.

Eventually Vice President Al Gore lost because he lost Florida. I don't doubt for a minute that he will go to his grave believing he won that state and consequently the whole election. I'm sure he really believes that he should have been president of the United States.

But eventually, after a Supreme Court ruling, he had to concede. He had to honor the ruling of the highest court in the land, no matter what he as an individual citizen thinks.

In North America, we don't talk much about honoring others. Other cultures do it far better. Take the Japanese, for example. In many Japanese homes people keep a "god shelf," a place for religious momentoes. That corner of the house is like a shrine; often it includes a place for pictures of parents and grandparents. Righteousness, in the Japanese tradition, includes honoring one's parents.

To honor one's parents means more than simply obeying them, even though obedience is part of honor since you can't honor parents by thumbing your nose at what they say. Vice President Gore honored the rule of law by admitting—not without biting his tongue, I'm sure—that his needs weren't as important as the needs of the whole nation. He honored the American people by giving in.

Sometimes honoring father and mother means giving in, not because they're right and you're wrong but because we have much bigger obligations. The fifth commandment doesn't require us to honor our parents because it's such a sweet thing to do. It's a directive from God's Supreme Court; God says it's right. We honor God by honoring our parents, and we dishonor God by dishonoring them. That raises the stakes.

What was tough for Gore is tough for all of us. Giving up ourselves can be painful. Maybe that's why God gave us commandments.

Dear Lord, sometimes it's hard for us to obey our parents and to honor them. But we know this is what you want from us. So help us to be willing to give up something of ourselves for them—and for you, O God, who has given us so much. In Jesus' name, Amen.

Respecting Mystery

Q&A 104

Be patient with their failings. . . .

Listen to your father, who gave you life, and do not despise your mother when she is old.

—Proverbs 23:22

My father served in the South Pacific during World War II. When he was still in training, he and my mother had their first child, a daughter. Then, before he shipped out, my mom became pregnant again with a second daughter, who was born when my dad was thousands of miles away.

When the war ended and my father returned, my mother must have been absolutely thrilled to meet him at the railroad station. He'd been away for more than a year. He hadn't seen her or the daughter he knew for a long, long time. What's more, he'd never even seen this second daughter, a little girl who was already almost a year old.

Then something funny happened. My mother got a little anxious about what was going to happen when her handsome sailor got off that train. She didn't know if she should offer him the little daughter in her arms, the little daughter at her side, or herself.

The more she thought about it, the more it bugged her. Was she somehow selfish for wanting to be the first one hugged? Shouldn't she be thrilled to hand over the baby? Wouldn't she love to watch him pick their oldest off the ground and swing her in the air? Was there something wrong with her for getting all anxious about it?

I love that story. Know why? Because it shows my mom overflowing with real human feelings. When I think about her getting all nervous about who was going to be hugged first, I see her as someone just like me, a mystery of a human being.

In his book *Mere Morality*, Lewis Smedes says that honoring parents means "respecting their mystery." We like to think we know our parents inside and out, but we don't. There's lots that you and I know nothing about.

The Catechism says we need to honor our parents no matter how old we are or they are, even when they fail. Why? Because we don't know everything. We don't know the whole story, even though we think we do.

Respecting our parents means honoring their mystery, their stories, their trials, their joys—the whole pageant of their lives. When we "respect their mystery" we honor them even in their failures.

I like that. And so, I believe, does the Lord.

Thank you for our parents, Lord. Sometimes we don't understand them. Sometimes they fail. Help us always to respect them, not for what they do but for who they are. In Jesus' name, Amen.

Growing Up

Q&A 104

For through them God chooses to rule us.

When I was a child, I talked like a child, I thought like a child, I reasoned like a child. When I became a man, I put childish ways behind me.

—1 Corinthians 13:11

It may be that the best-known visual artist in the world is Vincent van Gogh, a nineteenth-century Dutch painter whose canvases pulse with vivid colors. *Starry Night,* perhaps his most famous painting, is an explosion of stars in an inky night sky. He painted it while living in an asylum for the insane.

Vincent expressed the anguish you can feel in the painting in a letter to his brother, Theo. The experiences one gains in life, said Vincent, come, sadly enough, at the expense of childhood innocence. In other words, the more you know about the world, the less pretty the whole place seems.

That's as true for us as it was for Vincent.

My daughter and her husband are youth leaders in their church now, and they enjoy the job—sometimes. "What's amazing about kids," she told us not long ago, "is how much they think they know."

That remark made her mother and me giggle, because it doesn't seem that long ago that our daughter was in high school herself—and therefore in charge of the vault of the world's store of wisdom. Now she's older. She knows more. Oddly enough, she is confident of less. The world is bigger for her now, not necessarily more evil, but a whole lot more complex.

Think of it graphically. The bigger the world appears, the smaller we seem to ourselves. A two-year-old's world ends nearly at his or her fingertips. Lose a friend when you're sixteen, and the world seems like nothing but a black hole. Van Gogh was right—the more you learn about life, the less it seems like a cartoon.

The fifth commandment wasn't shoehorned into the ten by some dad or mom who wanted respect. God Almighty put it there. If all of us, mothers and fathers, grandparents and kids, keep in mind that there's always more to learn, getting along will be a whole lot easier. The moment any of us—grandparents, fathers, mothers, or kids—think we know the whole story, there's going to be trouble.

In the fifth commandment, God directs us to do what we know is right: honor our parents, even if and when we'd rather not. It's the way to live, God says. "For through them God chooses to rule us."

I know, I know—I sound like a parent, but trust me on this. Even if you don't today, someday you'll understand.

Lord, help all of us in the family to love each other, respect each other, and honor each other. Sometimes it's easy, but other times it can be so hard. Help us to love as you loved. In Jesus' name, Amen.

No Sweat

Q&A 105

What is God's will for you in the sixth commandment?
I am not to belittle, insult, hate, or kill my neighbor. . . .

"You shall not murder."
—Exodus 20:13

Benjamin Franklin was an American patriot. He was one of the authors of the Declaration of Independence, a scientist, a journalist, and the creator of clever little sayings that have become part of the way Americans think (God helps them that help themselves; Early to bed, early to rise, makes a man healthy, wealthy, and wise). His was the quintessential rags-to-riches story. But he was also, as people used to say, "stuck on himself."

At one point, Franklin determined that if he worked hard on it, he could nearly rid himself of sin. So he wrote down a list of good things (like sincerity and cleanliness) in a little book and then set out to live by those virtues, checking them off each day to be sure he'd practiced them. He figured he could systematically make himself into a good guy.

Of course we all do that in a way. Read through the Ten Commandments sometime. Most likely you won't pause long at all on number six: You shall not murder. No sweat. Haven't killed anybody today yet, though, of course, it's still early.

There's no small print on this commandment either, nothing to squint at, just four words. Easy enough. Like I said, no sweat.

Then why on earth does the Catechism spend three questions on the sixth commandment? Three questions on four words?

Listen to Jesus' words: "But anyone who says, 'You fool!' will be in danger of the fire of hell" (Matt. 5:22). Obeying the sixth commandment isn't as easy as it sounds.

Jesus Christ came to fulfill the law, to spell out its major truth. That truth is simple: love.

If you hate other people, Christ says, you break the sixth commandment, regardless of whether or not you pull a knife from your shirt or a handgun from your secret holster.

Know someone at school you just can't stand? Ever run away the moment you see someone in the hall? Feel your nerves sharpen whenever you hear this kid talk?

The sixth commandment says, "You shall not kill," but Jesus says if you honestly can't stand some other human being, you're as guilty as sin. Demean them, put them down, treat them like dirt, and you're not as pure as you think.

That's something to sweat about.

Lord, help us to love when it's so much easier not to. Help us to accept, not reject. Help us to be there for others, even when we'd rather not. In Jesus' name, Amen.

Loving Ourselves

Q&A 105

I am not to harm or recklessly endanger myself either.

How great is the love the Father has lavished on us, that we should be called children of God!

—1 John 3:1

Once, years ago, a student came up to my desk before school and just looked at me. He didn't say a thing because he expected me to say something. I must confess I didn't know what to tell him.

His brother had committed suicide about a week before. The word was that he hung himself because he was chubby. He hung himself because he got teased about his weight, because his weight made him feel worthless, and he figured that being no kid at all was better than the being the chubby kid he was.

Suicide stuns us, leaves us speechless. What can you say about despair so deep and overwhelming that people choose death over life? To those who've never felt that much rottenness inside, suicide is simply not understandable.

But it happens. Each year in the United States, thousands of teenagers commit suicide. It's the third leading cause of death among fifteen- to twenty-four-year-olds, and the sixth leading cause for five- to fourteen-year-olds.

Why the high suicide rate among teens? One reason (of many), I think, is that teenagers get wound up about everything; they get high on winning, high on buddies, high on good times. But when those highs sink, they plunge. Self-doubt comes in spades.

It's a confusing time of life, a time when people expect you to make plans for your entire life! What are you going to major in? What kind of job do you want? What do you want to be?

What's more, teenagers today often find themselves the victims of divorces that are not their fault, though they think they are. Guilt. Anger. Depression. Deep sadness. Among some kids they're as common as a cold.

The Catechism says "you shall not murder" applies to yourself too. Killing is killing, no matter who is the victim.

But remember how Christ turned this commandment inside out? Don't kill, don't hate, he said. Love. Love even yourself, hard as that may seem when you're too chubby.

Never, ever forget this. You are loved. I am. God our Father has lavished his love on us—amazingly, impossibly—even when we don't love ourselves. Amazing grace.

Lord, right now many people are grieving because someone they love ended his or her own life. Put your arms around them. Hug those who are thinking about ending their lives, Lord. Help us all to remember that you love us. In the name of Jesus, who loved us so much he died for our sins, Amen.

Capital Punishment

Q&A 105

Prevention of murder is also why government is armed with the sword.

But if you do wrong, be afraid, for [the one in authority] does not bear the sword for nothing. He is God's servant, an agent of wrath to bring punishment on the wrongdoer.

—Romans 13:4

On the afternoon of December 1, 1988, Wanda Jean Allen and Gloria Leathers got into an argument at a local grocery store, an argument that ended when Wanda shot Gloria—ironically, outside a police station. Gloria died four days later.

Wanda Allen's lawyer had never handled a first-degree murder/death penalty case before. Furthermore, Wanda's family had no money; they were able to pay the lawyer just $800 for his work. You could argue that if Wanda had come from a big bucks family, she would have had a stronger defense. Think of O. J.

What's more, three years after the trial, that lawyer swore that he'd never known Wanda Jean Allen's IQ had once been measured at 69. Some might call her mentally retarded. "I did not search for any medical or psychological records or seek expert assistance," he said.

At twelve, Wanda Allen had been hit by a truck and knocked unconscious; at fourteen or fifteen she had been stabbed in the left temple. When, several years later, a psychologist examined Wanda, he found her mental condition made her "more chronically vulnerable than others to becoming disorganized by everyday stresses—and thus more vulnerable to a loss of control under stress."

There's no doubt that Wanda Allen murdered Gloria Leathers, although there is some question about whether or not it was done in self-defense.

Should Wanda Allen have been put to death?

Those who argue for or against the death penalty on the basis of the sixth commandment alone are blindly leaping over immense hurdles.

A painful truth we all have to learn is that some questions in life don't have simple answers. Take Wanda Jean. She had a third-rate defense. She was really not totally in charge, mentally. But she was guilty as sin.

Shortly after midnight in the first minutes of January 11, 2001, Wanda Jean Allen was injected with three chemicals that, in effect, poisoned her to death. Could you have administered those shots?

Those in authority, says Paul, have the power of the sword. But when and why to use that sword are questions of life and death that have no easy answers.

Help us always, Lord, to balance our sense of righteousness with a full measure of love. Be near to those who wait on death row. Bring them the peace that only you can give. And be with us as we try to think through some of life's toughest problems. In Jesus' name, Amen.

Community

Q&A 107

God tells us to love our neighbors as ourselves. . . .

"And the second is like it, 'Love your neighbor as yourself.'"

—Matthew 22:39

I know of a kid in Japan who just sort of blew it one night. He was coming home from something or other, and he had a pack of matches in his pocket. For reasons that no one will ever know, he just started tossing lit matches into garbage cans. Some burned. No big deal—nobody was hurt, no houses burned down, no significant property damage.

But as it turns out, the Tokyo police tracked this kid down, came to his house, and pinned him with arson.

The kid didn't fight the charge, didn't try to lie his way out of it. He threw himself at the mercy of the court. He got fined—I don't remember how much—but one part of the kid's sentence just blew me away. Get this. The judge told him that he had to go to every one of his neighbors and apologize—that's right, go up to the door, knock, tell whoever came to the door that he was the criminal, then say he was sorry.

Maybe things like that happen in North America, but there's something very Japanese about what that judge required, because in Japan community is a really, really big deal. North Americans love to do their own thing; the Japanese do the community thing.

Just a tiny fraction of Japan is Christian, but it seems to me that the ethic out of which the judge was working in the case of the flaming garbage cans comes directly out of the Catechism's explanation of the sixth commandment. After all, loving our neighbors as ourselves means looking out for their interests, respecting them.

Most of us, even residents of small towns, don't really know our neighbors all that well, even though we live right beside them. But then, "neighbors" aren't only the people who live beside us. What's important, what's commanded, is that we care for our neighbors, all of them, that we love them as much as we do ourselves.

We all need community, need friends, need people to be there for us, just as surely as we need to be there for them. The commandment "You shall not murder," like the others to come, helps us create loving, nurturing communities.

How do we live? By love. The answer is that simple, but—as you already know—living by love isn't half as easy as it sounds.

Make us channels of your peace, Lord. Equip us to bring love where there isn't any, beginning with those who are closest—family and friends. Fill us with your love so it overflows on all those around us. In the name of him who loved us, Amen.

Adultery

Q&A 108

What is God's will for us in the seventh commandment?

"You shall not commit adultery."

—Exodus 20:14

Twenty-five years ago, a very good friend of mine left his wife for another woman. We were teachers at the same school; so was his new flame.

My wife and I knew his wife, but not well; we knew him much better. One night she came to visit us because she knew we were his friends; she came, crying, to ask what she could do to save their marriage. That was one of the saddest nights of my life, I think, because I was afraid to tell her the truth: There wasn't a thing she could do.

Thom (not his real name) and I had talked about the whole affair. "You know, Jim," he said once, "you've got no idea how wonderful it feels to get up in the morning, look in the closet, pick out clothes, and just know she's going to be looking at you. That's so great."

The *she* in that sentence wasn't his wife. It was his lover. His marriage, as the Righteous Brothers used to croon, had lost "that lovin' feeling." He'd found that with another woman.

Thom felt alive with the other woman. He felt like he was something, as if he really mattered. He could make someone else's day shine. That's how important he felt—with this other woman.

How can something that feels so good be so bad?

In the Protestant tradition, marriage isn't a sacrament as it is in the Roman Catholic tradition. But that doesn't mean marriage isn't important. God brought Adam and Eve together because he knew Adam wasn't complete, wasn't whole. There are tons of happy single people in the world, but a man and a woman together make some kind of circle, a line with no beginning and no end.

Marriages require commitment, even solemn vows. Most Christian couples marry in church before God and God's people, and when they do they pledge their faithfulness.

Thom's marriage broke up because he wanted that lovin' feeling more than he wanted to live by his commitment to his wife. Thom's marriage broke up because he wanted to *get* more than he wanted to *give,* because of his selfishness. That's the core of all sin.

You know, what Thom felt is understandable; it makes perfect human sense.

But it was wrong. That's what the commandment says.

Don't forget it.

Love is the word that we are supposed to live by. We know that. So teach us how to love selflessly, not selfishly. Teach us how to give, how to grow, how to nurture. Teach us to be more like you. Amen.

Commitment

Q&A 108

Married or single, live decent and chaste lives.

Husbands ought to love their wives as their own bodies.

—Ephesians 5:28

Every morning Werner Lode gets up at 4 A.M., not to go to work but to live. Werner is eighty-eight years old, and he lives in a small Iowa town named Sheldon. I read his story in a local newspaper.

Werner gets up at four because he's got things to do. He gets dressed, then heads downstairs and gets breakfast ready, along with his wife's insulin. His wife, Allie, needs it—she's a diabetic. In fact, Allie has other physical problems. Ten years ago she suffered a stroke while in the hospital for dizzy spells. That stroke left the entire left side of her body paralyzed. An eighty-year-old body requires more attention than a sixteen-year-old body, but an eighty-year-old body half paralyzed needs more attention than you can imagine.

Now you know why Werner Lode gets up at four. He's got lots to do.

His wife's plumbing system doesn't work the way it once did, so he's got plastic bags to empty and reaffix. He's got to help Allie into the wheelchair the two of them use to get her around the house. He's got to get her to the bathroom so she can get herself cleaned up.

It's probably not even 5:30 yet, but Werner's day—and Allie's—has only begun. Allie requires all-day care, of course, but the two of them prefer that Werner, not other people, does the work. "Allie didn't appreciate all those strange people working on her," Werner told the writer of the newspaper story. "She'd rather have me. She can kick me if I do something wrong . . . but not with her left leg."

There is nothing wrong with nursing homes or in-home nursing, but this couple of lovers prefers their care home-grown. "I've lost about forty pounds since I've been taking care of Allie," Werner says, "but I'm not going to put her in a nursing home as long as I can still help her. It's a good place, but not like home."

If I were Chairman of the World, I'd have every sixteen-year-old meet Werner and Allie Lode, because if you turned the seventh commandment inside out, it would read something like this: "You shall commit to the one you love."

God Almighty forbids adultery in the seventh commandment because God wants for all of us what Werner and Allie give each other: deep and loving commitment.

Lord, deepen our relationships, make our commitments strong and lasting. Thank you for people like Werner and Allie. Thank you for teaching us how to love. Throughout our lives make us better at it. In your Son's name, Amen.

Unfaithful

Q&A 109

Does God in this commandment, forbid only such scandalous sins as adultery?

Do not forsake your friend. . . .
—Proverbs 27:10

Kevin has been going with Laney for almost a year now. The other kids think of them as an old married couple—I mean, they've been a thing forever almost. Nobody ever gives either of them a second look; they're locked up, if you know what I mean.

Kevin's a star. He's the point guard on the basketball team, and since his sophomore year he's been getting calls from college coaches. He's quick, drives the lane as if no one else were there, and then kicks the ball out for his teammates' three-pointers. Of course, he hits his own, too—lots of them. Most games, he's a double-double—18 points, maybe, and 10 assists. He's good because he's got talent, but mostly because he's dedicated.

No one knows that more than Laney. From October through March she plays second fiddle to a round ball, and she knows it. All Kevin thinks about is practice and games—full court presses and a triangle offense.

That's why she was upset yesterday. Cedarville had two ball games last weekend, both of them important, both of them close. He was too tired to go out, he said. So for the most part she sat home. Tuesday was her birthday. He got her a box of chocolates, but what bugged her, what really blew her away, was the fact that he'd left the price tag on.

Big deal, you say. But that stupid price tag broke her heart—not because it was somehow dumb for him to leave it on, but because she knew in her heart that he'd picked it up on the way over to her house that night, just last-minute, you know? She knew because she knew him; she knew he wasn't thinking about her. He was thinking about basketball.

In the seventh commandment, God forbids adultery—the act—very clearly. Sometimes people use another word for adultery—*unfaithfulness.* And the sad fact of the matter is that married people, and people in committed relationships, can be unfaithful in more ways than one.

Marriages die for a ton of reasons. Sometimes it's adultery. But sometimes not. Sometimes people just aren't *faithful.* Sometimes all their passion goes into something—not just someone—else.

Maybe you're in a committed relationship right now, maybe not. If you are, remember not to forsake your friend (Proverbs 27:10). Remember that there's more than one way to be unfaithful.

Lord, in all ways keep us faithful in our relationships. When we've made commitments, help us keep them by making them stronger. Keep us faithful to you too. In Jesus' name, Amen.

Unchastity

Q&A 109

[God] forbids everything which incites unchastity, whether it be actions, looks, talk, thought, or desires.

"Anyone who looks at a woman lustfully has already committed adultery with her in his heart."

—Matthew 5:28

In the long line of American presidents, Jimmy Carter holds a unique place. His presidency was forever darkened by his inability to free several dozen Americans held hostage by Islamic fundamentalists and used as propaganda. While no one would deny that the small-town Georgia peanut farmer was a wonderful man, his fellow citizens voted him out of office after only four years.

But one of the most memorable stories of the Jimmy Carter presidency occurred before he was elected. *Playboy* magazine did an interview with him, and the interviewer asked if he'd ever committed adultery.

He admitted that he'd sinned. Even though he'd never committed adultery—that is, slept with a woman other than his wife—he told that reporter he'd certainly felt lust in his heart. In every possible way, that answer was the truth: he'd felt lust, and lust, even without acting on it, is sin.

Lust is sin? Yes, according to Jesus. "Anyone who looks at a woman lustfully has already committed adultery with her in his heart" (Matt. 5:28).

Most of America thought that Carter's answer was a scream.

I wouldn't be surprised if this book is being read by murderers; I've received letters from prisoners who've read some of my books. But the vast majority of those who are reading these words right now have never killed another human being. On the other hand, just about everyone I know—including me—has treated someone, sometime, very badly.

If we understand the commandments, there are no fewer adulterers in North America than there are killers. There are millions. Unless you're far more pure than most human beings, you and I are among them. That's what Jimmy Carter understood.

In the broadest sense, adultery, like hate, occurs whenever we want *our* way above all, when all we care about is loving ourselves. That's what Jesus said, and that's what Jimmy Carter believed.

If we define "religion" as something to which we are deeply devoted, then sex has become a religion in North America. Just watch TV. America laughed at Jimmy Carter because too many American people wouldn't buy his silly, archaic definitions.

Too bad. Jimmy Carter drew his definitions from the Lord God Almighty.

Create in me a clean heart, Lord. Keep your people chaste. Keep us faithful. Wash us, and we will be whiter than snow. Amen.

Trying to Manage Things

Q&A 109

God . . . forbids everything which incites unchastity. . . .

But the fruit of the Spirit is . . . self-control.
—Galatians 5:22–23

Kim Barnes grew up in a very religious home. Her parents were loving but immensely strict—she couldn't wear slacks to school, for instance, and her skirts had to be far below her knee. In the memoir of her childhood, *In the Wilderness,* she remembers a high school boyfriend, a member of her church, someone of whom her parents approved.

But this kid was insanely jealous. If she would as much as talk to another guy, he'd scream at her. Scream, as in shout hard in her face. The way she describes him, you'd really like to punch him out. Guess what? They broke up.

Now how do you figure that? He's a professing Christian, someone who wants to be good. He comes from a strict Christian home, reads his Bible, prays a lot, sings hymns, speaks in tongues—but he blows up like a cherry bomb at his girlfriend?

I'm no psychiatrist, but I've got a theory. The poor guy sat on every last shred of his human sexuality. He was so convinced that making out was sin that he pushed and shoved every bit into a flimsy container in the back of his mind that eventually just exploded. He lost it. His denial got so momentous it blew up.

There are probably other reasons why this guy's behavior seems so strange. But being brought up in quite a strict Christian home myself, I sometimes think the adjustment some kids go through can be more than a little difficult. I mean, Christian kids are told, "No, no, no, no," for all of their years until, suddenly, a few hours after one huge white ceremony, everything is "Yes, yes, yes, yes." Some people's switches just don't work that easily.

How to live with what you feel is especially difficult in a culture in which most movies require a sex scene, in which humor isn't funny unless it jiggles a body part. Our culture teems with sex—and yet it's off-limits. Stuff floats up into your consciousness, stuff you didn't ask to appear, but when it does, it's there in neon vivid enough to put Vegas to shame.

The seventh commandment, the Catechism says, "forbids everything which incites unchastity"—unfaithfulness, behavior unbecoming of believers. But sex in the right way, at the right time, isn't unhealthy or unbecoming. No way. Trust me on that.

May God grant all of us the strength to manage, kids and parents alike.

Lord Jesus, we want to be good and faithful, clean and chaste. Help us manage our joys, our fears, our ambitions, our sexuality. Give us the ability to enjoy everything you've given to us, to see it all as your gift. Forgive us when we fail—which we do, all too often. Thank you for your unceasing love. Amen.

A Little Number Crunching

Q&A 110

What does God forbid in the eighth commandment?

"You shall not steal."
—Exodus 20:15

Just for kicks, let's do a little number crunching. According to the United States Bureau of Justice Statistics, in 1990, 3,500,600 violent crimes were committed in the U.S. (including rape, robbery, aggravated assault, and homicide). That year, almost 2,000,000 of those crimes were reported to the police by the victims, and better than 1,500,000 were recorded by the police. That year, 722,400 arrests were made on those crimes. Seems like a ton of criminals got away.

Anyway, in 1999, the total number of violent crimes had fallen by almost one million to 2,530,000, close to a 28 percent drop. The number of crimes reported to police by victims fell to just over 1,400,000, while those crimes recorded by police fell to 1,130,700. In 1999, 636,000 arrests were made.

By my math, crime dropped as drastically as police work improved. On the basis of these statistics, life in the United States is getting better, or at least less violent. When people say society is falling apart and use violent crime to back up the argument, tell them that the numbers just don't crunch that way.

Today there's less robbery than there was a decade ago. Maybe people are starting to live by the "Ten Words."

I doubt that, I really do.

But—for whatever reason—it does seem that today fewer people need to sweat the eighth commandment; after all, fewer people steal.

By now you know where I'm going. Just as in each of the commandments we've looked at so far, there's more to "You shall not steal" than meets the eye. Not killing, remember, also means not hating; not committing adultery also means sticking with commitments.

"You shall not steal" doesn't only mean you shall not hold up some scared-to-death clerk at gunpoint at your local 7–11. The eighth commandment outlines how we are to live with . . . well, stuff. Things. Goods. In the eighth commandment God tells us how to live with things.

Ever been in a shopping mall three days before Christmas? Then you know that *things* are a really big deal in our society, a really, really big deal.

If you want to be happy in the land the Lord your God gives you, you better figure out what to love and what not to. Listen to the Lord.

Sometimes we'd rather not think that what we own—the stuff in our bedrooms, in our dreams—is really part of your rule in our lives, Lord. Be master of our lives, Lord. Help us not to be mastered by the stuff around us. Amen.

Loving Things

Q&A 110

In addition, [God] forbids all greed and pointless squandering of his gifts.

Then [Jesus] said to them, "Watch out! Be on your guard against all kinds of greed; a man's life does not consist in the abundance of his possessions."

—Luke 12:15

My father was always deeply opposed to gambling because he was sure that God Almighty was against it in every one of its forms.

In the village where I grew up, the Fourth of July was the biggest day of the year. The town park would fill up with people and the local American Legion would put up all kinds of tents with silly little games. Kids would put down quarters to try to pop three balloons with three darts. Get 'em all and win a teddy bear for your sweetie.

In addition, the Legion held a raffle. Buy a ticket and get a chance to win a snowmobile or a weekend at a resort in Lake Geneva.

My father hated that raffle. But once, his own brother—my uncle—won one of the big prizes. I remember hearing my uncle's name read off and feeling sorry for my dad because I knew how strongly he felt about gambling.

Today, the gambling casinos have grown like a fungus all over North America. The Legion raffle is child's play. I'm sure my father probably gets weary just thinking about all the gambling that goes on all over.

I don't gamble. I don't say that because I want you to know how righteous I am. I don't gamble, in part, because I remember how important *not* gambling was to my father. And, gambling is stupid.

I married the daughter of a farmer who is as opposed to gambling—the kind my father hated—as my father is. But he taught me a tough lesson.

In Iowa, farmers gamble for a living. They harvest soybeans, store them in an elevator, then wait for the price to rise. If it does and they sell, it's a gamble because the price could go higher. In a sense, farming requires playing the markets, which isn't much different from playing the slots.

"You shall not steal," as we've said, means more than not living by highway robbery. It means being responsible with what you own. My father would say—and so do I—it means staying away from gambling.

But what about a farmer who really has to gamble? "You shall not steal," turned inside out, means be responsible about things: your soybeans, your pocket change, your bank card. The real bottom line here isn't that tough, even if some of the specifics bring headaches.

As Andrew Kuyvenhoven says in *Comfort and Joy,* being faithful means *using* things and *loving* people—not *loving* things and *using* people.

Forgive us, Lord, when we love things and use people. Teach us to be responsible not only with each other but with all the good stuff that you give us. In Jesus' name, Amen.

The Love of Money

Q&A 110

In God's sight theft also includes cheating and swindling our neighbor by schemes made to appear legitimate. . . .

For the love of money is a root of all kinds of evil.

—1 Timothy 6:10

In the movie *Traffic*, Catherine Zeta-Jones plays Helena Ayala, the high-society wife of a handsome young entrepreneur with extensive holdings in several businesses. As the movie begins, she is happily munching on San Diego's most exclusive tea and crumpets while her darling son is taking golf lessons at some posh country club. She's not only take-your-breath-away beautiful, she's also take-your-breath-away rich.

Unfortunately, her husband, handsome and rich as he is, is a drug lord who never told his wife how he made his money. He'd told her about his several businesses, but when Mr. Ayala is hauled off to jail, she discovers that those businesses existed mainly to launder drug money.

Suddenly she's in big trouble. Her husband's creditors want their money, so they threaten her little boy's life. As a result, Mrs. Ayala begins to understand that in addition to being a high-society beauty and doting mother, she also has to protect her own and her son's interests. With a little help from her jail-bound husband, she discovers an insurance policy of sorts and starts a whole new life.

No, she doesn't become a schoolteacher or a nurse. She doesn't work in family counseling or detox centers. She becomes—guess what?—a drug lord.

Helena Ayala is a loving mother, and she's about to have another baby, but her horrible fall into drug trafficking is so believable because we know that she'll never be able to give up her easy life. The only way she can hold on to the mansion is to make big bucks like her husband. So that's what she does.

Helena Ayala's story is less about drugs than it is about the eighth commandment. The pregnant mom becomes a drug lord because she loves stuff more than people. She loves money, and the Bible says the love of money is the root of all kinds of evil.

"You shall not steal" means more than not picking a cheap watch off some guy walking down the street. Helena Ayala really doesn't need her San Diego mansion to raise her kids, but the mansion is more important to her than her little boy—or the baby that's coming—or the babies of the people down the street.

Helena Ayala is willing to hurt others to hold on to the posh parties on her palace porch. That's what's really sad.

Lord, all of us like the things we have that make us comfortable and allow us to look good. But don't let us forget that life isn't about toys—it's about you and the world you loved so much that you gave your only begotten Son. Amen.

Even in Our Families

Q&A 110

He forbids all greed. . . .

If we claim to be without sin, we deceive ourselves and the truth is not in us.

—1 John 1:8

The novel *A Thousand Acres* won lots and lots of literary prizes several years ago. It was even made into a movie. The author, Jane Smiley, lived in Iowa when she wrote the novel, and it shows because that story is all about Iowa farming and farm families.

Interestingly enough, Jane Smiley decided to borrow a story that had already existed for hundreds of years—Shakespeare's *King Lear,* a story about a king who divided up his kingdom into three parts for his three daughters. We don't have any kings in Iowa, so Smiley's take on the story features a successful farmer named Larry Cook who farms a thousand acres, which is not a pittance in rural Iowa.

But she kept the story line. Larry Cook decides, for odd reasons, to split up his farm three ways so that each of his daughters gets a parcel. Not smart. By the end of the novel, the family has lost the entire spread. Why? That's the guts of the novel.

Anyway, when *A Thousand Acres* was really hot stuff, the local library asked me to lead a discussion group.

The crowd was small, maybe seven or eight women, all of them farm folks (I'm not), all of them mothers. When we talked about the novel, I told them I figured that when a farmer and his wife retire in our area (where presumably people are Christians), dividing up the farm wouldn't be the home-wrecker it is in *A Thousand Acres.*

Those women looked at each other, their faces drawn like prunes. Then they looked at me strangely.

"Why are you looking at me like that?" I asked.

"Because it happens all the time, even in the best of families," one of them said, and the others nodded.

Don't be deceived by the simplicity of the Ten Commandments. "You shall not steal" sounds like a no-brainer, but life itself—even farm life among good Christian people—can overflow with greed, the love of *stuff.* Stealing isn't just grabbing a CD from a Wal-Mart. We steal because we love stuff—just got to have it.

"If we claim to be without sin," the apostle John says, "we deceive ourselves and the truth is not in us."

It's that simple.

Seeing things go wrong is always easy when we're looking at other people, Lord. Sometimes we can be blind to our own problems, our own sin. Thank you for reminding us—for commanding us—how to live. Give us your grace to help us live totally for you. In Christ's name, Amen.

Raisin Bread

Q&A 111

I do whatever I can for my neighbor's good. . . .

The Lord Jesus himself said, "It is more blessed to give than to receive."

—Acts 20:35

This morning for breakfast I had three pieces of raisin bread. That may sound like a lot but it wasn't, really. This loaf of bread, you see, is only about as round as a tube of sausage. Then again, this raisin bread isn't exactly the breakfast of champion dieters either. It's hardly light and fluffy, full as it is of raisins and nuts and sugar and a special prime ingredient I think is almost sublime—almond paste.

Now I honestly don't believe that the woman who baked it knows I'd die for almond paste. I think all she had in mind was that the bread would be a treat at our house. It was a surprise gift, a Christmas present. She and her family walked up to our door on Christmas Eve and gave it to me, all nicely wrapped.

Several months ago I visited her writing class because that class had just read a book I'd written. She wanted me to discuss the book with them. She thought it would be a good idea for students to get a peek at what happens behind the scenes when a writer writes a book.

So I went, and we had a good time. She thanked me a ton afterwards.

But then, months later, on Christmas Eve, she brought the raisin bread. It's wonderful. We froze it immediately because we had a Fort Knox of sweets around already that night, and I didn't thaw it out until this morning. That's when I had my first piece. Incredibly good.

I bring all of this up (oops! bad way of saying it) because I think that Christmas present of raisin bread typifies what "You shall not steal" really says when we turn the words inside out, as the Catechism does. "You shall not steal" means raisin bread. It means that I do whatever I can for my neighbor's good.

Now some people might try to build a case against raisin bread. If you know me, you know I don't need any more calories. But what's a holiday if you can't be joyful, right? I don't care if this stuff isn't lean cuisine. I love it.

A sweet loaf of bread, unexpected, on Christmas Eve—that's the real goods. Thinking of other people—that's the gospel truth.

I love raisin bread, and I adore almond paste, but this bread—this particular bread—tastes far better than the best; it was a gift from someone's heart.

Lord, thank you for blessing us with people who teach us the sheer joy of giving. Through all of our lives, help us to give, not take. And thank you for raisin bread. Amen.

False Witness

Q&A 112

What is God's will for you in the ninth commandment? That I never give false testimony against anyone. . . .

"You shall not give false testimony against your neighbor."

—Exodus 20:16

Murder? Nothing worse. Adultery? Awful stuff, breaks up families. Stealing? Totally stupid and wrong. Giving false witness? Sure, it's important, but is lying about people in the same league with the other big sins? Maybe there were lots of lawsuits in ancient Israel. Is giving false witness really that big of a deal?

"You know Miranda—she sits next to me in history. She's pregnant."

"No kidding!"

"It's what I heard. Mason told me. He doesn't usually make things up. He said he heard it from Paul—you know, Reggie's buddy." Pause. "Reggie's the father."

"No!"

"No lie. That's what I heard."

Miranda isn't pregnant. Reggie and Miranda don't even do what's got to be done for Miranda to get pregnant.

But the damage has been done. People think Miranda is going to have a baby, and they look at her differently. Some kids don't even talk to her—they don't know what to say. After all, if she's pregnant, it's got to be this really big deal.

Kids go home. Some of them mention to their parents the news on the street. If the parents know Reggie and Miranda—and their parents—there's even more trouble. After all, what do they say when they see her parents getting groceries? "Hey, tough news about your daughter"? How do you talk to people who are going through huge problems?

The rumor grew like some noxious weed, but nobody knows who planted it. What's more, some kids hinted that maybe there was an abortion.

"You're kidding!"

"No, that's what people said."

Giving false testimony kills something, even if it doesn't kill someone. The tongue, says James, is a fire (3:6). People get burned. Some kids will never look at Reggie and Miranda in quite the same way, even though there's no baby. What's more, Reggie and Miranda won't look at some friends the same way either.

Something dies—something important—when we give false witness. Character dies. Something else dies too: truth. That's why the ninth commandment is a big deal.

Lord, guard our tongues, lock our lips, keep our hearts pure. Help us to know the difference between concern and gossip. Help us know when to speak and when to remain silent. Build in us a deep regard for the truth. Keep us from sin. In Christ's name, Amen.

Reasons to Lie?

Q&A 112

God's will is that I never give false testimony against anyone. . . .

A truthful witness gives honest testimony, but a false witness tells lies.

—Proverbs 12:17

There were, of course, perfectly good reasons to lie. Jennifer had been a friend, maybe not the best of friends, but they'd had mutual friends. Had Julianne ratted, their friendship would have died.

And then there was Jennifer's future. If she'd have gotten kicked off the team, she might have lost her scholarship—and then who knows, maybe she wouldn't be able to go to college next year. And if that happens, what's ahead?

On top of that, there was a domino effect. The coach had only found out about Jennifer's being at the party—not Sarah or Josh or Sandy or Abby or any of the others. Jennifer's being there got around because she'd had too much to drink. That was the deal.

Besides, Jennifer's parents already knew. When she got home that night, she kicked in a window, trying to get into her bedroom without being heard. Her parents knew, and they didn't tell.

And if Julianne told, nobody would like her, right? I mean, turn yourself into the only rat in the pack sometime and see how many parties you get asked to. Lying meant nobody got kicked off the team and everything stayed cool.

Shoot, most kids thought lying was the right thing to do.

Even coach didn't want to know. When he sat there behind his desk, he had his hand up in front of his mouth as if he didn't want to say what he had to say. Think about it: Jennifer's worth eighteen points a game and maybe a dozen rebounds. Poof! There goes the season.

Besides, if Julianne ratted, the whole school would think she was in a snit because she didn't make the team.

All the way around, lying was the best policy, right?

If we turn the ninth commandment inside out, what turns up is a dedication to something called *truth*. Not lying means telling the truth. The ninth commandment—like commandments six, seven, and eight—looks like a piece of cake until you realize God Almighty wants the truth from us.

Was Julianne right in lying about Jennifer's being at this party? She saved her own hide, Jennifer's hide, the team's hide, the coach's hide, and even Jennifer's parents' hides. That's a ton of hides.

Telling the truth—like really loving others—is no snap. Believe me.

No, believe God Almighty.

Lord, help us to be people of the truth. Help us not to lie, not to spin the truth our way. Make our words really matter. In Jesus' name, Amen.

The Cynic

Q&A 112

I should love the truth, speak it candidly, and openly acknowledge it.

Love does not delight in evil but rejoices with the truth.

—1 Corinthians 13:6

I'm still smarting because I got chewed out yesterday. At lunch, my wife hammered me because I was being cynical about committees.

In my mind, on a scale from one to ten, committees come in at minus eight. They can be the most useless machines in the world because they have so many moving parts, any of which can be defective. Governing by committee means getting everybody's assent. For instance, where should we put the new Xerox machine? That can be tough, especially when the members all have to be heard, as they usually do.

I know someone who creates beautiful stained-glass windows, most of which end up in casinos or churches. He says he'd much rather work with casinos than churches because casinos don't form committees. When he works with churches, the whole project has to be supervised by eleventy-seven people.

Eleventy-seven. You can see why my wife chewed me out. I get cynical.

Cynicism happens when people like me—people who can, on occasion, be cynical—turn being cynical into a way of life. Add the *ism*, you see, and we make it into a 24/7 behavior. My wife wasn't disagreeing with me about committees; she just wanted me to admit that some jobs have to be done that way. Committees may be a necessary evil, but they're necessary.

Those who suffer from terminal cynicism can't really see the good in anything. When they see a silver lining, they immediately point out the black cloud. Cynics, and I can be one of them, are constantly turning good things over to try to find something rotten underneath, as if life were some ancient picnic table.

My wife told the truth yesterday at lunch. She told me I shouldn't be so negative. She wasn't bearing false witness; she didn't let me get away with my cynicism. My wife was living by the ninth commandment. She was telling the truth.

I wasn't. When I allow my cynical character to take over, when I stop believing in anything but my own vision of truth, I'm in trouble. It's a kind of pride, really, thinking that way. When I'm most cynical, it's difficult for me to love the truth, speak it candidly, and openly acknowledge it, as the Catechism says. In fact, it's not hard for me to take the ninth commandment and break it, as if it were something rotten.

I'm still smarting from my wife's scolding, but sometimes learning hurts a little. Know what I mean?

Protect us from ourselves, Lord. Create in us the desire to love the truth, to speak it candidly, and to openly acknowledge it. Keep us from the shadiness of cynicism. Help us never to lose the ability to love. In Jesus' name, Amen.

Strictly Speaking

Q&A 113

What is God's will for you in the tenth commandment?

"You shall not covet your neighbor's house . . . your neighbor's wife, or his manservant or maidservant, his ox or donkey, or anything that belongs to your neighbor."

—Exodus 20:17

We've arrived at the last of the Ten Commandments. Time to look back a bit.

The first five are about what we think about God, and how we act toward God. They're the foundation for everything else. Build your house on sand, and with a good rain it may end up slip-sliding down the block. The last five are about other human beings, starting with mom and dad, grandpa and grandma.

We've been turning these commandments inside out, trying to stress, as Christ did, that there's more here than meets the eye. But just for a minute, let's take them at face value, word for word.

There's murder—that means that somewhere there's a corpse, right? Break the most specific reading of the commandment, and somewhere there's a dead body. There's evidence. Are you with me so far?

Good. Adultery is also a public sin. There's no dead body, but there's another person involved. Strictly speaking, you can't violate this commandment alone. It takes two to tango.

Stealing also means goods, even if it's only paper. Not long ago in Iowa an ex-Quaker preacher just up and left with the holdings of his real estate company. He bought a yacht and got caught. Stealing is a public thing too, when you get caught.

Someone who tells lies about others needs others. I don't break the commandment by telling a lie about my wife to myself; it's got to be told to someone else. Strictly speaking, "bearing false witness" is a public sin.

Commandments six, seven, eight, nine—all of them require other people.

Not ten. Now we're in a new ball game.

You shall not covet, the commandment says in Exodus 20, and then goes on to list some "stuff" people in Bible times generally wished were in their own corrals. Say you wish you were Gwyneth Paltrow. You covet what she has—that's the extent of your sin.

There's no victim here, no public sin. The tenth commandment is a stealth bomber. Nobody sees it. Breaking it happens only between our ears and in the middle of our chests.

Really, the tenth commandment may be the most difficult, strictly speaking, because it is between only you and God.

But God knows. Count on it.

Father in heaven, keep us from believing that somehow we'd be better if we had this, that, or the other thing. We know that our joy is in you. In Jesus' name, Amen.

Desire

Q&A 113

That not even the slightest thought or desire contrary to any of God's commandments should ever arise in my heart. Rather . . . I should always hate sin and take pleasure in whatever is right.

Whatever is true, whatever is noble, whatever is right, whatever is pure . . . think about such things.

—Philippians 4:8

You want to see lust, go to a strip club.

Whoa! I don't mean that literally. Actually, all you have to do is turn on TV, where sex is used all the time for just about everything. When producers and advertisers undress a woman on screen, most red-blooded men can't turn away. That's the point.

See, a woman takes her clothes off and the forty-three men in the place (I know, I know—there are similar joints for women) become sexual robots. Their brains turn to mush; in fact, their heads could just as well flop from their shoulders and their tongues from their faces.

Get this—there is zero relationship between themselves and the woman. I mean, nothing. If they know her name, it's only an alias. They don't have a clue about whether she's a mom or somebody's girlfriend, whether she goes to school or has a day job. Furthermore, they don't give a hoot. Nobody asks. When a nearly naked woman parades in front of men, they aren't thinking about which word processing program she prefers.

Lust can't reason. It can't think, it can't moralize, but mostly it can't empathize—it can't put itself into another person's situation. It wants, it craves only what will satisfy itself. It has no problem imagining things; in fact, all it can do is imagine. Lust refuses to consider what's real.

Coveting really is a kind of strip club, except without the drinks and low lights. Coveting really means lusting, wanting something, tons of things, with the kind of reckless abandon you see on the faces of men in gentlemen's clubs.

Maybe you've heard this story. A woman in Texas had a girl murdered so that her own daughter could make the cheerleading squad. There goes the sixth commandment too, of course. But even if she hadn't actually killed someone, this woman was as guilty of coveting as the panting men in a strip club.

Oh, you say, but she wanted what was best for her daughter!

No way. She wanted her daughter to be a cheerleader for her own reasons. We covet when we lust. We lust when all we want to satisfy is ourselves. The truth is just this simple: Love is all about giving; lust is all about getting.

Taking pleasure in what is right—that's what's really inside the tenth commandment.

For that, Jesus Christ has to turn *us* inside out.

Come into my heart, Lord Jesus. Come in today; come in to stay. Come into my heart, Lord Jesus. Amen.

Media, Marketing, and Coveting

Q&A 113

What is God's will for you in the tenth commandment?

Be content with what you have, because God has said, "Never will I leave you, never will I forsake you."

—Hebrews 13:5

People think the Great Plains, where I live, are flat, but they aren't. Actually, we've got rolling hills—lots of them, enough so that the quiet quilt of land undulates like the sea. In fact, the first white folks here thought of the prairies as an ocean of grass.

When they came, there were no trees. The highest point on the landscape, almost inevitably, became their churches. Seen from a distance, a tall church in the middle of a huddle of buildings would have looked as if the entire town were pointing to God. I like that.

Then along came business. Soon enough, the tallest buildings weren't churches but grain silos, big and usually white. They towered over the churches. In a way, you might say that what the people aimed at, or so it looked, was storing up grain. Business may have become the strongest institution of society.

Today, however, the highest features on the horizon are communication towers. It's as if business isn't the heart of things anymore; media is.

It's fair to say—and I'm not alone in this—that today the most powerful institution is the media: TV, film, radio, and everything connected to the electronic revolution. And media exists, primarily, to make money.

Quick now—back to the tenth commandment. It tells us not to covet. But few in North America can easily pull away from the desire at the very heart of advertising. What every marketing genius covets is your covetousness; they want you to believe you've got to have what they're selling to feel like you're really living.

Marketing isn't evil, but we all need to remember that obeying the tenth commandment is likely made more difficult by those huge towers; by our love for media; by the sheer, incredible power of a system called capitalism.

Did those first settlers covet when they didn't have a TV? Of course. But in the world we live in today, coveting has become the way we live.

That means living by the tenth commandment is a tough, tough thing.

But then, that's what we've said about every other commandment too.

Thank goodness, there's a Savior.

Lord, keep us from thinking that sin only means doing bad things like stealing or killing. We confess that we also sin in ways that don't leave black eyes or empty shelves. Help us to withstand the lure of the advertising that comes into our homes every hour of the day. Make us content with what you have given us. Amen.

The GQ Christian (and Spouse)

Q&A 114

In this life even the holiest have only a small beginning of this obedience.

There is not a righteous man on earth who does what is right and never sins.

—Ecclesiastes 7:20

Barrett—let's give him a name with a little class. Everything he wears is from the Gap—or maybe Abercrombie and Fitch. Of course, Barrett would look good in sackcloth and ashes.

The thing is, Barrett, with his near-perfect beauty, is a Christian—a color-coordinated WWJD bracelet, a record of service projects as long as your arm. Every other Sunday he picks up adults who are mentally challenged and takes them to church (which they love, and so does he).

He drives a black SUV, expensive, a Lincoln, I think. And he's got dough that won't quit because he knows computers inside out and works for a company that rewards his knowledge big-time.

Why isn't he married? He is. (Remember, I'm making this up.) Wife's name is Josie, and she's in computers too. They're DINKs (double income, no kids), but they're starting to think seriously about a little Barrett or Josie.

Barrett and Josie visit Jesus, and when they do, they ask a peculiar question: "What must we do to live with you eternally?"

"Obey the commandments," Jesus says, smiling.

"Whew," Barrett says, and he wipes the back of his hand against his forehead.

"One thing more," Jesus says. "That SUV, those clothes, the big house, the boat, the good jobs? They've all got to go." He looks at Barrett's forehead. "And the Rogaine, too—everything. Give away everything you own."

At this, their faces fall.

Barrett and Josie get in the SUV and drive home. They don't talk for the next half hour.

You know this one, right? The point of the story is *not* that every last one of us have to do everything right. The point of the story isn't about being perfect.

It's the opposite. The point is that we *can't* do it all right.

Nobody does the commandments perfectly. In this life even the holiest have only begun real obedience. Nobody behaves their way into God's love. Christ bought all our tickets. He paid our way with nothing less than his blood.

There are things even Barrett and Josie can't do—big things.

They've already been done. Praise the Lord.

It hurts, Lord, to know that even our best deeds don't earn us a thing. We'd rather earn our own way. But that's not the way it works, Lord. Thank you for giving us your love even though we don't keep the commandments you've given us. Thank you for grace. Amen.

198

Billy Graham

Q&A 114

They do begin to live according to all, not only some, of God's commandments.

Not that I have already . . . been made perfect, but I press on to take hold of that for which Christ Jesus took hold of me.

—Philippians 3:12

Billy Graham is perhaps the most respected Christian in the world today. But he's an old man now. One of these days he'll have gone to the other side of time, where he'll probably be less prominent but even more happy. If some of the most persistent visions of heaven are right, he'll be singing in the kind of mass choir he's had at hundreds of revivals all around the world.

Billy Graham is respected because of his crusades to millions around the world. But that's not all. He is respected because he has been faithful to what he preached. Billy Graham lives what he believes.

Yet even Billy Graham can't obey all the commandments all of the time. He'd be the first to admit that himself. Not even the best of us are perfect.

That doesn't mean we can't be faithful or good. It doesn't mean we can't do right. All kinds of people around the world, not just Christians, respect Billy Graham because he practices what he preaches, because he lives by the Ten Commandments.

The Catechism simply won't allow us to take anything for granted. The fact is, Christians *can* be different. Christians *can* love each other; Christians *can* turn away from idols; Christians *can* stay committed in marriages; Christians *can* put Christ and not things foremost in their lives.

But nobody will ever do it all right. Nobody earns God's love. But that doesn't mean we should hang it all up and just live and let live.

I'm not perfect, says Paul, but I press on, I keep trying, I don't give up on doing good.

I once confronted a married man about taking sexual advantage of a young woman. "She came on to me," he said in his defense. "What do you expect me to do?"

God expects obedience.

Billy Graham would agree—nobody does everything right. But Billy Graham is a magnificent witness to the world because he tries in every way to be obedient.

And so should we.

We know we can't do it all, Lord. In fact, we can't do anything without you. Come into our hearts and help us to live in love and truth. Thank you for people like Billy Graham who show us how to live. Help us be obedient. Amen.

Losers and Winners

Q&A 115

So that . . . we may come to know our sinfulness and . . . more eagerly look to Christ for forgiveness. . . .

If we confess our sins, he is faithful and just and will . . . purify us from all unrighteousness.

—1 John 1:9

If you're sticking with the program, you've just read about thirty-five devotions on the Ten Commandments. Yet, as Christ himself says, we really can't do all of that perfectly anyway.

Even if you don't have a pinch of cynicism in you, you can't help but think, "So what's the big deal? If nobody can keep the Ten Commandments anyway, what's all the fuss?"

That's exactly what the Catechism asks in question 115: "No one in this life can obey the Ten Commandments perfectly; why then does God want them preached so pointedly?"

The first half of the answer goes like this: Those commandments we can't keep? They let us know we are sinful so that we'll look to Christ for forgiveness.

Let's see if we can understand that by way of a little example.

Yesterday, the Minnesota Vikings got thumped horribly by the New York Giants in the NFC Championship. Now, I'm no Vikings fan, but even here in Iowa you can feel the sadness ooze over the northern border. Right now, happiness is as hard to come by in Minnesota as a suntan.

In sports, as in life, you have to lose to appreciate winning. One of these years the Vikings will take the Super Bowl, and when they do, January in Minnesota will be as warm as Miami, because Minnesota knows all too well right now (and for the last several years, in fact), the bitterness of losing.

This is a stretch, but stick with me. The Catechism makes it pretty clear we haven't walked off with the Super Bowl either. We're losers. Heart and soul, we go down fast because we can't keep the law.

But if we know that we can't do it, then we've got no choice but to look for help. When we're really down, we look up—it's the only direction left.

The commandments remind us not only that we can't win on our own, but also that we'll need divine help. Every time we go over the commandments we're reminded that we're winners only with Jesus' blood.

Once we know that in our hearts and souls, we're no longer losers. We're winners. Forever winners. Eternal winners. Christ's blood has made us champions in life itself.

That's what the Ten Commandments teach us. That's the big deal.

Lord, thank you for the commandments. We confess that we can't keep them as we should; we are sinners. Thank you that Jesus did what we couldn't do. Thank you for making us your champions through Jesus' blood. In his name, Amen.

Bar Mitzvah

Q&A 115

We may never stop striving to be renewed. . . .

Oh, how I love your law! . . . How sweet are your words to my taste, sweeter than honey to my mouth!

—Psalm 119:97, 103

In the Jewish tradition, thirteen-year-old boys and twelve-year-old girls (I'm not sure why there's an age difference) are brought into the synagogue to accept their role as mature members of the family of believers. In our church, we call a similar ritual profession of faith; in other Protestant traditions it's called confirmation. These important rites often signify that a child is no longer a child.

In one way, though, bar mitzvah (bat mitzvah if you're female) isn't like profession of faith or confirmation, because the Jews still await the Messiah; to them, Christ, a Jew, was not the Savior of mankind.

So when kids come into the Jewish fellowship, they don't "profess" Christ as their Savior. *Bar mitzvah* literally means "son of the commandments." *Bat mitzvah* means "daughter of the commandments."

Traditionally, Jewish children aren't obligated to observe the commandments until they reach the age where they know what they're doing, twelve or thirteen. At that point, they too must live by the commandments. Their coming into the fellowship of believers means they promise to live by the commandments. They become "children of the commandments."

Bar mitzvah and bat mitzvah are big-time celebrations. Once the ceremony is over, there's often a big party. Sometimes, I'm told, the congregation gathers on the steps of the synagogue and throws candy at the one who just became a "child of the commandments." Why candy? Because the congregation wants to symbolically tell the brand-new son or daughter of the commandments that the commandments are sweet.

Check out Psalm 119 and you'll see that the psalmist sang to God about his love for the commandments. He said they were as sweet as honey because the commandments give life and structure to our lives. Think of a world without law, a world where nobody cared if the bullies beat the tar out of everybody. It would be awful. Maybe you've experienced a little of that if you've had a teacher who didn't know how to control the class. It's fun for a day or so, but then nobody learns anything and things get ugly.

The law brings life and joy and harmony. It keeps us from the jungle. The law means our lives make sense.

Look out! Here comes a roll of Life Savers.

Thank you for your law, Lord. Thank you for pointing us in directions that will make our lives meaningful and filled with peace. Help us always to strive to keep your law and to be children of the commandments. In Jesus' name, Amen.

When to Pray

Q&A 116

Prayer is the most important part of the thankfulness God requires of us.

Be joyful always; pray continually; give thanks in all circumstances, for this is God's will for you in Christ Jesus.

—1 Thessalonians 5:16–18

Jewish people claim that the Temple Mount, which stands at the heart of the old city of Jerusalem, is the holiest place on earth. Some Jewish sages believe it's the place where creation began.

But there's more. The Temple Mount is also the place where King Solomon built the first temple. When it was destroyed, the second temple was rebuilt on its ruins. Sadly, that temple went down too, but eventually King Herod renovated it once again and built the Western Wall to support the western side. Then the Romans demolished the third temple, and today all that's left is this Western Wall, sometimes called *Kotel* or the Wailing Wall.

Go there and you'll see people standing beside the wall and reading psalms or praying their own personal prayers or saying formal prayers. The people at the wall—often Orthodox Jewish men with hats and beards and long, spiraling side-burns—are quite expressive. They bob their heads back and forth toward the wall almost madly. It's what people do at the Wailing Wall.

Islamic people, who also inhabit Jerusalem, have their own age-old prayer traditions with specific names: *fagr* before sunrise, *zohr* at noon, *asr* between noon and sunset, *maghreb* at sunset, and *eshaa* after sunset. What's more, each of these prayers has its own prescribed rituals. In Islamic countries, throughout the day each and every Muslim simply stops working to pray.

In our family we pray before and after meals, but not always. Otherwise, nobody in our family sticks by any ancient traditions. When I was a boy, the local radio station used to broadcast the Roman Catholic rosary prayers. I remember thinking a half dozen "Hail Marys" were more than a little silly.

But now I wonder sometimes about traditions and formal rites. The fact of the matter is—and I'm not proud to admit this—I don't pray as much as the Muslims. I've got freedom. I'm not tied to traditions that force a person to do some things.

The downside of freedom is that sometimes we don't do the things we should—like pray. The Catechism doesn't mince words. Prayer, it says, is "the most important part of the thankfulness God requires of us."

Whether we do it voluntarily or by way of ritual or tradition, prayer is a big deal. Why? Simple. Because prayer is talking to God.

Lord, you want our attention. You want us to ask you for your blessing, to thank you for giving us life. And we know very well that we can't have a relationship with you without speaking. Bring us closer to you, Lord, by bringing us to our knees more often. In Jesus' name, Amen.

Close to God

Q&A 116

Why do Christians need to pray?

The LORD has sought out a man after his own heart and appointed him leader of his people. . . .

—1 Samuel 13:14

David, son of Jesse"—his brothers, all-pro line-backers, the little guy something of a wimp, yet chosen by God to be king. "David and Goliath"—head-hunting for the Lord. "David and Jonathan"—best of friends. "David dancing nearly naked before the Lord"—wild man. "David and Absalom"—grief and guilt. "David the poet"—singing songs to the Lord.

Sometimes the Bible refers to David as a man after God's own heart. Could there by any more awesome recommendation? I don't know of any other biblical character described that way.

David, King David. What a believer!

Wait a minute. Didn't he sneak a peek at a bathing beauty, then call her over for a little extracurricular activity? Yes, he did. Even worse, when she got pregnant and her husband wouldn't, for noble reasons, play along with David's treachery, King David arranged her husband's death. Furthermore, it took Nathan the prophet and a slap upside the head to get David to recognize that what he'd done.

David—adulterer and murderer, blind to his own sin. Yet the Bible says God called him "a man after my own heart."

Shocking, isn't it? Amazing.

I've got a theory. I'm going out on a limb, but here's what I think. If you read David's songs, his poems, his psalms to God, you get the picture of someone who went to the Lord with everything—literally everything. When he was depressed, he told God as much. When he overflowed with joy, all his praise flew to the throne. When he was worried, he begged for help. When he was afraid, he called in the Lord's legions.

Here's my theory. King David talked to God constantly. He prayed without ceasing. He and the Lord were, as they say, like this (twist your first two fingers together).

King David's life wasn't all peaches and cream. But always, even in his misery, he talked to God. David was constantly on-line to the throne. David never stopped touching the Lord. I may be wrong, but that's why I think God considered him "a man after my own heart." He prayed, it seems, almost without ceasing.

Doesn't take a rocket scientist to see a lesson here, a lesson about prayer.

Thank you for the example of King David, Lord, a man after your own heart. Help us to remember that you want our attention. You want our prayer. You want us to talk to you. Amen.

Beggars to Givers

Q&A 116

Prayer is the most important part of the thankfulness God requires of us. . . .

How can I repay the Lord *for all his goodness to me?*

—Psalm 116:12

Every Sunday before prayer our church passes around microphones to allow people to tell others about their joys and concerns. It can be a wonderful time. Sometimes people tell very moving stories about someone—or themselves—being healed. Other times, real fears come out in real tears.

But sometimes I wonder if this sharing of joys and concerns is a bit of a mixed blessing. Because if we were to do a tally, most of the things people bring up are requests: "I'm going for surgery this week, so please pray for me." "My aunt was hurt in a car accident, so please pray for her family." "We're leaving on a service project, so please pray for all of us."

There's nothing wrong with those requests, but the Catechism is talking here about more than bringing God all our requests. Of course, our requests are important, and God wants to hear each and every one of them. But there's more to prayer than asking.

In his book *Comfort and Joy* Andrew Kuyvenhoven says that we grow as believers when our prayers take us from being beggars to givers. I think he's right on the money on that one.

There's no question in the world (or out of it) that God wants to hear our requests. "Ask and you shall receive," the Bible says. On the other hand, God wants us not only to ask but also to give—give God praise for being our God, give thanks for God's love in every day of our lives, give our pledge to work for God throughout our whole lives. "How can I repay the Lord for all his goodness to me?" is the question we all ought to be thinking about, along with the psalmist.

Don't get me wrong. There's nothing wrong with making requests. But if we remember God's greatness, if we remember what God has saved us from, if we consider what we'd be without God, then our prayers won't *only* be wish lists, as important as those are. When we speak to God, we'll be givers and not just askers.

Confession time. The most fervent prayers of my life happened when I asked for things, when I knew I needed God, when I thought myself as filthy as a junkyard dog. It's always easier, I think, to ask than to give.

But giving is just about all the Lord God Almighty has ever done.

And I need to give too. So do you.

You alone are worthy, Lord. You alone make the morning sing, the night coo. You bring life to our souls and our eyes and our ears. You are King of the universe. And you love us. Thanks so very, very much. In your Son's name, Amen.

Keep in Touch

Q&A 116

God gives his grace and Holy Spirit only to those who pray continually. . . .

Pray continually.

—1 Thessalonians 5:17

Felicia's dad is an engineer in charge of this huge building project downtown. He's super busy. The customer wants the place up in two years, and it's going to be nip-and-tuck, if you know what I mean.

So Felicia's dad spends most of his time working, and sometimes it hurts. Felicia plays a fair-to-middlin' clarinet in the civic orchestra. Throughout her life both her parents have supported her music. For years, her mom's been driving her back and forth to lessons on the other side of the city. They usually come to concerts too.

Felicia's dad doesn't know that Felicia—not to mention her mom—has this sense lately that she isn't anywhere near the top of his "to do" list. Not that she wants every last moment, but she and her mom do want to register on his radar screen somewhere. In the middle of all this big-time downtown building, they feel as if they've fallen off.

So Felicia's dad missed her concert last week. Too busy. He'd asked her before the concert whether she really wanted him to go, but she lied. "It's no big deal, Dad," she said.

Well, the fact of the matter is, it *was* a big deal. And when her father decided to stay at the office and hammer out plans for the next week, she got mad. Rightly so.

After the concert, she went out with her friends. They did stuff they shouldn't have. They got caught smoking dope.

Felicia's father was super ticked, but when he tried to tell her so, she screamed at him. She told him he didn't care about her life.

That blew him away. It wasn't a pretty scene. Felicia's mom sided with her. What happened between them is what family counselors call "a breakdown in communications."

What happened between Felicia and her father can happen to us. There are times—sometimes prolonged times—in our lives when we do not ask, when we do not talk, when we are not open with God. And when that happens, there's trouble, believe me.

"God gives his grace and Holy Spirit only (get that, *only*) to those who pray continually." So keep in touch, hear?

Lord, we know what's right, we know what's good, we know what's going to bring us joy and peace and love. But we don't always do them. Stay close to us, even when we choose not to stay close to you. Remind us to keep in touch every day of our lives. In Jesus' name, Amen.

How to Pray

Q&A 117

How does God want us to pray?

"Lord, teach us to pray."

—Luke 11:1

I'm teaching a course on-line this year. Some of my students are going to do the assignments, discuss the things I want them to in a chat room, and hand in their stories—all in cyberspace.

"I'm impressed," a student told me last night after class in real time—in a classroom. I'd just explained to them their options in taking the course—on-line or in class—and he thought the whole arrangement was pretty cool. "Most guys your age aren't into this stuff," he said.

I felt like Methuselah.

But I know what he meant because, honestly, I'd still rather have my son around when I set the VCR. The truth is, I've had to learn tons of stuff to put together this on-line course.

How-tos are absolutely essential these days. Many of my ex-students, good writers, work for computer outfits that need page after page of instructions to go with their software or hardware (and they make better money than their old teacher, I might add). Every appliance needs instructions; every building project needs a guide. Bookstores are jam-packed with how-to books on everything from caring for fingernails to redoing a Harley. Wondering about that first kiss? There's gotta be a how-to.

But you wouldn't expect such a thing for prayer. After all, some of our prayers don't even use words. King David used to ask God to hear "the sound of his groaning." I've always loved that idea because I'm convinced some of our very best prayers are groans.

The Catechism insists, however, that we learn how to pray, even if prayer is, in the words of an old hymn, "the soul's sincere desire, unuttered or expressed." The Catechism says that there's a right way and wrong way to pray. In response to his disciples' request to teach them to pray (Luke 11:1), Jesus said, "When you pray . . ." And then he gave his disciples—and all of us—the Lord's Prayer.

That was the first how-to on prayer.

One of the more comforting truths in life is that God hears our groaning. But that doesn't mean all our groans are prayers. When we pray, there are a few guidelines we'd best not forget.

Don't throw away the instructions.

Teach us to pray, Lord. Teach us to speak to you, our loving Father, through your Son. Teach us to know ourselves. For the rest of our lives, teach us more and more about you. Amen.

Chums

Q&A 117

How does God want us to pray? First, we must pray from the heart to no other than the one true God. . . .

Great is the LORD and most worthy of praise; his greatness no one can fathom.

—Psalm 145:3

Funny little word, isn't it? *Chums*. Sounds almost like a fish, but I guess I say that because I remember my mother buying *chubs*. Not the same thing.

Even though nobody uses that word anymore, everybody knows what it means. Chums are buddies. Chums are really, really close friends, the only ones to whom you tell all your secrets—well, at least most of them.

I bring up the word because of a prayer I heard from a kid I know. It went something like this:

God, I'm just asking you to be there, God, because, God, without you we're zeros. And with you, God, we can move mountains. At least, God, that's what you say in your Word, so, God, please just be there for us. We just ask, God, that when things get rough, God, you'll be there walking in our shoes. Amen.

Is that a real prayer? Yep. Is it sincere, from the heart? Yep. Did God hear it? Yep.

The why do Grandpa's eyebrows get crooked when he hears a prayer like that? Because the language is not his. Grandpa and grandma were brought up with phrases like "It behooves us to have fellowship with thee."

Grandpa doesn't like the idea that his grandson and God are chums, a perception he gets from the way the kid tosses in the word *God* so often. It's as if his grandson were talking to a buddy.

Is God our buddy? In a way, sure.

But God's a whole lot more than that. Think of the infinitude of space. Think of the flight of a hummingbird. Think of a white-tailed deer hurdling a hedge. Think of whales singing. God's not just a chum; he's the Creator of the universe.

God's probably not as tough on language as Grandpa, not if God listens even to our groaning. God wants us to pray from our hearts. But when we pray, we've got to remember who God is. God's a friend, all right, but a whole lot more. "His greatness no one can fathom," says David.

God is more than a chum—God is the Creator.

Dear God, you are so very great. It seems incredible to think that you are somewhere on every city street throughout the world right now. To think this minute you're hearing hundreds of thousands of prayers simultaneously. And to know you love us too, each of us. Thank you, Lord. Amen.

"Know Thyself"

Q&A 117

How does God want us to pray? We must acknowledge our need and misery, hiding nothing. . . .

"God, have mercy on me, a sinner."
—Luke 18:13

How to pray. That's what we're talking about, strange as it may sound. The first thing to do, says the Catechism, is to pray from the heart to the one true God. When we pray, we need to remember who God is. We should remember that God judges our lives but also gives us grace. We should remember that God is our friend but is also the almighty Creator.

The second thing to do, says the Catechism, is to know ourselves.

An ancient philosopher named Socrates said many smart things, one of which has never faded from use: "Know thyself." Sounds so simple, right? I live on a certain street, in a certain town; I like donuts, the Iowa Hawkeyes, and motorcycles. I am married, the father of two. Done. I know myself.

Hardly. The fact is, any one of us could spend a lifetime searching our own dark corners—our own mystery. Why do some of us hate cats? How come Alicia smokes? Why do I believe in God?

Tell you what, let's create a profile. Take Amanda. Amanda's ancestors on her father's side immigrated from Scotland in the late eighteenth century soon after the American revolution. They lived in South Carolina for a couple of generations, and then, after the Civil War, the family moved to Missouri, where her great-grandfather made wood barrels for the wagon trains going west. Her grandmother was a teacher; her father an accountant. She likes to dance, probably more than anything else. She's a Christian, raised in an Assemblies of God church.

On her mother's side, she's the great-granddaughter of German immigrants who lived in Illinois, a farm family. When her grandmother grew up, she became a nurse; her mother is a doctor (she met her dad at college), and Amanda herself—well, she doesn't know what she wants to be, and she's getting tired of telling people that.

We've just been through a genealogy. Does all of that define Amanda? Of course not. There's more to her than a family album.

Then what is it exactly that we need to know about ourselves when we pray? Does God care about a pedigree? Not a bit.

To answer Socrates and to approach God's throne in prayer we really need to know just one truth: We need to know that we need God.

Tell God you're a sinner and you need him. Hide nothing about yourself.

That's how to pray.

Dear God, we know that we need you. Every day. All day. We know that we are sinners saved by your amazing grace. Please help us to be honest about ourselves, hiding nothing when we talk to you. In Jesus' name, Amen.

The Bottom Line—It's Simple

Q&A 117

How does God want us to pray? We must rest on this unshakable foundation: . . . God will surely listen to our prayer because of Christ our Lord.

Everyone who calls on the name of the Lord will be saved.

—Romans 10:13

Just for a moment, feel this book. (You've got an advantage because I don't have a book, just a computer screen.) Lift it. Flip through its pages. Pretty good size, huh? Lots of words. Too many, maybe you're thinking.

I'm fifty-two years old, and I've gone to church for just about my whole life. I've probably heard (that is, really listened) to thousands of sermons, read umpteen pages about the Christian faith, and written a shelf full of books of meditations.

Too much, someone might say. We can think and explore and analyze and rip apart—endlessly so, it seems. Yet the bottom line is very, very simple. Jesus loves us.

Look, little kids pray. Do they know God? Sure, after a fashion. Do they know themselves? Maybe—in fact, maybe that's all they know. Do they know they need God? In a way, but that's a stretch. Are they cute when they pray? No kidding.

Do we really have to know all this stuff? After all, anybody can pray. Almost anybody can feel God's love. Why the huge book? I'm sick of all the fuss.

Understandable. Right now, even to me it seems a little pushy to think that we have to know three things before we can pray. That goes a little too far, doesn't it?

Here's what we have to know, the Catechism says. We have to know God; we have to know ourselves and our need of God; and, finally, we have to know what Jesus Christ did, so that when we pray we can know for sure that God hears us.

If you want to know how to pray, the Catechism says, you have to know that Jesus Christ, God Almighty, slipped into human skin for our sake. You have to know he suffered and died and walked out of a grave, killing all of our sin in one fell swoop.

That's it. We're home free. That's what we have to know. Our only comfort in life and in death. I belong to my faithful Savior, Jesus Christ.

Talk to God. You can, and you can know God hears you because of what Jesus did.

Thank you, Lord, for saving my soul. Thank you, Lord, for making me whole. Thank you, Lord, for giving to me your great salvation, so rich and free. Amen.

Everything We Need

Q&A 118

What did God command us to pray for? Everything we need, spiritually and physically. . . .

For your Father knows what you need before you ask him.

—Matthew 6:8

Years ago, a good friend of mine was here, visiting. He said he wanted to teach my class. I didn't know what he'd say to my class because he doesn't teach writing, and this was a writing class. But you can't really say no to this guy. I like him, I really do. But he can be kind of a bully—at least that's what my students thought.

I think, in a way, he wanted to kill them, though not literally. "OK," he bellowed, "what do you know about joy?" He poked his finger in one young woman's face. "When were you really happy?" he said.

I swear that young woman looked as if she were going to cry. "When our volleyball team won the championship?" she said, hoping he'd leave.

"Are you kidding?" he roared.

It wasn't pretty.

But I've never forgotten her answer. She would give him a different answer today, I'm sure, but back then her definition of happiness was her team winning the state championship.

Last night, the Iowa Hawkeyes came to the University of Wisconsin undefeated in the Big Ten. They left with their first loss. I'm a fan. I wanted them to win. When it was clear they weren't going to, I slapped the TV off because I couldn't stand to watch the blood at the end. Really, most of the night I felt terrible.

I don't like to feel awful, do you? Last Saturday I saw a dad come out of the local gym with his arms around his bawling daughter, a girl in volleyball pads.

I've never forgotten the answer my student gave to my pushy friend because I wonder sometimes whether athletics don't really become a religion for some people (including me!).

I can understand why people pray to win games. Nobody wants the agony of losing. Everybody wants the thrill of victory. Most of us will do anything to avoid getting beat—even pray.

"What did God command us to pray for?" asks today's question, and the answer comes bouncing right back, simple and short: "Everything we need."

What do you think—do we really *need* to win a ball game? You'll have to answer that one yourself.

Praying is all about needs, not wants. We can want all kinds of things very badly. In fact, sometimes we believe our wants are our needs.

But they aren't, and knowing the difference helps us when we pray.

Help us separate what we want from what we need, Lord. We confess that sometimes we can't tell the difference. Thank you for loving us. Amen.

How, Not What

Q&A 119

What is this prayer? Our Father in heaven . . .

"This, then, is how you should pray: 'Our Father in heaven . . .'"

—Matthew 6:9

When I was a boy, I remember listening to my parents' little radio in the kitchen. One program created by a Roman Catholic church featured recitals of "Our Fathers" and "Hail Marys." To a kid born and reared in a Protestant church, those endless repetitions of the Lord's Prayer and "Hail, Mary, full of grace; the Lord is with thee; blessed art thou among women, and blessed is the fruit of thy womb, Jesus" seemed funny and weird.

I'm older now, and I don't think repeating those words is as strange as I used to. In many parts of Christendom, meditation begins with repetitions, lots of them. Still, it's important for us to realize that when Jesus first uttered the words of the Lord's Prayer, he didn't say, "This is *what* you should pray"; instead he said, "This is *how* you should pray."

Just a few weeks ago, I was part of a group of Christians who worshiped with a Jewish man and his wife, two people who were part of the Jewish renewal movement. In essence, what they did is explain to us some things about their faith.

In one of the exercises, we separated into pairs. Then we took a psalm, broke it into separate verses, and paraphrased them to each other. We put those verses into our own words and used our own lives to say the things David had written. It was an amazing exercise because it made each of us think deeply about the words and the meaning of the psalm. Try it for a moment: "The LORD is my shepherd, I shall not be in want." How would you say that in your own words and your own life?

Now I'm not suggesting that the whole church adopt the practice we learned from these loving Jewish people. I am suggesting, though, that it was something like what Jesus Christ did when he said, "This is how to pray" and then taught his disciples the prayer that Christians have since repeated gadzillions of times.

Jesus was showing us *how* to pray—it's that simple. He wasn't telling us *what* to say; he was showing us *how* to do it.

We're going to go through this familiar prayer phrase by phrase, trying to unpack its meaning. It's a prayer that's blessed by having come from Jesus Christ himself.

It's the divine model. The Lord's Prayer teaches us how to pray.

Every bit of what we need to know about talking to you, Lord, is in the prayer you've given us. Thank you for teaching us the Lord's Prayer. Thank you that it's been a blessing for so many, for so many years. In the name of the One who gave us this prayer, Amen.

Kids

Q&A 120

Why did Christ command us to call God "our Father"? To kindle in us . . . the childlike awe and trust that God through Christ has become our Father.

Yet to all who received him, to those who believed in his name, he gave the right to become children of God.

—John 1:12

You want to know what kids are like? Listen.

> On the first day of school, the kindergarten teacher said, "If anyone has to go to the bathroom, hold up two fingers." A little voice from the back of the room asked, "But Teacher, how will that help?"

Being a kid, I suppose, means never having to say you're sorry for saying what's right there on your mind. Being a kid means being incredibly innocent. Now listen to this one.

> A mother was preparing pancakes for her sons, Kevin and Ryan. When the boys began to argue over who would get the first pancake, their mom saw the opportunity for a moral lesson. "Now boys," she told them, "if Jesus were sitting here, he would say, 'Let my brother have the first pancake because I can wait.'" Kevin turned to his little brother. "Ryan," he said, "you be Jesus!"

Now that little story would be awful if it weren't about a kid, right? The truth is, kids get away with all sorts of stuff because they don't know any better.

> A father was at the beach with his children when his four-year-old son ran up to him, grabbed his hand, and led him to the shore, where a seagull lay dead in the sand. "Daddy, what happened to him?" the son asked. The father wasn't sure what to say. "That seagull died and went to heaven," he told his son. The kid's eyes scrunched. "Did God throw him back down?" the boy said.

A perfectly logical question, really—if you're a kid. There's something forever innocent and sweet about kids. Life seems so uncomplicated, the world little more than a cartoon. But kids grow up.

The Catechism says the Lord's Prayer begins with "Our Father" because we are God's children. God has become our Father—through Christ. And God would like us to be, in his presence, kids. God wants us to believe in him completely with the unsullied trust of a child.

In faith, God wants us to be kids.

Help us to be children, Lord. In your presence, make us innocent, give us trust, strengthen our faith, erase whatever doubt we've ever felt. Father, help us love honestly and truly. Amen.

"'Death Spiral' Around a Black Hole"

Q&A 121

Why the words "in heaven?"

"Our Father in heaven . . ."

—Matthew 6:9

Here's an actual title of an article I saw recently: "'Death Spiral' Around a Black Hole Yields Tantalizing Evidence of an Event Horizon." Quite a title! Here's the story behind it.

Just last week, NASA's Hubble space telescope may have, for the first time, revealed factual evidence for the existence of black holes. NASA's Joseph F. Dolan actually saw pulses of ultraviolet light from clumps of hot gas seemingly die out in intensity and then disappear as they swirled around Cygnus XR–1, some kind of space object.

This activity appeared to occur at what scientists call an "event horizon," the mysterious region around a black hole that traps light and matter straying nearby, or so the NASA scientists say.

That's this week's news from outer space.

Tomorrow there will be more, I'm sure. Ever since the Hubble space telescope rocketed into space in 1990, it has been discovering new "events" all around the universe.

Imagine growing up centuries ago, when the best way of viewing the stars and planets was simply lying on your back and looking up. Imagine how much easier it would be to say, "Our Father in heaven."

Let's face it: The Hubble space telescope makes believing in heaven as a real place a whole lot more difficult. If heaven is a place, like Chicago, it must be infinitely farther away.

The Catechism says that Christ wanted us to remember that his Father hasn't set up residence in Chicago, at the River Ganges, or somewhere in Jerusalem. Jesus Christ told us to start our prayer with "Our Father in heaven" because our Father is heavenly huge, too big to register on the Hubble.

Wherever heaven exists, God rules, looking out over stars and planets and black holes and event horizons. He watches Singapore and Sioux Center, not to mention Saturn, without blinking. Our God is heavenly. Our God rules. Our God reigns.

The God who spun black holes like little eddies from a canoe paddle, that God can play chess with mountain ranges. That God is ready to hear our prayer.

Our Father in heaven, imagining your greatness almost blows us away. You range above everything, watching and directing. And you love us. Help us to thank you with all of our lives. In your Son's name, Amen.

Definition

Q&A 122

What does the first request mean?

"Hallowed be your name . . ."

—Matthew 6:9

I'm a sucker. Here I am, over fifty years old, and whenever I watch certain ads on television, I still think I can be somebody I'm not. I think if I buy some fancy gizmo I can tighten my abs, slim my belly, or pump my quads. "Buns of steel," right? Sure.

Watch gymnasts for a while, and you begin to wonder if you were born defective. Ever see the arms on a power forward? Thick muscles hanging off their frames like bridge cable, every last sinew startling.

It's called *definition.* Definition is what anybody who works out really wants. It's what's visible when some buff guy slips off a T-shirt and every last muscle makes a statement.

Definition—what's there is clearly visible.

We've already been through the commandments. Remember number one? The Creator of heaven and earth doesn't need beefy biceps, but God does want definition. God wants to stand out, vividly and startlingly. Human beings worship a thousand gods, but this one—the God of the universe—wants definition: "You shall have no other gods before me."

So I suppose we shouldn't be surprised that when Jesus Christ taught us all how to pray, he started with definition, just like the commandments: "Hallowed be your name." How do we pray? Start with definition, says Jesus. "Our Father in heaven"—mine and yours—above all gods. That's the way to start. We're not praying to a rock or the sun. We're setting out with definition: "Hallowed be your name."

If you're like me, your most deeply felt prayers don't start that way. Instead they start with what we want. "Please, Lord, please, please, pretty please . . ."

That's not the way, Jesus says. When you pray, start with definitions: "Hallowed be your name." Not ours. Your will, God; not ours. Your way; not mine.

I suppose it's human for us to forget to bless God's name. All of us, me included, want what we think we need, right?

Remember this: God is God. So when you pray, don't just ask. Praise.

In the gym or anywhere else, when we drop our sweats and show the world our definition, we want the world to see the Lord because God's name must be hallowed. That's the definition most blessed.

Not because it blesses us, but because it blesses God.

Hallowed be your name, Lord. In all the earth, in all the cosmos, in the vast reaches of a universe we can't even measure—hallowed be your name. Amen.

Like the Hypocrites

Q&A 122

Help us to really know you, to bless, worship, and praise you for all your works. . . .

"When you pray, do not be like the hypocrites. . . ."

—Matthew 6:5

It's too easy for us to want to be liked for being nice. Apparently the disciples had the same problem.

A few verses back in Matthew 6, Jesus tells the disciples it's not a good idea to make a big show of being nice to other people. "Be careful not to do your acts of righteousness before men," he says, "to be seen by them." When you give to the needy, Christ says, "don't announce it with trumpets."

"And when you pray," he says (v. 5), "do not be like the hypocrites, for they love to pray standing in the streets." And more: "Do not keep on babbling like pagans, for they think they will be heard because of their many words" (v. 7).

"This is how you should pray," he says, and then we get the Lord's Prayer.

Now don't get me wrong. I think it's a good thing my parents taught me a little ditty prayer when I was a little bitty kid: "Now I lay me down to sleep . . ." My parents taught me to pray.

But if our prayers are only something we recite—say, a standard mealtime blessing or even the Lord's Prayer—then we're not getting much farther down the pike than the hypocrites who go on endlessly with the same words, as if they don't know any others.

For a long time already, a big fight has been going on in the U.S. about prayer in schools. For a long time, good Christian people have been working to get schools to allow a prayer to be said every day in class, a prayer that will offend no one but will teach kids to pray (they hope). It's a notable goal.

But endless repetition mostly ends up a blur, and blur is not definition. Remember, it's definition that God wants. When we riffle through the words—whether it's in silence, in a crowd, or in a classroom—and we don't really think about what we're saying, we're not hallowing God's name, we're cheapening it like some flea market cast-off.

You can't hallow God's name, I'm saying, if your mind is on the barbequed ribs.

"Hallowed be your name" is not a throwaway line, not a cliché, not a ditty. If you don't mean it, you demean it.

Here's what Jesus said, "Don't be a hypocrite."

Hallowed be your name, Lord, in all the earth, in all the skies, in all the seas. Hallowed be your name, Lord, in every one of your children. Hallowed be your name, Lord, in every prayer we bring to you. Amen.

Whatever You Do

Q&A 122

Help us to direct all our living . . . so that your name will never be blasphemed because of us, but always honored and praised.

So whether you eat or drink or whatever you do, do it all for the glory of God.

—1 Corinthians 10:31

Alex is his name. Nice guy, married to a sweet girl. They've got one child, a daughter, cutest kid in town. A decade ago Alex went to work for his uncle as a mason. He worries a little about his arms giving out someday, but he loves his work.

You see, masonry isn't just brick on brick; it's creation, in a way. The idea is to lay stone or block or brick with such precision that everything fits. That's what Alex loves about it, making the whole thing sing.

Mr. Bronson, a client, is building a place on the lakeshore, a beautiful place. Alex put in a fireplace, stone by stone, from a pile Bronson had shipped in from Australia, because his wife loved the place when they visited five years ago. The guy's got bucks.

The fireplace was one thing, but Bronson came by one day and said he wanted a balcony built out over the second floor of this dream house—stone by precious stone.

Now Alex knows he can make mega-bucks if he says OK. But here's what Alex is thinking. Constructing this whole huge balcony, a painstakingly slow task, out of that incredibly expensive stone is really excessive.

Alex isn't poor. But he wonders, really, whether the Lord God Almighty, creator of heaven and earth, wants him spending the next two months of his time piecing together a beautiful stone balcony for some guy who doesn't need it. He wonders if he's using his talents for the Lord or for sheer ostentation.

Last night he told his wife he was thinking of telling Bronson to get somebody else. He just couldn't do it, not when he knew that he could be building things that had much more use.

Would you do it? Should he?

There are no easy answers to questions like this, believe me. We all make choices every day of our lives, and often enough those choices are tough.

But if we take the profession "Hallowed be your name" seriously—and it is a profession—then what we profess comes out not only in our words but deeds.

In a sense, my life, like yours, is a profession of faith. It's a form of evangelism. Alex wants his life to witness for Christ.

"Help us to direct all our living so that your name may be always honored and praised." That's a prayer to live by.

"Help us, Lord, to direct all our living—what we say, think, and do—so that your name will never be blasphemed because of us but always honored and praised." Amen.

The Battle and the War

Q&A 123

What does the second request mean?

"Your kingdom come. . . ."

—Matthew 6:10

We were standing in the town square at Bastogne, Belgium, reading an ancient, yellowing map pinned up behind glass when an elderly man and his wife walked up. They were speaking English, as we were. The map traced the lines of the Battle of the Bulge, Hitler's last great offensive in his attempt to thwart the march of Allied troops toward Germany and Berlin.

This man had been there. He remembered being wounded. He remembered trying to stay warm in snow holes he dug with frozen hands. He remembered numbing cold and heart-wrenching fear.

The Battle of the Bulge, the largest land battle of World War II, raged from December 16, 1944, to January 28, 1945. What did it look like? Think endless miles of snow on an open landscape. Think blood, lots of it. More than a million troops participated, and when it was over there were 81,000 United States casualties, 19,000 dead; Nazi casualties included 100,000 killed, wounded, or captured.

This old man we met had lived through it. When we went with him to the museum in the middle of that broad battle plain, he couldn't say much because what he remembered tore his heart out, even though the battle had happened a half century before.

Germany was losing the war. The Battle of the Bulge was Hitler's last-ditch effort to turn the tide. If you know your history, the end of the war didn't come for another year, a year in which that elderly man at the Battle of the Bulge was nearly killed.

When you pray, Jesus said, say this: "Your kingdom come."

But isn't God already King, right now? Absolutely. Victory over death and sin is already in the bank.

But that doesn't mean there is no more fighting. Every day is a Battle of the Bulge; like Hitler, Satan isn't going down without a fight.

"Your kingdom come." When we pray that, we're asking God, who's already won the war, to end the final battle.

Your kingdom come, Lord. Bring peace eternally.

Lord, we know that with the resurrection, death itself was destroyed. Still, every day of our lives sin—ours and others'—presents us with problems and headaches. Your kingdom come, Lord. Bring us peace, forever. In your Son's name, Amen.

Couch Potato

Q&A 123

Rule us by your Word and Spirit in such a way that more and more we submit to you.

Teach me to do your will, for you are my God; may your good Spirit lead me on level ground.

—Psalm 143:10

Leonard Lazy-Boy gets everything he knows from the tube. Not that he really likes sitcoms or game shows or anything else; he doesn't. It's just that at the end of the day, he's tired. All day long he's busy stacking shelves in the store where's he's worked for ages. He doesn't like his job much either.

The best place on earth, he thinks, is the couch in the family room, where his dog, who loves him, circles up around his cold toes while he's watching TV. Sports are a big deal too. In fact, during the NCAA tournaments he cannot be moved.

Mostly he hates the President, thinks he's just another one of those rich guys who get all the breaks when the working stiffs (like him) get nothing. His wife works as an orderly in the hospital; she's gone most nights. Their marriage isn't all that hot. The two of them have three kids, but for some odd reason they don't hang around the house much. That's OK with him because, often as not, they seem like a pain, you know?

Leonard thinks of himself as a Christian, sort of. He goes to church most every Sunday. Sometimes the singing lights a fire or two, but mostly going to church is just something he does because it's good for him and good for the kids. To Leonard, the Christian faith is like a flu shot: they stick a needle in you and make your arm sore so that you won't get laid up later on.

As he has for years, he prays the Lord's Prayer before whatever meals the family eats together. "Your kingdom come," he says, and all the rest of the words too.

Poor Leonard Lazy-Boy. He's probably never more an unbeliever than he is when he says those three little words: "Your kingdom come." He doesn't mean it, because if he did, he'd have to get off the couch.

"Your kingdom come" means signing up on the dotted line of the Creator's draft notice. We are God's, out there in the world at work for our Maker.

"Your kingdom come" commits us to Christian service in every area of our lives, commits us to work for God's kingdom.

So what are you going to do when you get out of school? "Your kingdom come." Do you mean it? Get up off the couch and sign on the dotted line.

God, to you be the glory forever and ever. Empower us to take your love into absolutely everything we do at home, at work, at school, even in front of the TV. Rule in our lives. Your kingdom come. Amen.

Listening for God's Voice

Q&A 123

Rule us by your Word and Spirit . . .

Choose life . . . that you may love the Lord your God, listen to his voice, and hold fast to him. For the Lord is your life. . . .

—Deuteronomy 30:19–20

She came into my office—very small, blonde hair, dimples, a great smile. She wanted to visit the college where I teach because she wanted to enroll.

Lots of high school kids visit colleges, of course, and I end up talking to many of those who are interested in majoring in English here. This young lady already had her mind made up, or that's what she told me.

"So," I asked, "what convinced you to come here?"

"When I saw an ad in a magazine," she told me, full of joy, "God told me this was the place."

I winced.

Some alarm goes off in my head when someone says God told him or her to do a certain something like enroll in this, that, or the other college. I just don't trust it. It sounds looney.

But then, maybe that's because I've never heard God's voice in just that way. People used to sing a hymn titled "In the Garden." Maybe you've heard it; it used to be hugely popular. The second stanza goes like this: "He speaks, and the sound of his voice/is so sweet the birds hush their singing."

The fact that I don't recognize it as God's voice doesn't mean God doesn't speak to me or nudge me on toward destinations. That I don't hear a thunderous command or a melodic articulation and recognize it as God's voice doesn't mean I don't pick up that voice.

This morning, for instance, a fresh blanket of snow covers the neighborhood; God speaks to me in beauty. Someone asks me to do a writing job for them; God calls me to a mission. Some student loses her grandma; God speaks to me in her heartache.

When we say "Your kingdom come," we're asking the Lord to "rule us by his *Word* and *Spirit*," by what we read in the Bible and what we hear in stunning garden voices and the urgent whispers of real human need.

When we say "Your kingdom come," we're asking for God's rule in our lives; we're asking God to help us determine, among other things, which college we're going to attend. We're asking God to have a hand in all the big decisions of our lives. We're asking God to help us, guide us, speak to us, see us through.

We're asking God to be the King of our lives.

Be there for us, Lord, in every tough decision we will ever make. We know we can count on you because we know you are King of all of creation in this world and the next. Thank you for loving us. Your kingdom come. Amen.

The Iron-Pumping Church

Q&A 123

Keep your church strong, and add to it.

"I will build my church, and the gates of Hades will not overcome it."

—Matthew 16:18

Take your best friends, the kids you hang out with, the ones who tell the same kinds of jokes, love the same movies, follow the same baseball team, the ones who'd walk through fire for a great burrito. Take all of those kids and stick them together in a building somewhere and call it a church.

Want to go there?

Most of us would. If we could surround ourselves only with people we like and call it a church, we'd be happy campers. We'd be at peace.

An old preacher friend of mine used to think that same thing. But then, he said, he'd stand at the back of his church after his sermon and shake hands with all the real people who'd file by, among them dozens of folks he really wouldn't care to go fishing with.

There's a story about a basketball coach who had a line drawn on the doorsill of his office, along with a sign that read, "If your vertical jump doesn't go this high, don't bother knocking." He may have been a good coach, but he's not God. And his team isn't the church, because the church is what people used to call "a five-and-dime store"—a place where you can find just about everything on two legs. Church is a sanctified junk drawer.

Get a hundred Christians together and a bunch of them will want to sing only praise and worship songs. Another bunch will want only the old hymns. Some will speak in tongues. Some won't go to movies on Sunday; some won't dance; and a few from every camp won't be sure the others should even be there.

"Your kingdom come" isn't a line for the weak-kneed. When we say it, we're asking God to make the church pump iron, to make it strong and make it grow despite the differences between us.

After all, the church knows more about the kingdom than anybody else. In part, that's why it's the church. But the church is not the kingdom. It's part of the kingdom, a very special part of it—the soul. And that soul needs to be strong because the church has work to do. "Your kingdom come" means, Build us up, Lord, for the work you call us to do in the bigger world of your kingdom.

Jesus says "I will build my church." And he wants you and me to join the construction crew.

Strengthen us for the work you've given us to do for your kingdom. Help us to love each other, despite our differences. Make us family, your family. In Jesus' name, Amen.

"Marching Along"

Q&A 123

Destroy the devil's work. . . .

The God of peace will soon crush Satan under your feet.

—Romans 16:20

It's maybe a sign of my age, but old songs keep popping into my head. This morning, while shoveling snow, I found myself singing a ditty I haven't heard for forty years, a song no Sunday school teacher would think of singing now (well, maybe I'm overstating).

Here it is. "Little soldiers of Jesus are marching along,/marching along, marching along;/little soldiers of Jesus are marching;/joyfully, joyfully, marching along."

Crazy, huh? Imagine thousands, even millions of pajama-ed little kids in perfect rows, flapping their arms in strict time, marching on toward what? Toward some big battle, I guess.

I was born after World War II, so war, to my parents, was very real. There was a real enemy, a demonic enemy with a funny little mustache, a man who built factories to kill millions of people. Marching to war wasn't at all strange to my parents' generation, a generation that taught us as kids to sing those songs.

But today the picture of cute little kids marching to war may well remind us of something called the Children's Crusade, a pathetic military march undertaken by children (how many will never be known) in 1212 to recover the Holy Sepulcher from the Muslims. Thousands of children followed two visionary boys who promised a glorious victory; thousands died from hunger and disease during the march.

Most Christians are not into war these days; they're into love—rightly so. But according to the Catechism, when we pray, "Your kingdom come," we're asking God to blast away at his enemy, the Devil. We're asking God to turn us into soldiers, to gear us up for war with the powers of darkness.

These days, that's hard to swallow. C. S. Lewis used to say that when it comes to Satan, we can get it wrong in two ways: We can take him so seriously that we see him behind every last bush in the yard; or we can laugh him off as some medieval silliness. Both attitudes fall short of the truth.

Personally, I'm very comfortable with soft-pedaling the war stuff. But the moment I believe there are no powers of darkness is the moment I'm living in a make-believe world. Jesus himself came into our world to destroy the devil's work, says 1 John 3:8.

When we say "Your kingdom come," we're really asking God to fight and to help us fight the powers hell-bent against God's kingdom.

"Joyfully, joyfully, marching along."

Give us wisdom, Lord. Help us to know when to fight and how to fight against the powers in our world that deny your kingdom. Your kingdom come. Amen.

Lord Jesus, Come Quickly

Q&A 123

Do this until your kingdom is so complete and perfect that in it you are all in all.

[God] will wipe every tear from their eyes. There will be no more death or mourning or crying or pain. . . .

—Revelation 21:4

I once knew a man who was dying.

I guess that's a stupid thing to say, isn't it? Everybody I know is dying.

I once knew a man who knew he had less than a year to live. He had cancer. On a warm April day during the last year of his life, I asked him to come over for a cup of coffee. The two of us sat on the deck he himself had built on our house and talked for a long time.

I really wanted to know what it felt like to be dying. How does it feel to know you're going to leave, to know that when you get up in the morning, there aren't going to be many more?

Ken didn't want to talk about that. Instead, he wanted to tell me how loving God was, how much joy God had given him, what he imagined heaven would be like.

In a way, I was disappointed. All he could talk about was where he was going. But that's when it struck me that he was making perfect sense.

Think of it this way. It's the night before you leave for college for the first time. Guess what? You're not thinking about old times in high school because you're focused on where you're going. Sure, the past is important; sure, you'll miss your high school friends. But there's a whole other world for you now, and you know it. My friend Ken was thinking about where he was going to be tomorrow. That's all he could talk about. He was, in a way, planning his trip.

"Lord Jesus," Ken might have said, "come quickly." Not because he didn't care about what he was leaving behind, but because he was thrilled about what was ahead.

"Your kingdom come" has nothing to do with death; it has everything to do with eternal completeness. "Your kingdom come" asks God to knock out cancer forever, to heal this broken world, to pull off a miracle with all our suffering, to end the groaning of all the world's pain, along with war and hate and death and sin itself.

"Your kingdom come" asks for the eternal peace God promises. "Your kingdom come" helps us plan for the greatest day of our lives.

"Your kingdom come" is a profession of our faith that God Almighty is our eternal King, whose eternity will bring all of us, like Ken, home at last.

Lord, take us to that day when we won't hurt, we won't sin, we won't die. Bring it on, Lord. Take us to that day when we won't go to war, we won't pick on others. Bring it on, Lord. Your kingdom come. Amen.

Obedience

Q&A 124

What does the third request mean?

"Your will be done on earth as it is in heaven."

—Matthew 6:10

For the past couple of months, Margie and Eric have ended most of their dates having sex in Eric's apartment. Both of them were raised as Christians, raised to believe that sex is for marriage. But they've been going out for four years, and it won't be long until they're married. Then it will be official, they figure; but meanwhile, they're having a great time. How can anything so great be so wrong? That's what they tell each other.

Obedience isn't easy.

Shandra has been running the human management side of Arteros for about three years. She loves the job. But when her boss said he wanted a woman named Franzen fired, Shandra guessed she knew why. The boss had come on to Ann Franzen and she hadn't played along. Tomorrow morning, Shandra tells herself, she's going to walk into her boss's office and tell him she can't fire Franzen. Tonight, she can't sleep.

Obedience isn't easy.

Mark's job pays him well, and he's tired of the Honda he's been driving since he was in college. It's got a million miles on it, and the driver's seat is shredded. He's always had this thing for the environment, but a coworker named Ron is trying to sell his Explorer. Mark loves the outdoors; if he had that Explorer he could go off-road and all that, just like in the ads. Besides, he could get it cheap from Ron. What he pays extra for the gas the Explorer gobbles, he could get back from the deal. What should he do?

Obedience isn't easy.

Lisa would rather write new computer programs than do most anything else. A big company recently offered her $75,000 a year to do nothing more than check out other companies' software and write a few reports. It would be so easy, and the money would be so good. But her gifts are in programming, not just checking someone else's work. She wonders what to do.

Obedience isn't easy.

When we pray "your will be done," we're throwing our own will into God's. We're promising that what *we* want will be what God wants. "Your will be done" shoves our wills back into second place or worse.

The thing is, what we want isn't always what God wants. "Your will be done" may well mean ours won't.

Don't let anybody kid you—obedience isn't easy.

Lord, help us let go of our wills so that your will may be done. Help us to give everything we are to you. We know it's not easy. Your will be done, Lord. Amen.

Self-Denial

Q&A 124

Help us and all people to reject our own wills and to obey your will without any back talk.

Then Jesus said to his disciples, "If anyone would come after me, he must deny himself. . . ."

—Matthew 16:24

My back went out. I had to have surgery. It took a long time before I could stand up straight without wincing. Not fun.

The old chair I used down here in the basement behind my computer didn't exactly fit the new shape of my refinished back. I'd sit here awhile and get sore. Lumbar support, that's what I needed, and that's got nothing to do with two-by-fours.

So I got a new chair, a good one, a factory-second right from the place it was made in Michigan. Great chair, but suddenly I didn't fit under the old desk.

So I needed a new desk. I could get a good used desk from a guy in town I knew, so I sold my old one, and the new one cost less than a candlelight dinner.

But then I needed a new computer to go with my new desk and chair. The old one's memory was like mine—not so hot. And while I was at it, I needed a laptop for when I travel. I'd also really like to have my own digital camera instead of having to borrow the one from school.

You know, I've come to a point in life where buying stuff isn't all that tough. If I need something, as long as it doesn't break the bank, I go out and get it. It's just that easy.

You know what else? I don't think I'm all that different from most people in North America. Sure, I know there's poverty here, but if you contrast our wealth with, say, Somalia's or India's, we've got it made.

So what do I know about self-denial? Not a thing, really. Not a thing.

Self-denial. An awful word. Almost un-American. Look, everybody needs a new DVD player. If no one buys them, thousands of people will be out of work. We've got to buy things just to keep people happy.

Self-denial. Loren is an incredible skater, but he quit. He dropped the sport because, he said, it had become his god. He said he couldn't love God and skating at the same time. He could have gone to the Olympics. We thought he was nuts.

Self-denial. When we say "your will be done," we're denying ourselves, sometimes even our wants, our dreams, our fantasies. We're denying ourselves and giving ourselves to God.

Jesus said if we want to follow him, we've got to deny ourselves.

That's what he wants. Can you do it? Want to try?

"Help us and all people to reject our own wills and to obey your will without any back talk. Your will alone is good." Amen.

Zaniken

Q&A 124

Help us . . . to obey your will without any back talk . . . as willingly and faithfully as the angels in heaven.

So the people grumbled against Moses, saying, "What are we to drink?"

—Exodus 15:24

One of the few Dutch words that have come down to me through five generations of American life is the verb *zaniken* (pronounced zah-ni-ken). Like other foreign words that feel just right, it hasn't disappeared because it's somehow better than its English equivalents.

Zaniken means grousing, but not just grousing. People who grouse are generally grouchy; *zanik*ers are whiners, and whining is different from grouching. *Zaniken* is worse than pouting. Pouters generally don't say much; they're experts at the silent treatment. People who *zanik* let you know by *zaniken*. Tell you what—say it this way and you get the whole effect: zaaaaaaaaaaahniken. See what I mean. People who *zanik* cry without tears.

The fact is, you don't have to be Dutch to *zanik*. We all do it. We just had three inches of snow. Mom yells up at Junior, "Markie, you're going to have to shovel the driveway."

"Awwwwhhhh Mom," Markie *zanik*s.

Your little sister has her piano lesson in two days, and she hasn't sat on the bench all week long. Mom reminds her that she hasn't practiced.

"Awwwwhhhh Mom," she *zanik*s.

You've got a history paper due on Friday. There's a ball game tonight, and what do you care about the Peloponnesian wars anyway? Dad says, "Don't you think you better get that paper done?"

"Awwwwhhh Dad," you *zanik*.

We're all *zanik*ers, really.

The people of Israel were world-class *zanik*ers. Moses is up on the mountain getting the Ten Commandments, and they start *zaniken* to Aaron. "Give us something to worship," they say. "We don't want to wait around. We want to dance."

And more. "Can't you give us some food?" God gives manna.

"I'm sick of this white stuff." God gives them a cloud of quail.

"Awwwwhhhh, Moses"—time and time again they *zanik*.

So do we.

Even the Catechism understands *zaniken*. When we say, "Your will be done," we're asking for God's help to deny ourselves and to obey—"without any back talk," it says. That means no *zaniken*.

And that's what we promise—a real mouthful—when we say, "Your will be done."

Lord, mold us and shape us to your will so that we can take your love into all the world with joy in our hearts. Help us not to zanik. *Your will be done, Lord. Amen.*

Modesty

Q&A 125

What does the fourth request mean?

"Give us today our daily bread."
—Matthew 6:11

He comes in a hooded gown. Often he's holding a scythe, one of those long-handled blades people used to use to cut down long grass. Know him?

Maybe not. You don't see much of him on TV or in movies. He's not that nice of a guy. He's Death, and few human beings want to see him.

He's got a starring role in a play that's at least five hundred years old, a short little drama called *Everyman.* Chances are, you haven't heard of the play either.

This character, Death, who usually has a skull for a face, comes to a guy with the generic name Everyman. Death tells him, quite simply, that the clock of his life has only a few ticks left. As any of us would be, Everyman is shocked. "Will you let me get my life in order?" he begs. Death says he'll give him some time.

So Everyman scrambles to find somebody to come along on this horrible journey to death. First he goes to his friends, who aren't overjoyed at the prospect of coming with him, so they take off.

Then he goes to his family. "I'd feel a lot better," he tells them, "if one of my loved ones would come along."

"What loved ones?" they say, and skedaddle.

So Everyman turns to a character named Worldly Goods, a huge guy whose pockets bulge with so many coins he can hardly move. "How about you?" Everyman says, pleading. "Can't I take you with me?"

"Forget it," the big guy says.

"But I loved you," Everyman says.

"That's your problem," says Worldly Goods.

"I was deceived!" Everyman says.

"What else is new?" says the massive master, and he lumbers away.

Neither you, nor me, nor Madonna, nor Bill Gates will take a dime along when the fat lady sings. That's the truth, hard as it is to swallow for Everyman—and for us.

The Lord's Prayer says nothing more or less than "Give us today our daily bread." The Lord's Prayer teaches us modesty. It teaches us not to buddy up to Worldly Goods.

"Our daily bread." It's a daily reminder of our only comfort.

The truth is, we really don't need much at all.

Lord, give us today our daily bread. You are the only source of everything good. Neither our work and worry nor your gifts can do us any good without your blessing. Amen.

Compassion

Q&A 125

Do take care of all our physical needs. . . .

"I have compassion for these people; they have already been with me three days and have nothing to eat. I do not want to send them away hungry. . . ."

—Matthew 15:32

It's hard to even imagine this, but it's true, so let's try. It's Republic Day in India, a holiday celebrating Indian independence. Four hundred kids from a school in Anjar, a small town with narrow streets, are out marching and singing patriotic songs.

Suddenly the earth begins to shake. In the very center of those narrow streets, those kids huddle together as they fall to the ground, unable to stand. The walls around them fall in like stacks of dominoes.

Thousands of people die in a massive heave of the earth that measures 7.9 on the Richter scale. In less than a minute, more than three hundred of those kids celebrating Republic Day are dead. The city is destroyed. Those who remain alive are huddling in tents. One of the major concerns is getting enough firewood to burn the dead bodies to prevent disease.

That's what's happening in a western province of India today, as I write.

And here I sit in my warm basement. If I get hungry, I'll go upstairs and get a bagel. What to spread on it? Cream cheese, jelly, or peanut butter? That's maybe the toughest decision I face right now.

If I put my ear to the ground, I wonder if I could hear crying on the other side of the world. Probably not. But if I were there, I couldn't miss it.

Suffering, real suffering, sometimes seems very far away. What do I have to do with those poor Indian people, most of whom aren't even Christians? Why should I care? I've even got a choice of bagels—cinnamon raisin, plain, or sunflower seed. I'm OK.

Notice that "Give us today our daily bread" uses the pronoun *our,* not *my*. Just think how much different it would sound if Jesus had said, "Give *me* today *my* daily bread." But he didn't. Christ wants us to care, to show compassion, just as he had compassion on the hungry crowds who came to hear him preach.

It's hard to show love to suffering people of India on the other side of the world. But when we say "Give us today our daily bread," it's clear God wants us to think about more than just ourselves.

God wants us, every day, to think of all of God's children, to act with compassion when and where we can.

"Give us today *our* daily bread."

Lord, don't let us shut our doors to your children wherever they suffer. Help us to show compassion when and where we can. Give all of us today, Lord, our daily bread. Amen.

Confidence

Q&A 125

Help us to . . . put trust in you alone.

Cast your cares on the LORD and he will sustain you.

—Psalm 55:22

Ms. Barrows chose the play *Up the Down Staircase* because she thought the kids would like it—and they do. It's about a school. Right from the beginning, the cast giggled and laughed all the way through. But the truth is, the play's headed for big trouble.

Performance is three weeks away, and at least four of the major characters still don't know their lines. What's more, the set crew has been sitting on their hands. And publicity should be out, but that committee isn't getting their work done either. The poster is made, but guess what? Nobody took it to the printer.

Time for Ms. Barrows to kick some butt.

Only thing is, she doesn't like to kick butt. She wishes she were more like Coach Meyers. He yells at his players as if they were a mule train, and they seem to love him for it. Ms. Barrows hates to raise her voice. But she knows she's got to start yelling soon or the play's going to be a full-fledged disaster.

At night, she dreams she's standing in a packed theater yelling out lines because the cast doesn't know a thing. She can't sleep. She can't teach either. She can't eat. She can't get in a workout because she doesn't have time. It's driving her nuts. She thinks she's going to explode.

Like Ms. Barrows, we're all too busy. And so we worry and fret our way into bad dreams.

"Give us today our daily bread" says nothing about school plays, of course, but it does offer some help for our busyness. For starters, we can learn a ton about standing up straight by getting on our knees, right? That's what we do when we ask God to give us what we need, not once a week, not now and then, but every day.

You know as well as I do that Ms. Barrows can't just pray her problems away. She can't just say, "Well, Lord, I'll trust in you and everything will turn out OK." She may still have to kick butt.

But when we pray "Give us today our daily bread," we're confessing that God can do what has to be done to meet our needs. What's more, we're trusting God to do it.

God Almighty. "Cast your cares on the LORD and he will sustain you." God will supply everything you need.

Dear Lord, sometimes we feel really stressed out by all the stuff we've got to do. Sometimes it feels as if the clock just goes too fast. Give us the confidence to know that you'll take us through. Give us today, Lord, our daily bread. Amen.

The Miracle of Forgiveness

Q&A 126

What does the fifth request mean? Because of Christ's blood, do not hold against us, poor sinners that we are, any of the sins we do or the evil that constantly clings to us.

"Forgive us our debts, as we also have forgiven our debtors."
—Matthew 6:12

You probably know Jesus' parable of the Prodigal Son, the one about the kid who demands his inheritance, leaves home, blows it all, then returns (see Luke 15 for details). Just for kicks, let's get into the mind of his brother, the good kid who worked hard and never left the farm. Junior's back. Here's what big brother might be thinking.

> Let me get this straight. Junior makes a fool out of the old man by demanding money that isn't yet his. Then he's off to the races or Las Vegas or wherever. Of course the money disappears. Duh, I wonder why.
>
> That's not all. While he's out there shooting craps and chasing women, I'm left here with a pitchfork and way too many barns. Junior's livin' the high life, and I'm barely able to drag my sorry rear end into bed, that's how hard I'm working.
>
> So is it my fault he drains his cash? Is it Vegas's fault? No way. Junior could have turned his back on all that sinful living any time he wanted to, but no. He waits until he doesn't have a nickel, then comes crying home to Papa.
>
> And what does the old man do? Hauls out the best steaks in the freezer and turns the whole place into New Year's Eve. Why? Because my jerk brother came home.
>
> My old man's a wuss. He should have made Junior clean barns for ten years before talking to him. That's what Junior deserved. But what does he get? A party. Shoot, the old man never gave me a party, and I've given him every last year of my life. It's not fair, you know what I mean? It's just not fair.

The Prodigal Son is a parable that can make good Christians wince. God's love really doesn't make sense. The faithful brother in the parable spent most of his life trying to live right, but it's the problem child who gets the fatted calf. Go figure.

When we talk about forgiveness, we have to think "miracle." The facts are clear: We're poor sinners, all of us, even the faithful brother. Just listen to him.

But here's the miracle: God forgives. God deletes everything, the sins we do and the evils that cling to us. We're loved by God Almighty. By the gift of the Son, our sin is rolled away forever.

Like I said, when you say "forgiveness," think "miracle." That's what it is. Nothing less than a miracle.

Lord, do not hold against us, poor sinners that we are, any of the sins we do or the evil that constantly clings to us. In the name of Jesus, who paid for all our sins, Amen.

The Forgiven Forgive

Q&A 126

Forgive us just as we are fully determined . . . to forgive our neighbors.

"Forgive, and you will be forgiven."
—Luke 6:37

I'd been invited to speak somewhere. I read a story or two, and people seemed to appreciate it. When it was over, some of those who'd listened wanted to talk.

The person I want to tell you about was a woman, not young. She had fancy hair and lots of jewelry. She waited until everyone else was finished saying what they had to say, and then she unloosed something within her and the whole story came pouring out.

Her husband left her, she said, for another woman, someone much, much younger. It had happened ten years ago already, but the way she talked about it made me think she'd taken a knife just that afternoon. She said that his leaving was terrible, something no one should ever have to live through; but even worse than that were the aftershocks, the rumbling horrors she still faced.

Family reunions, for example. She and her husband had several children, and every holiday was awkward. Weddings were too difficult to get through; when her son got married, his father had insisted that his new young wife sit in the pew beside him. Their son didn't know what to do, she said. She felt as if she were on display at that wedding, an abandoned, pitiful soul, sitting there alone. She felt worthless, absolutely worthless.

There was more. Her husband was a big man in the church somewhere, she said. Didn't I think there was something wrong with a church that made an adulterer into a saint? she wanted to know.

I felt sorry for her, I really did. I could have kicked her husband if he'd been standing there.

Even as I listened to her, however, I knew the real problem. I didn't tell her, because sometimes there are things you simply can't say. This woman needed, more than anything, to forgive her husband.

The fifth request of the Lord's Prayer makes it very clear that there is some kind of relationship between our asking God for forgiveness and our forgiving others. That woman will not be able to go on with her life until she forgives. She'll never forget, of course. That's not what we're talking about. But if she wants any peace, she'll have to forgive her ex-husband.

It takes a miracle for that kind of forgiveness to happen.

What we pledge in our request for forgiveness is that we too will try to forgive.

Giving and receiving forgiveness—it's all a miracle. Praise the Lord.

Comfort all those, Lord, who have been horribly sinned against. Help them—like all of us—learn from you to forgive. Forgive us our debts as we forgive our debtors. Amen.

Forgiveness and Godliness

Q&A 126

We are fully determined . . . to forgive our neighbors.

Then Peter came to Jesus and asked, "Lord, how many times shall I forgive my brother when he sins against me? Up to seven times?" Jesus answered, "I tell you, not seven times, but seventy-seven times."

—Matthew 18:21–22

We've already talked about Mr. Ives, the hero of Oscar Hijuelos's wonderful novel *Mr. Ives' Christmas,* an unforgettable story of miracles.

Just exactly who Mr. Ives is isn't all that clear. We know that he lives in New York City, that he seems to have Spanish blood, and that he is, without a doubt, a deeply religious man. But as an orphan, he has no immediate family.

Eventually Mr. Ives gains a family. He marries and has a son, Robert. Throughout his childhood, Robert picks up his father's strong faith and eventually sets out to become a priest. Then one December afternoon after choir practice, Robert's life ends when a fourteen-year-old boy shoots him in the face at point-blank range on the steps of the church.

A man as devoted to God as Mr. Ives has to ask himself really difficult questions at a time like that—questions like Why, God? In the darkness after his son's murder, Mr. Ives's faith nearly evaporates in grief and anger.

Slowly, inch by gracious inch, his doubt and fear and grief and anger begin to fade away. Why? Because he knows what is required of him. He knows he must forgive as he has been forgiven.

Oscar Hijuelos's novel is a fable of forgiveness. Eventually, years later, on the invitation of a local priest, Mr. Ives goes to the cramped tenement apartment where the killer, Danny Gomez, now lives. Gomez, afraid of the meeting, spends most of the morning throwing up. But when he looks into Mr. Ives's eyes, he sees "a face filled with compassion." Meanwhile, Mr. Ives feels a definite urge to strangle the man, but instead hugs him. "In those moments," Hijuelos writes, "Ives knew his son was somewhere in that room, approving of what he beheld."

It's a marvelous story because forgiveness is a miracle.

God wants us to be more like him. How? Well, we know certain things about God. For instance, we know that he loves more than we ever can, and we know he forgives.

When we do what we know God does, we come to know God better. When we forgive—hard as that may seem—we actually come to know God far better than we ever would without forgiving.

"Forgive us our debts, as we forgive our debtors" is a plea and a pledge. We ask and we give, and in the process we grow near unto God.

Forgive us, Lord, just as we are fully determined, as evidence of your grace in us, to forgive our neighbors. Amen.

Lead Us Not

"And lead us not into temptation, but deliver us from the evil one."

—Matthew 6:13

Q&A 127

What does the sixth request mean? By ourselves we are too weak to hold our own even for a moment. . . . And so, Lord, uphold us and make us strong. . . .

Football is by far the most important thing in Mitch's life. That's what he thinks about most all the time. Football is the reason he spends half his life in the weight room. What's more, he's good at it. Coach tells him if he beefs up, he's got a shot at Division I.

His cousin, Seth, is a computer whiz who has mega bucks. Seth has two tickets to this year's Super Bowl. "Game's on Sunday but we drive down on Friday," Seth told him. "It'll be a weekend you'll never forget."

The ticket is free, but Mitch figures the whole weekend will cost him around five hundred bucks, which he really can't afford. His parents aren't thrilled about his going either.

He'll miss some school and his Saturday job, and he won't go to church. All totaled, he figures, that's not a big deal. It's the chance of a lifetime.

For some of us at least, real temptations can be far more enticing than pornography or drugs. It's almost impossible not to be tempted; if you're alive, you're tempted. Take a step out your door and feast your eyes on that Mustang across the street. Or stay at home and watch the endless parade of goodies advertised on TV. Or face your little sister's whining about how mean you are—without badmouthing her right back.

But where's the devil in the decision Mitch faces? In the Super Bowl itself? In Mitch's choosing it over church? In Mitch's not doing what his parents would prefer? You might argue for any one of these, but I think the devil is in Mitch himself. Because Mitch—though he may not know it—worships football more than the God he says he loves.

When we ask God to "lead us not into temptation," we're asking God to beef us up for what's coming, to make us strong enough to make the right choices, fast enough to run away from evil, agile enough to avoid those lovely offerings Satan lays before us. Because he will.

Really, we're asking God not to let us fall. We're asking God for strength because—and this is the part that really hurts—we know we need it. We are too weak to hold our own, even for a moment, says the Catechism. We can't do it ourselves.

We belong to God.
Be there for us, Lord.

Lord, make us strong with the strength of your Holy Spirit, so that we may not go down to defeat in this spiritual struggle. Lead us not into temptation but deliver us from evil. Amen.

232

The Devil

Q&A 127

Our sworn enemies—the devil, the world, and our own flesh . . .

Be self-controlled and alert. Your enemy the devil prowls around like a roaring lion looking for someone to devour.

—1 Peter 5:8

Several years ago in a small town near here, a two-year-old girl named Shelby was murdered. Charged in the death were her mother and her mother's live-in boyfriend. Most people thought the boyfriend guilty of actually killing Shelby, but a jury said there wasn't enough evidence to convict him. He went free. Nobody was happy.

Shelby's mother was convicted of child endangerment. She'd serve time, but just about everyone felt angry. Shelby was murdered, but according to the law nobody did it.

Last night in my writing class, we read a story—fiction, not a news story—about a mother who had abused her little boy by breaking some of his bones. It was a good story because it brought us deeply into the mother's life—the mother told the story. In fact, several of my students claimed they really came to like the woman.

You know, if I spent a day with Shelby's mother, I don't doubt I could like her too. All I know about that woman, after all, is that she was charged with the death of her daughter. My guess is that she did some sweet things during her life. Nobody's all bad.

Nobody's all bad. Some armed robbers can be nice guys—ask prison guards. I once told a social worker I'd like to meet a sexual predator because I couldn't begin to imagine what they were like. "No, you wouldn't," he said. "You'd probably think he was a nice guy." And I don't doubt that's true.

I say all this because the Catechism lists the devil as one of our "sworn enemies." But who, really, is the devil?

Honestly, the devil is not all that easy to spot, in part because he's unique in all the world. There's no one else like him.

You see, the very worst person we know isn't all bad, but the devil is. One idea drives him: to make us believe there is no God. That's what he lives for. There's not a dime of goodness in him. He's the only total liar.

Behind every miscue, mishap, mistake, misstep, misdeed, and misery, he's there.

So, as the apostle Peter says, be alert.

It's scary, Lord, to think about the power of Satan. Thank you for winning the war against him. Please give us strength for the battles against him that we still have to fight. In Jesus' name, Amen.

Temptation Island

Q&A 127

Our sworn enemies—the devil, the world, and the flesh—never stop attacking us.

Watch and pray so that you will not fall into temptation.

—Matthew 26:41

By the time you read this, Fox network's TV show *Temptation Island* will be history. At least I hope so. I hope the show has vanished like the Wicked Witch of the West. But as I'm writing this, it's headlines. There's a big article about it in today's newspaper.

Let's presume it's history. That means I have to tell you what it was about. The show took four committed but unmarried couples to a Caribbean island, where a couple dozen beautiful singles were ready and willing to test their commitment. A real tropical meat market.

Once those committed couples got on the island, they were separated from each other and then introduced to those beautiful singles to see if those committed relationships would become, well, uncommitted.

Honestly and truly, I never watched the show. I don't know what happened. I do know some people claim the ads are much wilder than the show itself. Initially at least, the show wasn't so hot when it came to ratings.

Cry me a river. *Temptation Island* was scumbag low when it comes to entertainment. Sad to say, down there at the bottom of the TV barrel with Jerry Springer, it's got lots of company.

The Catechism lists three sworn enemies of all believers: the devil, the world, and the flesh. It doesn't take a rocket scientist to understand that anybody who says "Lead us not into temptation" and then signs up for *Temptation Island* is suffering a major disconnect. Fact is, anybody who prays "Lead us not into temptation" and then watches the show ought to have his or her battery checked too.

Why? Because watching beautiful people in thongs isn't spiritually enriching? Yeah, that's true.

But there's more. *Temptation Island* appeals to what's most glandular in us, most sheer instinct, most animal, really. It proclaims a gospel of bosoms and butts.

Why? Simple. To sell stuff. *Temptation Island* is really all about ads. Bigger audiences mean bigger bucks.

When we say "the world" is our enemy, we mean the culture of *Temptation Island,* the culture of television, the culture that says if you want to be happy you've got to buy, buy, buy. And that's the culture all around us, the world of the lie.

That world is our enemy. "Watch and pray that you do not fall into temptation." Don't fall for the lie.

Lord Jesus, help us deny the world that tells us our glory is in skin cream and skinny thighs. Strengthen our souls in the knowledge that you love us. Help us carry your love into your world. Amen.

"The Flesh and the Spirit"

Q&A 127

Our sworn enemies—the devil, the world, and our own flesh . . .

May God himself, the God of peace, sanctify you through and through. May your whole spirit, soul and body be kept blameless at the coming of our Lord Jesus Christ.

—1 Thessalonians 5:23

In 1630, when she was just eighteen years old, Anne Bradstreet and her husband immigrated from England to the Massachusetts Bay Colony, where together they raised a family on a frontier farm.

Anne found time to write poems people still read today. Among them is one titled "The Flesh and the Spirit." Actually, it's a conversation: Flesh talks to Spirit, and Spirit talks to Flesh. Here's the way she introduces her characters:

> One Flesh was called, who had her eye
> On worldly wealth and vanity;
> The other Spirit, who did rear
> Her thoughts unto a higher sphere.

I happen to like Anne Bradstreet's poetry, but I don't really like the way this particular poem rather bloodlessly cuts us in two pieces: We are flesh (bad, bad, bad) and spirit (good, good, good).

Sometimes it seems that way, of course. Our spirits get ticked off about what our bodies want (chocolate ice cream, diamond studs, a romp in the hay), and we start to think that if we didn't have to lug around these bodily desires, we'd be angels. Anne Bradstreet is saying what lots of religious people think: Our bodies are tar pits.

Even the Catechism says our own flesh can be our enemy, an evil we need to ask God to deliver us from. Seems that the devil can nest quite comfortably in our bodies.

But we can't be dissected as easily as frogs. Our souls aren't always trustworthy either, you know. Sometimes when we think we're doing blessedness, our best stinks. "Our righteous acts are like filthy rags," says Isaiah (64:6).

Besides, our bodies can be beautiful, buff or not. A smile can be a blessing.

When we use our bodies badly—and it happens a lot—then our flesh becomes the enemy. When we listen to the voice of what is worst in us—and it happens a lot—our spirit belongs to evil.

Deliver us, Lord, from the total liar, the devil; rescue us from the world's Temptation Islands; and lift us up—body and soul—from sin deep within.

That's what we're asking when we pray, "Deliver us from evil."

Deliver us from evil in all its forms, we pray. Keep us safe and keep us pure. And when we fall, please forgive us. In your Son's name, Amen.

Our Only Comfort

Q&A 128

What does your conclusion to this prayer mean? *For yours is the kingdom and the power and the glory forever* means, Your holy name . . . should receive all the praise, forever.

I will praise you, O Lord, with all my heart. . . . When I called, you answered me.

—Psalm 138:1, 3

When it comes right down to it, what God wants from us is that we want God. That's the whole package.

That's why God loves to hear us pray. If we don't talk to God, it seems that we don't like him. Makes sense, doesn't it? If you deliberately choose not to talk to someone, it usually means you don't like that person, right? You talk to people you like. You talk to people you want to be with.

God wants our prayers. God wants us to talk to him.

It so happens that I have a bad head cold, one that sticks like third-rate peanut butter. I've been eating so many oranges and grapefruit, I feel like a Florida fruit stand.

In that earthquake in India last week, reports say as many as 100,000 people were killed. When I contrast my head cold with the devastation in India, then I'm tempted to say, "Why bother the Lord with my runny nose?" All I need is another box of Kleenex.

But that's not the point, is it? The point is God *wants* to hear us, *wants* our attention, *wants* our trust. Even if my head cold is trivial stuff, God wants me to want God.

So we pray, you and I, about head colds and ball games and piano recitals. We talk to God. We wouldn't ask God to lug our burdens if we didn't believe he would. We bother God because we trust God cares. We pray because we believe in God.

That's why the Lord's Prayer ends with praise—because we believe. When we ask God about head colds, we speak for ourselves, but when we believe, we praise God's name with millions of other believers. When we tell God we trust him, we're a choir, we're the church—all believers, all the body of Christ, all the members of God's family.

Praise brings us together.

"For yours is the kingdom, and the power, and the glory, forever." When I say that, I can live with a head cold. God's my only comfort, in life, in death, and even with this lousy sore throat.

Praise the Lord, as David says, with all your heart. When you call, he answers. Praise God. Look around—everybody's doing it.

Thank you, Lord, for listening to everything. Thank you for being with us every moment of our lives. Thank you for giving us faith that you are our God. For yours is the kingdom, the power, and the glory, forever. Amen.

Grumbling and Singing

Q&A 128

For yours is the kingdom and the power and the glory. . . .

"Yours, O LORD, is the greatness and the power and the glory and the majesty and the splendor. . . . Yours, O LORD is the kingdom. . . .

—1 Chronicles 29:11

I hate to admit it, but I've seen more than my share of church wars. They're not pretty, and they're not fun, but they happen.

Maybe you've heard this one. A man is rescued from a deserted island. He's been there alone for forty years, and when the rescuers find him, they're amazed at the great buildings he's created.

"That right there," he says, "that's my steak house." He leans to the left. "And over there," he says, "that's the post office." He giggles with a little pride. "And up there on the hill is my church. Isn't it beautiful?"

"But what's that domed thing over there?" the rescuers ask.

"Well," the bearded guy says, "that's the church I used to go to."

If you don't get it, ask your parents.

I used to think only my church argued, but everyone's does.

This line at the end of the Lord's Prayer doesn't appear in the Bible passages where Jesus teaches the disciples to pray. But the church has used lines like this for years. They're called "doxologies," which means, after a fashion, words of praise. That's really what the final phrasing of the prayer is all about: words of praise.

Doxologies have a long history. From the very beginning, even the Old Testament church used doxologies—a kind of praise song—to conclude its prayers. This one probably comes from a doxology of King David (1 Chronicles 29:11).

The fact is, doxologies are often sung. For years in my church, we used to end the service with "Praise God from Whom All Blessings Flow." I still love to end a service with that one.

I may not be the best singer on the face of the earth, but I agree with Andrew Kuyvenhoven, who says you and I are far better people when we sing than when we fight. Grousers don't harmonize; their monotone will never light the place up. Think about the most quarrelsome person you know. Can you imagine this person singing? Sort of hard, isn't it?

Praise, especially by way of music, brings us, I think, closer to the angels.

When we end the Lord's Prayer, the doxology "for yours is the kingdom" almost begs to be sung. You can't grumble that line out. You can only praise.

Maybe we all ought to sing a little more. Sing praise.

Yours is the kingdom and the power and the glory forever. Receive our praise, Lord. Bless your holy name. Amen.

Raised Hands

Q&A 129

Amen means . . . it is even more sure that God listens to my prayer, than that I really desire what I pray for.

For no matter how many promises God has made, they are "Yes" in Christ. And so through him the "Amen" is spoken by us to the glory of God.

—2 Corinthians 1:20

I'm not big on raising hands in worship. I don't know why. Maybe I'm just an old fogie. Sometimes I think it becomes a show, a human test of righteousness maybe. Yeah, I know, when I say that I'm sounding more like a grumbler than a singer.

Despite my personal reservations, I do believe that raising hands in prayer is a great gesture.

But before we go into that, let's look at the answer to the final question of the Catechism: What do we mean by "Amen"? Easy enough.

It's the answer I don't like. It's certainly not wrong, but you have to read the sentence three times to begin to understand. Listen: "It is even more sure that God listens to my prayer, than that I really desire what I pray for."

That whole sentence suffers, I think, from "pronoun-itis," especially the *that* in the second half. That word is really foggy, making haze of the whole sentence. Try to put the idea in your own words. You have to work at it.

Here's what it suggests: We believe more in God's answers than we do in our own requests. But even that isn't so clear. Why don't we just say it this way? When we say "Amen," what we mean to say is "to God be the glory." That's what the answer suggests, I think. It's also what Paul suggests when he says the "Amen" is spoken by us to God's glory (2 Corinthians 1:20).

But now, back to raised hands in worship. What I like about this gesture is that it suggests we're making an offering of ourselves. Some people feel they're receiving when they lift their hands, opening their arms to catch blessings. But I personally see it more as a picture of offering ourselves to God. Really, the very heart of true faith is giving yourself away, every bit of who you are. Right from the start, the Catechism says our only comfort is that "I am not my own, but belong."

The picture of a believer raising hands as an offering of self is as perfect an image of what the Christian life is all about as we'll ever find on earth.

"To God be the glory." Not to me. Not to you.

That's at least part of what we affirm when we say, "Amen."

Take every bit of who we are, Lord. Use us in your kingdom. Help us listen when you call and answer when you speak. To you be the glory, forever and ever. Amen and Amen.

Amen

Q&A 129

This is sure to be!

The grace of the Lord Jesus be with God's people. Amen.
—Revelation 22:21

My father is the only person I know who says "Amen" with a certain oomph, even in prayers around the dinner table. He always says, "Ah-MEN," with a kaboom on "men." The reason has nothing to do with gender, with *men* as opposed to *women.* It has everything to do with the Catechism.

I can learn something from the way my dad hits that word hard every time he prays. When we say Amen perhaps too easily, it becomes a word like, say, *the,* something we call an "article." The power of the English language is in nouns and verbs, I always tell my students. *A* or *an* or *the* don't light up a sentence.

What my father wants to do is say "Amen!" with an exclamation point, not just an everyday period. And he's right.

So what do we mean when we say "Amen"? The Catechism says it means "This is sure to be!" Did you notice the exclamation point?

The word *Amen* may be one of the most universal words amid the world's thousands of languages. It's said every day by millions of people in millions of places using thousands of tongues. And they all mean the exact same thing: "This is sure to be."

That's a wonderful answer, and I certainly wouldn't suggest changing a word of it. But come back with me for a moment to old England—the English are the ones who created our language, after all—and consider a certain situation.

Mr. Barrington is speaking to Ms. Courtland. They're on the veranda after concluding a wonderful date. Mr. Barrington says, "It was, don't you think, a most extraordinary afternoon?"

Ms. Courtland looks back at him. "Indeed!" she says, nodding invitingly.

Indeed! I love it. When we say "Amen," what we mean, in the English fashion, is "Indeed!" I'll tell you why.

Something is embedded in that word. When we say "Indeed," we're not only saying "definitely," we're also pledging that we mean "definitely" not only in our words but also—surprise, surprise—in our deeds. In-deed.

To God be the glory. For yours is the kingdom and the power and the glory, because we are not our own and you are our only comfort.

Indeed! This is sure to be! Amen! As my father says, "Ah-MEN!"

Exclamation point. World without end.

Take every bit of who we are, Lord. May our lives sing your grace. Nothing means as much to us as your gift of love. We raise our hands to you. For yours is the kingdom and the power and the glory, forever. Amen.

Afterword: "Every Bit of Who We Are"

Once the car carrying him and his friends stopped rolling, it ended upside down in the middle of the road—not hidden in the bottom of a ditch or out in a stubbled cornfield where it might have been missed by carloads of his friends returning to campus, as he had been, from a hockey game.

When other cars came upon the accident scene that night, some of his friends, frantic with the realization that their buddy was still inside, tried madly to right that car and get him out. But it didn't work. There were no miracles. By the time the rescue squad came, dozens of kids saw them remove his body.

His name was Khamko Baccam, a Laotian-American, a soccer star here at the college where I teach, and a good, good kid. He died that night in an accident that was made even more horrible by the fact that it was all so very public. An hour later, more than fifty of his friends stood in the waiting room at the local hospital, praying and hoping they wouldn't hear the words every last one of them feared, the words they eventually heard anyway in the darkness of a November night.

He was a local kid, born in Laos but reared here in town, so his funeral, bilingual, was held in a local church and was attended by hundreds of students. Had he been from somewhere far away, maybe the ordeal would have been out of sight and out of mind earlier. But the funeral was here, and his body and the casket were lowered into the ground of the local cemetery, whitened that morning by an early winter snow.

Event after event after event happened right here—his public death, the hospital waiting room, the blanket of sadness that spread like a plague over the campus on Saturday morning, the flow of grief in a totally unscheduled gathering in the chapel, Sunday worship together, Monday's funeral, Tuesday's final memorial chapel on campus—all of it happened right here, creating the impression that nothing else was happening anywhere in the world. For several days the whole campus walked slowly, face to the ground, hand in hand, many wiping their faces. On the wide prairie landscape out here where I live, there was no hiding from Khamko's death.

On Saturday night, two hundred kids held each other and cried, huddled on the stage of the auditorium in an impromptu gathering of the wounded.

Some of them read Bible passages they'd picked out. Some prayed. All of them sat together up on stage, more crying in public than I'd ever seen.

They sang "When Peace Like a River" in a way that at any other time you would have considered to be very much less than a full effort. One of them played piano, and really, no one sang—not if *singing* means raising their voices. As music, it was totally unspectacular. But I'll never forget their song because it was the most moving rendition of that old hymn I've ever heard. "It is well, it is well with my soul. . . ." It was sung with inner voices that never really reached throats parched from a night and a day of grief that none of them will ever forget.

Again on Tuesday, at Khamko's memorial chapel on campus, grief brooded over everything. Some professors talked about Khamko. A history prof everyone knew spoke a few words, then took off his glasses up in front of the biggest chapel crowd I've ever seen, stepped back from the mike, and wiped his eyes. Another told the crowd how he'd written in his grade book that Khamko had withdrawn from class and transferred to heaven.

At the end of that memorial chapel, one of Khamko's roommates stood behind the podium and told us how his roommates had gone out for supper together after the funeral on Monday, and how one of them had just mentioned that reading the first question and answer of the Heidelberg Catechism would be comforting, and how they did, and how it was very comforting.

So, he said, they had thought it would be good to do the same thing at that chapel service with all of their friends, with all who knew Khamko—how it would be fitting if the whole bunch of us, a chapel full of students and faculty and staff, would stand and repeat the answer. "You can find it in the hymnal," he said, pointing at his, "page 861."

And we did. Everyone turned to that page, and then Khamko's roommate read the question, and just like he said, we all responded with the answer about comfort. "I am not my own . . . I belong to my faithful Savior, Jesus Christ . . ."

And that was the end of the chapel—not the end of grief and sadness, but the end of that memorial chapel service. We left quietly and walked out into the soft snow that fell over both the campus and the cemetery not far away, where many of them had stood beside an open grave just an afternoon before.

I don't know about the rest of them in the chapel that day, but I will never forget that particular recitation of the first question and answer. It comes back to me now, eleven years later, as clear as yesterday, because there is every bit of comfort the question promises in the words of the answer "that I am not my own." There's comfort for eternity in the realization that every bit of who we are and what we are belongs to God.

I hope you remember that too.

Jim Schaap